New Hand
British Pottery &

New Handbook
of
British Pottery &
Porcelain Marks

Geoffrey A. Godden

BARRIE & JENKINS

LONDON

Every effort has been made to verify the information contained in this book. However, the author and publishers are not liable for any loss incurred as a consequence of reliance upon it.

Barrie & Jenkins Ltd
Random House
20 Vauxhall Bridge Road
London SW1V 2SA

Copyright © 1968, 1999 by Geoffrey A. Godden
First published 1968 by Herbert Jenkins Ltd
Reprinted 1968, 1969, 1972 (with revisions), 1975, 1977, 1978, 1981, 1982, 1985, 1986, 1987, 1988, 1989, 1990 (with revisions), 1992, 1993, 1994, 1995

Second edition, revised and enlarged, 1999

A CIP catalogue record for this book is available from the British Library.

Random House UK Limited Reg. No. 954009

ISBN 0 09 186580 8

Designed and typeset by Behram Kapadia
Printed and bound in Great Britain
by Mackays of Chatham

Contents

Preface 7

Introduction 8

Pictorial Glossary 12

THE MARKS 39

Potters' Initial Marks 151

Registered Designs 1839–1883 168

Registration Numbers 1884–1999 245

Collectors' Clubs, Societies and Groups 247

Selected Bibliography 250

Index 252

Preface

For this revised, new edition, dates and details of the major manufacturers have been rechecked and may well differ from those given in earlier non-Godden works! In the case of the more important manufacturers the reader is informed of specialist books which can offer fuller information or a range of illustrations. A most helpful feature is the warning offered in the cases where reproductions can be expected and the original marks copied. Guidance is also offered on the rarity or the commercial desirability of certain makes or types – although this, like value, can vary with time and be dependent on quality and condition.

The key, identifying, initials of nearly a thousand British ceramic manufacturers from the end of the 18th century onwards are listed, together with the name of the firm and its working period.

A new valuable feature is the chronological listing of the registration entries for new British ceramic shapes or designs, as entered in the official Design Registry files between 1839 and 1883. A list of collectors' clubs and societies has also been added.

Whilst this Handbook cannot compete for comprehensive cover with the large Godden 'bible', the *Encyclopaedia of British Pottery and Porcelain Marks* (first published in 1964) or with the *Encyclopaedia of British Porcelain Manufacturers* (Barrie & Jenkins, 1988), it does provide a convenient, inexpensive, and helpful guide to the markings to be found on collectable British pottery and porcelains, and will lead the reader on to more detailed works of reference.

Every effort has been made to verify the information contained in this book. However, the author and publishers are not liable for any loss incurred as a consequence of reliance upon it.

GEOFFREY GODDEN
The Square, Findon, West Sussex

Introduction

The object of a ceramic trade mark is to enable at least the retailer to know the name of the manufacturer of the object, so that re-orders, etc. can be correctly addressed. In the case of the larger firms the mark also has publicity value and shows the buyer that the object was made by a long-established firm with a reputation to uphold; such clear name-marks as Minton, Wedgwood, Royal Crown Derby and Royal Worcester are typical examples.

To collectors the mark has greater importance, for not only can they trace the manufacturer of any marked object, but they can also ascertain the approximate date of manufacture and in several cases the exact year of production, particularly in the case of 19th- and 20th-century wares from the leading firms which employed private dating systems.

With the increasing use of ceramic marks in the 19th century, a large proportion of British pottery and porcelain can be accurately identified and often dated. With the many hundreds of different manufacturers' marks it is quite impossible to remember all the various devices, sets of initials, or the working periods of the firms concerned. Hence the need for a concise pocket-book such as this, to give the collector basic facts and to lead on to works giving detailed information and illustrations of typical examples. In the few cases where popular marks are known to have been reproduced on forgeries, the reader is warned of this fact.

Ceramic marks are applied in four basic ways:

(a) *Incised* into the still soft clay during manufacture, in which case the mark will show a slight ploughed-up effect and have a free spontaneous appearance.

(b) *Impressed* into the soft clay during manufacture; many name-marks such as Wedgwood are produced in this way from metal or clay stamps or seals. These have a neat mechanical appearance.

(c) *Painted* marks, usually name or initial marks, added over the glaze at the time of ornamentation, as were some stencilled marks.

(d) *Printed* marks transferred from engraved copper plates at the time of decoration. Most 19th-century marks are printed, often in blue under the glaze when the main design is also in underglaze blue.

Information on the method of applying each mark is given in this book, and the information can be of vital importance. For instance the early Chelsea triangle mark must be *incised* not impressed, as it can be on 19th-century fakes. Photographs of typical incised and other basic mark forms are given in my *Encyclopaedia of British Pottery and Porcelain Marks* (1964), Plates 1–8.

There are several general 'Godden' rules for dating ceramic marks, attention to which will avoid several common errors:

(1) Printed marks incorporating the Royal Arms supported by the lion and the unicorn are of 19th- or 20th-century date. The Royal Arms with the inescutcheon, or extra central small shield, are the pre-1837 version. It should be noted that copies of this device can occur on non-British wares!

(2) Marks incorporating the name of a pattern will be post-1830, and are often very much later.

(3) Marks incorporating the diamond-shape design registration device will be between 1842 and 1883. See pp. 168–9 for a full explanation of this device.

(4) Printed, garter-type marks, incorporating the maker's name or initials etc., were popular from about 1840.

(5) Marks incorporating the word 'Royal' tend to postdate about 1850.

(6) Marks incorporating the word or various abbreviations for 'Limited' must postdate the 1861 Limited Liability Act.

(7) Marks incorporating the words 'Trade Mark' must postdate the 1862 Trade Mark Act.

(8) The addition of the word 'England' in a mark indicates a date after 1880 and in general after 1891 when the American Tariff Act came into force. However, the absence of such a designation does not necessarily show that the piece is of an earlier date! Whilst 'England' was the usual description, as it included all the Staffordshire wares, alternative country-names were sometimes used. Scottish firms used 'Scotland' or the earlier name 'North Britain' or simply 'Britain'.

(9) The abbreviation 'UK' or 'United Kingdom' is usually only found on recent productions.

(10) Marks incorporating a registration number, which is usually prefixed

'R^D N^o', will postdate 1883. The key to these numbers is given on p. 245.

(11) The wording 'Made in England' (etc.) tends to occur on marks after about 1910. However, this is far from being an inflexible rule and many post-1945 marks do not include it.

(12) Marks incorporating the word 'Copyright' will postdate c.1920.

(13) Marks bearing the description 'Bone China' tend to postdate the 1920s and can be very recent.

(14) Marks incorporating the letter 'R' (usually within a small circle) postdate 1955.

(15) Marks incorporating wording relating to dish-washers, detergents etc. are obviously of a relatively recent period.

(16) Marks incorporating the initials 'PLC' postdate the mid-1970s.

(17) Marks or pattern descriptions incorporating the word 'old' or 'olde' are generally reasonable modern reissues of 19th-century designs or are based on such former patterns. They are nostalgic essays in salesmanship!

(18) Marks incorporating the initials 'BS' followed by a number denote a British Standard quality or performance showing that the object or the body has passed tests. A BS number again denotes a recent date for that mark or product.

These 'Godden' rules relate to the age of a piece, but remember that age in itself is not a virtue! Do not worship age alone.

A high proportion of English pottery and porcelain was made in the district known as the Staffordshire Potteries centred on the present city of Stoke-on-Trent. The Potteries are basically made up of seven separate towns – Burslem, Cobridge, Fenton, Hanley (incorporating Shelton), Longton (also Lane End), Stoke and Tunstall. These towns will be found in the addresses of many firms listed in this book. The initial letters of these towns may be incorporated in several 19th-century initial marks, e.g.

H & G
   B   (Heath & Greatbatch of Burslem)

J & G
   L   (Jackson & Gosling of Longton) etc.

It may be useful at this point to advise readers that the Stoke-on-Trent City Museum at Hanley recently changed its name to The Potteries Museum while this book was in press, and the text has only been altered when convenient.

Remember that many marks relate to the retailer, wholesaler or agent, not to the manufacturer. Such name or initial marks that include the name of a non-pottery-producing city or town will fall into this category. Typical non-ceramic place-names include London, Birmingham, Manchester and Dublin, although most towns had their own retailers, who might specify in their orders the requirement to include their own name rather than that of the maker.

As I have included under each entry in the mark section details of the standard or latest specialist books, it will be helpful to make some general comments on such works. First, one should obtain the most recent work on any factory or subjects, as it may be expected to contain the latest information. This is particularly important if you wish to resort to Price Guides. Secondly, a reference book is not prime source material: it will only include the author's interpretation of available source material or gleanings from other works. It is always worth checking so-called facts. Errors once made tend to be copied by a succession of authors.

Specialist reference books are often published in short runs, so they may well become unavailable within a few years. Of course, we enjoy a splendid Library Service whereby out-of-print books may be obtained, on loan, for a small charge. Various book dealers also specialize in new and out-of-print books on ceramics or on other collecting subjects. Although I cannot mention any one such firm, they tend to advertise from time to time in collectors' magazines such as *Collectors' Guide*, or they may have a stand at a specialist Antiques Fair. Certainly a good, well researched and illustrated reference book should be of lasting value and prove a good investment for the serious collector. On the other hand, general books on a wide variety of subjects cannot be very detailed on any one facet of collecting. Apart from the specialist books listed in the mark section I have also included a general bibliography at the end.

Pictorial Glossary

This helpful feature shows and gives a brief outline of the various basic types of British ceramics produced from the 17th century onwards.

It is arranged in alphabetical order. It is, however, essential to bear in mind the approximate periods within which these differing bodies or styles were popular. One should also note that certain types were very seldom marked. These generally unmarked types include 17th-century and early 18th-century Delft-type tin-glazed earthenwares, the glossy, black-glazed Jackfield type wares, early slip-decorated earthenwares, salt-glazed stonewares and 19th-century lustred wares. Also British ceramics produced before about 1770 will rarely bear a maker's name. This is to be expected and the lack of a mark will hardly affect the commercial value of these types, although in general the presence of a mark will enhance the desirability of a piece.

British ceramic types featured in the Pictorial Glossary

DELFT-TYPE TIN-GLAZED EARTHENWARES
17th and 18th centuries

SLIP-DECORATED EARTHENWARE 17th century onwards

STONEWARES 17th century onwards

SALT-GLAZED STONEWARES c.1720 onwards

JACKFIELD c.1720–1770

BLUE AND WHITE (PORCELAIN) c.1748 onwards

CREAMWARE c.1760 onwards

BASALT c.1770 onwards

BISQUE PORCELAINS c.1770 onwards

JASPER WARES c.1770 onwards

PEARLWARE c.1780 onwards

CASTLEFORD c.1800–1820

BONE CHINA c.1800 onwards

LUSTRED WARES c.1805 onwards

IRONSTONE BODIES c.1813 onwards

STONE CHINA BODIES c.1813 onwards

GRANITE CHINA c.1830 onwards

TERRA-COTTA c.1840–1900

PARIAN PORCELAIN c.1842 onwards

REGISTERED DESIGNS c.1842–1883

MAJOLICA c.1850 onwards

PÂTE-SUR-PÂTE c.1870–1939

ART POTTERY c.1870–1920s

ART DECO c.1925–1930s

ART DECO

The British 'Art Deco' styled wares of the mid-1920s and 1930s are typified by the well-known Clarice Cliff designs and the angular forms made to suit the jazz age, broad, colourful patterns. Like jazz and Odeon cinemas the new style spread rapidly and soon most middle-market potters were following the fashion.

In post-war years these once inexpensive wares, usually earthenwares, have returned to fashion and have become highly collectable. Collectors of such wares have taken the subject seriously and a mini-library is growing to fund the increasing interest in these fashionable and so typically 1930s designs. So-called 'Antique Fairs' now abound with these smart designs and the style is in some cases being revived in current replicas.

Specialist works include *Art Deco Source Book*, by P. Bayer (Phaidon, 1988); *Lyle Price Guide Art Deco Ceramics* (Ebury Press, 1999); *Art Deco & Modernist Ceramics*, by K. McCready (Thames & Hudson, revised edition 1997); *Art Deco China*, by J. Hay (Little Brown, 1996); *Collecting Art Deco Ceramics*, by H. & P. Watson (Francis Joseph, 2nd edition 1997) and *Clarice Cliff and her Contemporaries* by Helen C. Cunningham (Schiffer Publishing, 1999).

Art Deco

ART POTTERY

It is very difficult to precisely define 'Art Pottery' which can differ from Art Potteries! In essence we are concerned with wares (usually earthenwares) made within the approximate period 1870–1920. These ideally should be individually made and hand-decorated, as the William De Morgan earthenware vases shown here. Art Pottery is usually of a decorative type, not table services. Again, usually but not invariably, the wares would be made by individuals or by small groups or firms. There are obvious exceptions, such as the individual signed stonewares made at the Art Pottery Studio, within the large Doulton works at Lambeth.

Because of their decorative and individual qualities, or because the Victorian Art Potteries are typical of their period and can be produced by leading artists or designers, much Art Pottery is highly collectable. Important examples by fashionable artists, craftsmen or designers can be expected to be commercially desirable.

Several of the new entries in this Handbook relate to Art Pottery, and reference books on the different types are listed in the individual sections. General works on Art Pottery and the Art Pottery movement in general

Art Pottery

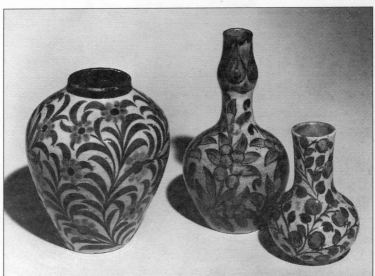

include *Victorian Art Pottery* by E. Lloyd Thomas (Guildart, 1974), and *Encyclopaedia of British Art Pottery* by Victoria Bergesen (Barrie & Jenkins, 1991).

BASALT

The basalt body was also known as 'Egyptian black'. The black body has a matt (unglazed) exterior and was popular for both useful and ornamental ware from the 1760s into the 19th century. Josiah Wedgwood improved the original body and termed it 'basalt' (c.1773). Wedgwood also adapted it for the manufacture of classical formed vases, relief moulded plaques, etc. Very many 18th and early 19th-century manufacturers produced 'basalt' or 'Egyptian black'. Except for the major makers such as Wedgwood, basalt wares are seldom marked.

The modern standard book on these wares is *Black Basalt, Wedgwood and Contemporary Manufacturers*, by Diana Edwards (Antique Collectors' Club, 1994).

Basalt

Bisque

BISQUE

'Bisque' or 'biscuit' porcelain is simply the once-fired body without the addition of glaze. Bisque figures and groups were popular on the Continent in the 18th century, and in England the Derby factory produced tasteful examples from c.1770. It is noteworthy that such pieces were more expensive than the same model which had been glazed and coloured, because the bisque examples had to be perfect in every respect. Several early 19th-century factories produced charming biscuit figures, groups and animals, until the new, creamy-coloured, Parian body became fashionable in the 1840s. Later Continental biscuit porcelains (often coloured) were popular and generally inexpensive. English bisque porcelain is seldom marked, except for Derby examples.

BLUE AND WHITE

This term relates to a very large class of pottery and porcelain decorated in cobalt blue applied to the bisque body before glazing, giving rise to the description 'underglaze blue'. Much imported Chinese porcelain was of this type and most, if not all of our early porcelain manufacturers produced Oriental-style blue and white. The teapot here shown is Worcester c.1760, painted by hand with a very popular Oriental-taste design.

18th-century British blue and white porcelains are very collectable and can be costly, especially for rare patterns or unusual objects. Specialist books on our main porcelain factories – Bow, Bristol, Caughley, Derby, Limehouse, Liverpool, Longton Hall, Lowestoft and Worcester – will feature a good range of blue and white specimens, as will modern general works.

Apart from the standard book, Dr Bernard Watney's *English Blue & White Porcelain of the 18th Century* (Faber & Faber, revised edition 1973), the reader could consult my *Eighteenth-Century English Porcelain* (Granada Publishing, 1985).

Blue and white

Blue and white (printed)

BLUE AND WHITE (PRINTED)

Apart from the hand-painted underglaze blue porcelain (and some earthenwares) much blue and white from about 1760 onwards was transfer-printed. In these cases the cobalt pigment was applied to the once-fired but still unglazed body, by means of transfer paper charged from engraved copper-plates.

This obviously speeded up the decorating process and gave a uniformity where large runs of, say, plates were required. The pair of openwork baskets here shown are Worcester c.1770. The reversed example shows the blue-printed shaded or hatched crescent mark. Most of our 18th-century porcelain (and earthenware) factories produced printed designs. In general these are not as highly regarded as the often earlier and more individual hand-painted examples.

Underglaze blue prints on 18th-century porcelains were made at most British factories, notably at Caughley, Worcester, the Liverpool factories, Isleworth, Derby, Lowestoft and New Hall. Although in general hand-painted designs are more highly regarded some printed designs are scarce and are highly desirable.

General books on early underglaze blue printed porcelains include Dr Bernard Watney's *English Blue & White Porcelain of the 18th Century* (Faber & Faber, revised edition 1973) and specialist works on the individual factories. It is impossible to cover the vast subject of blue-printed earthenwares in this brief glossary.

BONE CHINA

English bone china is a superbly strong and pleasing ceramic body. It is basically similar to hard-paste porcelain (containing China Stone and China Clay) plus up to 50 per cent of calcined animal bones. Various manufacturers favoured different receipts and within a factory different mixes would be employed to produce different sized articles. A different mix would be required for hand-turned objects, to that needed for the slip-casting process.

It is generally conceded that the body was perfected at the Spode factory at Stoke, in about 1800, although bone-ash had been used in other porcelain mixes from the 1740s. By about 1820 all British porcelain manufacturers were using bone china, of various qualities. The name Bone China was not however, generally used before the mid-1840s. Printed marks incorporating this term will usually be of 20th-century date.

The reader is referred to the late Reginald G. Haggar's chapter 'Bone China, a general survey', in *Staffordshire Porcelain*, edited by Geoffrey Godden (Granada Publishing, 1983). This book illustrates a varied feast of Staffordshire bone china objects.

Bone China

Castleford

CASTLEFORD

'Castleford' is a generic term, covering a large class of early 19th-century white (or slightly creamy) semi-porcelainous stoneware, displaying some translucency. It usually has a slight smear-glaze and various designs are moulded in relief. Sets of teapots, covered sugar basins and cream or milk jugs were popular in this body – as they were in the black basalt. Teapots often have hinged or sliding covers and such (usually unmarked) wares were certainly not confined to the Castleford factory or to other Yorkshire potteries. Many seem to have been produced in the Staffordshire Potteries. Most seem to relate to the 1800–20 period. Examples are attractive and not unduly expensive.

CREAMWARE

Creamware is a light cream-coloured earthenware, introduced, tentatively, in about 1740. After perfection by Josiah Wedgwood it had become by the 1760s the standard refined British earthenware body, largely replacing the earlier tin-glazed (delft-type) earthenwares and salt-glazed white stonewares.

Creamware

The potter's term 'cream colour' (abbreviated to C.C.) was replaced for sales purposes by Wedgwood's apt name 'Queens Ware'. It is light in weight, pleasant to use, neatly potted and lends itself to various forms of decoration. Much, however, was sold in an undecorated state, as the 'W(xxx)' marked, pierced-edged plate here shown. The body and glaze was often whitened after about 1785 giving rise to 'Pearlware', better suited to underglaze blue decoration.

The standard specialist book is Donald Towner's *Creamware* (Faber & Faber, 1978), although the 1986 Northern Ceramic Society exhibition catalogue, *Creamware and Pearlware* (Stoke-on-Trent City Museum, 1986) is an invaluable well-illustrated guide and gives details of specialist books on individual types and cites some factory pattern books.

Creamware can be highly interesting and collectable although comparatively few pieces bear a maker's mark. Commercial prices are very variable. The reader is warned of recent creamwares produced in old styles and shapes, underlining the lasting decorative appeal of even undecorated creamware.

DELFT

Delft-type, or tin-glazed, earthenwares have a clay-coloured rather low-fired body which has been coated with an opaque, whitish glaze, usually incorporating oxide of tin. This glaze was intended to give the general appearance of porcelain and to serve as a base for any added decoration. It is, however, prone to chipping at the edges, so exposing the underlying body. Delft-type wares (a small 'd' when referring to British 'delft') are liable to cracking or other damage and were, in general, superseded by the creamware body.

The Delft technique was widely used on the Continent but the British essays were made at several centres including London, Bristol, Glasgow, Liverpool and Wincanton, from the 17th century into the middle of the 18th century.

Examples can be charming, interesting and highly collectable. Commercial value depends on the object, its decoration, its condition and other factors. A simply decorated, chipped plate can be purchased for a modest outlay but a special article such as the dated 1732 Royal subject large bowl here featured would command several thousand pounds. Most old British delft ware is unmarked.

Specialist books on tin-glazed earthenwares include *Tin-Glazed Pottery*

English delft

in Europe and the Islamic World, by A. Caiger-Smith (Faber & Faber, 1973); *English Delftware in the Bristol Collection*, by F. Britton (Sotheby, 1982); *Dated English Delftware*, by L. Lipski & M. Archer (Sotheby, 1984); *London Delftware*, by F. Britton (Jonathan Horne, 1987); *British Delft in Williamsburg*, by J. C. Austin (USA, 1994); *Tin-Glazed Earthenwares – from Maiolica, Faience and Delftware to the Contemporary*, by D. Carnegy (A. & C. Black, 1995); and *Delftware. The Tin-Glazed Earthenware of the British Isles*, by M. Archer (HMSO, 1997).

IRONSTONE-TYPE BODIES

The ironstone body was patented by Charles James Mason (the son of Miles Mason) in 1813. The strong, durable, body quickly established itself, firstly for tablewares, dinner services etc., usually decorated with colourful Oriental-styled designs. It was cheaper than porcelain, but stronger in use and colourful. Ornamental as well as tablewares were soon

Ironstone

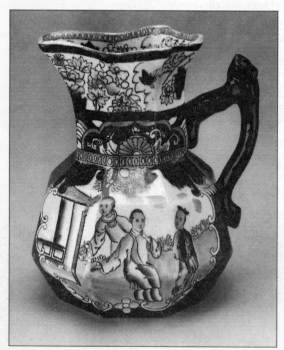

made ranging from toy or miniature pieces to huge vases or even fire sur-
rounds! Jugs in various sizes and decorated like the example here shown
are amongst the best-known examples but ironstone-type wares have
been made up to the present time.

Many firms apart from Masons produced ironstone or the similar
'Stone China' or 'Granite China' wares. Various factory marks can occur.
Desirability varies according to quality, age, condition, the type of object,
the standing of the maker, etc., but in general colourful old ironstone is
very collectable.

Various specialist reference books include *Godden's Guide to Mason's
China and the Ironstone Wares* (Antique Collectors' Club, 1980) and the
general guide to ironstone wares, *Godden's Guide to Ironstone, Stone and
Granite Wares* (Antique Collectors' Club, 1999).

JACKFIELD

'Jackfield' is largely a generic name for a class of British earthenware of a
reddish-brick body, which has been coated with a glossy black glaze –
giving the opposite effect to white coated delft wares.

Many of the pieces were originally decorated with low-fired enamel
decoration or non-permanent gilding. Some examples, like those here

Jackfield

shown, are of good form with relief motifs. Such Jackfield type black-glazed wares were produced at various centres, not only in Shropshire. Indeed, most examples certainly have a Staffordshire origin. No marked examples seem to be recorded.

Most examples will have been produced in the approximate period 1720–70. Such 18th-century examples are collectable but seldom very costly unless dated or of extreme importance. As yet no specialist book is devoted to these attractive pieces, which in the main comprise tea or coffee wares and jugs.

JASPER

Jasper is a decorative fine-grained hard earthenware (really a porcelain as it can be translucent) which can be stained to various tints – usually blue. This serves as a wonderful ground for added white motifs.

Josiah Wedgwood experimented with and perfected the jasper body in the 1770s and his name is rightly always associated with it. It was, however, so successful that various other 18th-century potters sought to emulate

Jasper

Wedgwood's success. Some non-Wedgwood jasper wares reached very high standards. Marked examples by Adams, Neale, and Turner are particularly noteworthy and were often decorated with sprigged white-relief motifs, in the well-known Wedgwood manner. Similar wares were made throughout the 19th century but with a falling-off in quality. Messrs Josiah Wedgwood & Sons Ltd still produce their traditional jasper wares.

All jasper has decorative merits. Commercial considerations include the importance, attractiveness or rarity of the object, the quality of potting, the desirability of the maker and the age of the piece.

All books on Wedgwood will give a good account of the jasper wares, as will specialist books on the main makers mentioned above. There is a section on jasper wares in my *British Pottery. An Illustrated Guide* (Barrie & Jenkins, 1974).

LUSTRE

British lustre ware basically comprises earthenwares covered with an extremely thin metallic based wash, to emulate silver (or silver-plated)

Lustre

wares or copper articles. Such metallic decoration can also be applied to porcelains but usually as a border or edge trim, or as pink-lustre decoration, rather than as a total covering as was often applied to earthenwares. The so-called silver-lustre has a platinum coating, not silver which would oxidise. Copper lustre is based on gold.

Most lustre was made in the 1805–80 period but some can be present-century – often made to old shapes or styles. All lustre has a decorative charm but prices vary greatly, depending on the form, condition, age or general desirability of the piece. The copper-lustre jug here shown is a good quality Staffordshire example with printed panels datable to c.1835. Very few 19th-century pieces bear a maker's mark. The splash-lustre style is traditionally associated with Sunderland, but was also made in Staffordshire.

The standard book on this vast subject is *Collecting Lustreware* by Geoffrey Godden & Michael Gibson (Barrie & Jenkins, 1991).

MAJOLICA
Victorian majolica (as opposed to earlier Italian Maiolica) was introduced to this country by Minton's French Art Director, Leon Arnoux, just prior to the 1851 Exhibition. In essence it is a fine earthenware body normally moulded into intricate decorative forms. The coloured and glazed deco-

Majolica

ration gives the effect of pleasing semi-translucent tinted glazes. The leading manufacturers such as Mintons, Wedgwood and George Jones employed talented and often well-known modellers to supply the initial master-models. Good examples by the leading English firms are very desirable and are highly valued today.

Several specialist books feature these earthenwares, including *Majolica – British, Continental and American Wares, 1851–1915* by V. Bergesen (Barrie & Jenkins, 1989); *Majolica. A Complete History and Illustrated Survey*, by M. Karmason & J. Stacke (Harry N. Abrahams, NY, 1989); *Majolica*, by N. M. Dawes (Crown Publishers, NY, 1990); *Majolica: European & American Wares*, by J. B. Snyder & L. Bockol (Schiffer, USA, 1994); and *European Majolica, with Values* by D. M. Murrey (Schiffer, USA, 1997). This is not a complete listing but most of the books on majolica are published in the USA – where, it should be stated, the very keen and seemingly wealthy collectors are based.

PARIAN

Parian is a typically Victorian ceramic body. It was introduced by Copeland & Garrett and by Mintons almost simultaneously in the early 1840s. It largely replaced the earlier whiter biscuit porcelain for figures, groups and busts. The new body could be readily slip-moulded, had a pleasing slightly creamy tint and a very slight surface sheen.

The original idea was to mass-produce at low cost reduced copies of famous marble statuary, indeed Copeland & Garrett's original name for the new body was 'Statuary Porcelain'. Within a short period, however, it was employed to produce all manner of objects, from small trinkets to large objects, such as fireplaces. Moulded jugs by the tens of thousands were produced.

Generally the body was left undecorated to show its marble-like quality but it could be glazed, tinted or slightly gilt. The leading firms, such as Copelands, Mintons, Wedgwood marked their wares but a host of small firms issued unmarked examples. Some firms specialized in parian producing no other types.

Specialist reference books include *The Illustrated Guide to Victorian Parian China*, by C. & D. Shinn (Barrie & Jenkins, 1971) and the multi-authored work *The Parian Phenomenon*, edited by Paul Atterbury (Richard Dennis, 1989). *The Encyclopaedia of British Porcelain Manufacturers*, by G. Godden (Barrie & Jenkins, 1988) gives details of the various manufacturers, large and small, as parian is a class of porcelain.

Parian

PÂTE-SUR-PÂTE

Pâte-sur-Pâte is the most expensive 19th-century form of ceramic decoration. Leading specialist artists slowly built up the white porcelain or parian relief-decoration in individual designs over a contrasting ground. Such designs were in effect sculptures. It was a slow, painstaking process and the best work was always expensive. The master in this technique was the Frenchman M. L. Solon (1835–1913), who worked for Mintons in the 1870–1904 period. Some plaques were produced in his own time up to his death in 1913. Solon trained various apprentices who worked for Mintons into the 1900s. Their work is not so valued as Solon's figure compositions, a modest example of which is here shown.

Various firms, other than Mintons, also produced decorative articles in the same style – Royal Worcester, Grainger of Worcester, George Jones of

Pâte-sur-Pâte

Stoke being the most familiar. Some of these designs can be duplicated as they were worked up from a moulded base work. Such pieces are very decorative but are not valued so highly as the unique designs of the leading (mainly Minton) artists. Some Continental firms also produced very good examples.

The specialist reference book is *Pâte-sur-Pâte. The Art of Ceramic Relief Decoration, 1849–1992*, by Bernard Bumpus (Barrie & Jenkins, 1992).

PEARLWARE

Pearlware was developed in the latter part of the 18th century as a new basic earthenware body, nearer in appearance to porcelain than to the then standard creamware. It was termed 'Pearl White' by Josiah Wedgwood who mentioned this name in 1779. In essence it was the old creamware mix with the addition of china clay but further whitened by the addition of a small amount of cobalt added to the glaze. An alternative term much used by the potters was 'China Glaze'.

The new whiter body retained the benefits of creamware, it was light in weight, reasonably easy and inexpensive to produce and fire. But most

Pearlware

importantly the colour approached that of porcelain and underglaze decoration looked far more attractive on pearlware than on the former creamware.

Underglaze blue printing was applied to pearlware from the 1780s onwards. The early examples in a dark blue usually comprised Oriental-styled designs and in dinner services especially vied with the Chinese porcelain imports. Most of the leading British potters produced pearlwares of various types, enhanced in different styles. It was by the 1790s the standard British earthenware body. Consequently specimens are plentiful and standard patterns on plates need not be costly.

Many modern books illustrate pearlwares, particularly those relating to blue-printed earthenwares. Of special interest is the Northern Ceramic Society 1986 exhibition catalogue *Creamware and Pearlware* published by the City Museum & Art Gallery, Stoke-on-Trent.

PORCELAIN

Porcelain, as can here be seen, is or should be translucent, as opposed to earthenware or pottery which is usually opaque. However, the translucency of porcelain can be variable. It depends on the thickness of the object and the firing temperature, as underfired porcelain will not show much translucency.

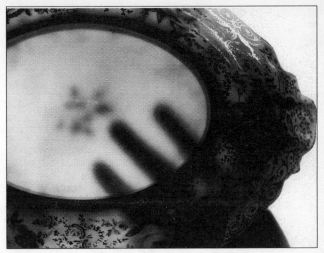

Porcelain

18th-century British porcelains are of the soft-paste type, with the exception of Plymouth and Bristol. Various other types (New Hall, Coalport, Chamberlain-Worcester, Miles Mason, etc.) of the approximate period 1780–1810 are of intermediate type, termed hybrid hard-paste porcelain.

Bone china is a type of porcelain, as is the marble-like parian body. The general term china is normally used to indicate porcelain but it is not an exact term!

In contrast, pottery and earthenwares are opaque (unless very thinly potted and fired to a vitrifying temperature). These general terms cover basic British types of ceramic body, such as creamware, pearlware, delft-type tin-glazed wares or terra-cotta. Terms such as 'Semi China', 'Opaque Porcelain' as used in several marks are fanciful marketing terms for earthenware bodies.

Ironstone wares and the related stone china or granite wares are considered to be pottery rather than porcelain although they can display some translucency.

REGISTERED DESIGNS
This otherwise unmarked plate (overleaf) can be accurately identified and dated to narrow limits by means of the diamond-shaped registration

Registered designs

device it bears. This device appears on tens of thousands of articles introduced between 1842 and 1883. In this case the plate shape with its moulded and pierced edging was registered by John Rose & Co. of the Coalport Porcelain Works, on November 30th, 1849.

The key to thousands of these British registered devices, with a brief description of the subjects, is uniquely given in this Handbook. This long listing is arranged in chronological order from p. 171, after the important introduction to that section.

SALT-GLAZED STONEWARE
British salt-glazed stoneware is one of the basic 18th-century types produced at our main ceramic centres. It is, however, not marked, although very rare examples may be inscribed and dated. Much was sold in the white as a porcelain look-alike. Other examples, as the teapot here shown, were originally decorated with low-fired gilding which has worn away in use.

Other types may be decorated with raised motifs or with incised decoration. This scratched decoration was sometimes accentuated with

Salt-glazed stoneware

pigment, usually cobalt blue. Other more costly examples were enamelled with floral, landscape or figure subjects.

All 18th-century (c.1720–70) salt-glaze is collectable and can be delightful in its simplicity. Prices vary greatly; undecorated plates are inexpensive, whilst an important enamelled example can run into thousands of pounds. This fact has led to a few white pieces being decorated at a later period!

Some clay-coloured salt-glaze stoneware was produced in later periods by firms such as Doultons and some is produced by studio potters today. These later wares can be highly interesting and of value but references to salt-glaze stoneware normally relate to 18th-century whitish-bodied articles.

The standard book is the late A. R. Mountford's *Illustrated Guide to Staffordshire Salt-glazed Stoneware* (Barrie & Jenkins, 1971).

SLIP-DECORATED WARES

Slip wares, or earthenwares decorated by trailing diluted, perhaps coloured, clay (called 'slip') form an old and traditional mode of ceramic

Slip-decorated wares

decoration. Certainly, not one confined to Great Britain.

The technique is similar to that of decorating an iced cake. The design may be broad or rudimentary but it has a spontaneous charm and simplicity. Some now rare and costly examples were especially made and bear names or dates.

17th and early 18th-century examples are highly desirable and some damage can be overlooked, for the pieces were in the main of a useful nature. Old examples will not bear an impressed mark but some rare pieces bear a slip-trailed name, such as Thomas Toft, indeed the whole class could almost be called Toft ware! A group of potters working at Wrotham in Kent often added their name or initials to the face of the pot.

General books on early British pottery will include illustrations of typical (if rather special) slip wares. It should be noted, however, that not all examples are old. Reproductions, which may be antique in their own right, occur and some modern potters still practise their traditional skills with the slip-trailer.

Specialist books on British slip-decorated earthenwares include *English Slip-Ware Dishes 1650–1850*, by R. G. Cooper (Tiranti, 1968) and *Mary Wondrausch on Slipware*, by M. Wondrausch (A. & C. Black, 1986).

STONEWARE

Stonewares comprise several types of normally salt-glazed high-fired clay-bodied useful wares, of which mugs and jugs were the most popular and successful products.

The surface colour can vary, depending on the firing or on any dip added to the surface. Traditional British stonewares were made at many centres including Nottingham and London. 18th-century examples seldom bear a maker's mark, although an inscription may indicate the locality of production.

Utilitarian stonewares depend on their appeal on the turned shape, its surface sheen or colour. Added decoration may be incised or applied in relief – a very popular form of decoration continued into the present century. Some Nottingham stoneware was attractively carved or pierced.

Apart from very important early examples, or documentary inscribed and dated pieces, most stoneware is modestly priced. Doultons in particular continued the tradition into the twentieth century. This firm did not close its Lambeth stoneware factory until 1956.

The standard specialist reference book is *English Brown Stoneware 1670–1900,* by A. Oswald, R. Hildyard & R. Hughes (Faber & Faber, 1982).

Stoneware

Terra-cotta

TERRA-COTTA

Terra-cotta is a very ancient form of pottery – basically a fired clay left in its unglazed state. In the Victorian era, however, it was perfected and used to produce in commercial quantities moulded figures or busts and a large array of jugs, pots and other ceramic objects.

Some of these were hand-fired to give a good body appearance and shapes could be turned to give a polished look. F. & R. Pratt of Fenton produced notable terra-cotta type objects usually enhanced with printed decoration. Other firms, not necessarily in Staffordshire, produced graceful terra-cotta forms but relatively few examples bear a maker's mark.

Terra-cotta is rather neglected by collectors, perhaps because of the sameness of texture and colour and consequently unmarked examples are not costly.

THE MARKS

It will be appreciated that a convenient Handbook such as this cannot include all the thousands of recorded British marks found on pottery and porcelain. The selection does, however, include the main, collectable, markings which the dealer or collector may come across. It does not include very rare or obscure marks which will be found included in the comprehensive encyclopaedias, such as my *Encyclopaedia of British Pottery and Porcelain Marks* or the specialist *Encyclopaedia of British Porcelain Manufacturers*, both published by Barrie & Jenkins.

The selected entries will, however, where appropriate give details of specialist works, give reliable dates and suggest if the products are currently desirable from the collector's viewpoint.

The arrangement is in alphabetical order of the main factory or personal name from Adams to Worcester.

WILLIAM ADAMS (& Co.) or (& SONS)

A leading manufacturer of good quality earthenwares, basalt, jasper, porcelains and ironstone-type wares. There were at different times several Adams potteries, mainly situated at Tunstall and Stoke in the Staffordshire Potteries. Production ranges from c.1769 to the present day (within the Wedgwood group). Early wares made before about 1780 are unlikely to be marked.

ADAMS Early impressed mark, c.1785–1819.

Various fancy marks occur impressed or printed from c.1800 onwards, incorporating the simple name – Adams.

W. ADAMS & SONS Various impressed or printed marks incorporating the new '& Sons' or '& S' style, sometimes using 'Stoke-upon-Trent', c.1819–64. Rare Adams parian bears this impressed name.

ADAMS
W. ADAMS Various mid-19th-century wares can bear these simple marks in various forms.

W. ADAMS & Co.   Various impressed or printed marks incorporating the new style or the initials W. A. & Co, can usually be dated c.1893–1917.

ADAMS
ESTBᴰ 1657
TUNSTALL,
ENGLAND

Standard mark found on Wedgwood-type jasper wares, c.1896+.

Standard mark on Adams stonewares and 'ivory' bodied wares, c.1890s+.

Standard printed mark widely used with slight variations from c.1914 onwards.

Early Adams earthenwares and the 19th-century porcelains are certainly rare and collectable. The later pieces are more plentiful but are always of good quality and have decorative merit.

A standard specialist book is *William Adams, an Old English Potter*, by W. Turner (Chapman & Hall, 1904). Standard works on blue-printed wares will feature this important aspect of the Adams production. The reader should note that there were several other potters of this name active in the 19th century, see G. Godden's *Encyclopaedia of British Pottery and Porcelain Marks*.

SAMUEL ALCOCK & CO.

Manufacturers of porcelain, parian and earthenware at Cobridge and Burslem, Staffordshire, c.1828–59. Much Alcock porcelain is unmarked. It is generally of good quality and of a decorative nature. As a grouping it is not rare but pieces are collectable and decorative. Prices are generally rather less than those for better-known contemporary firms such as Rockingham, Minton or Derby.

SAML. ALCOCK & CO.
COBRIDGE

Various name-marks with place-name 'Cobridge' employed during the 1828–53 period.

PUBLISHED BY
S. ALCOCK & CO.
BURSLEM

ALCOCK & CO.
HILL POTTERY
BURSLEM

Numerous name-marks with place-name 'Burslem' were employed during the 1830–59 period. Other marks incorporate, or consist of, the initials 'S. A. & Co.'

ALCOCK'S
INDIAN IRONSTONE

Impressed marks on ironstone earthenwares, recently found on the factory site; one piece is dated 1839.

For further information see 'The Samuel Alcock Porcelains', ch. 21, *Staffordshire Porcelain* (Granada, 1983).

CHARLES ALLERTON & SONS

Manufacturers of earthenwares and china, at Longton, lustre decoration a speciality, c.1859–1942. Many marks occur with the name or initials of this firm. The printed marks reproduced here cause confusion on account of the date incorporated in the marks; they were not used until the 20th century. Most marked examples are not antique. Prices and demand rests on the decorative merit of the piece.

G. L. ASHWORTH & BROS (LTD)

Manufacturers of earthenwares at Hanley, c.1861 to 1968 when retitled Mason's Ironstone China Ltd.

ASHWORTH

A. BROS

G. L. A. BROS

Many different printed marks incorporate the name 'Ashworth(s)' or the initials given. c.1861+. Ashworth possessed the original Mason Ironstone designs and moulds and produced 'Mason's Ironstone' to a considerable extent, sometimes reusing the Mason printed marks (see under Mason). The Ashworth impressed name-mark may also occur on these Mason-marked examples. Impressed year numbers can occur on Ashworth wares.

Although Ashworth wares can be decorative their Mason's-type ironstone wares are not at present as highly valued as the earlier Mason's examples. For further information, see *Godden's Guide to Mason's China and the Ironstone Wares* (1980) and *Godden's Guide to Ironstone, Stone and Granite Wares* (1999).

J. AYNSLEY & SONS

John Aynsley established a porcelain works at Longton in c.1856, trading firstly as Aynsley & Co. This prospered and in about 1879 the style was changed to Aynsley & Sons. The Aynsley porcelains are of good quality and typical of their period. They are respectable collectable wares that are not costly. The firm has traded since 1971 as Aynsley China Ltd.

AYNSLEY

Various, mainly printed, marks incorporate this trade-name. Such porcelains are usually of 20th-century date, often post-1920.

B

WILLIAM BADDELEY

EASTWOOD

Manufacturer of earthenwares, often in Wedgwood style, at Eastwood, Hanley, c.1802–22. Impressed mark, the place-name 'Eastwood'. Examples are now rarely found but are not as desirable as those of the better-known makers such as Adams, Davenport or Spode.

BAKER, BEVANS & IRWIN

Manufacturers of earthenwares at the Glamorgan Pottery, Swansea, Wales, c.1813–38. Although these Glamorgan earthenwares are of a routine type, mainly restricted to blue-printed tablewares, they are in demand by collectors of Welsh ceramics. Marked examples will command a premium over most Staffordshire examples.

BAKER BEVANS & IRWIN
SWANSEA

Standard impressed name-mark, c.1813–38.

B. B. & I.

B. B. & Co.

G. P. Co.

Several different printed marks incorporate the initials B. B. & I, B. B. & Co. or G. P. Co. (for Glamorgan Pottery Co.), c.1813–38.

As with all aspects of Welsh pottery and porcelain the standard work is still E. Morton Nance's now costly book *The Pottery & Porcelain of Swansea & Nantgarw* (B. T. Batsford, 1942). Robert Pugh's slim guide *Welsh Pottery* (Towy Publishing, 1995) is also of interest.

FRANK BEARDMORE & CO.

This firm produced a large range of useful and decorative wares at their Sutherland Pottery, Fenton, between 1903 and 1914.

F. B. & Co.

F. B. & Co.

F

Various initial marks, c.1903–14.

Standard printed mark, found with or without the trade name Sutherland Art Ware.

Victoria Bergesen's *Encyclopaedia of British Art Pottery* (Barrie & Jenkins, 1991) gives further information.

BELLEEK

This famous pottery in County Fermanagh, Northern Ireland was established c.1863 by David McBirney & Co. and has continued to the present day under various changing ownerships. Earthenwares, parian and porcelains have been produced but Belleek is best associated with delicately potted glazed parian, often in marine-based forms.

BELLEEK

BELLEEK
CO. FERMANAGH

Various impressed or printed name marks have been employed.

BELLEEK
POTTERY

An impressed or printed harp device is a rare early mark. This can be crowned or uncrowned, c.1863–90.

The wolf-hound, tower and harp printed mark is the standard basic mark. The first version, c.1863–90, is normally printed in black.

Second, black-printed version, c.1891–1926, with additional wording 'Co Fermanagh Ireland'.

The third, black-printed, version has the words 'Deanta in Eirinn' (Made in Ireland) with the registered number of the new trade-mark device, c.1926–46. The fourth mark was printed in green, not black, c.1946–55. The fifth mark has the addition of ® signifying that the mark was registered, c.1955–65. Later versions were smaller in size and 'Co Fermanagh' was deleted from the scroll leaving only the word 'Ireland', c.1965–81. The colour of the basic printed mark became gold, c.1981–92. From 1993 the earlier black mark (with ®) has been used but printed in blue.

Delicate woven baskets normally have an applied pad-mark; the country of origin IRELAND should appear on post-1890 examples.

Early Belleek and rare or imposing shapes and designs are highly collectable. There is a Belleek Collectors' Society with an international membership. Specialist reference books include *Belleek*, by Richard K. Degenhardt (revised edition, Batsford, 1994); *Belleek Porcelain & Pottery*, by G. M. Smith (Toucan Press, 1979); and *Belleek Irish Porcelain*, by M. Langham (privately published, 1992).

NB. Some American potters used the name Belleek on Irish-styled wares.

J. BESWICK (LTD)

John Beswick company was established at Gold Street, Longton in 1936, in succession to J. W. Beswick. The firm was taken over by Doulton & Co. and an extended range of porcelains have been produced.

**BESWICK
ENGLAND**

Various printed Beswick name marks have been used from 1936 onwards and an interesting range of decorative models have been produced.

The Beswick models have become very collectable and numerous price guides feature these non-antique wares. Such often non-British books include the Charlton *Standard Catalogue of Beswick Pottery*, by D. & J. Callow (Charlton Publishers, Canada, 1997).

JOHN BEVINGTON

Manufacturer of decorative (Dresden-style) porcelain at Hanley, c.1872–92.

Blue painted mark, often on floral-encrusted porcelains or figures, c.1872–92. Examples are illustrated in my *Staffordshire Porcelain*.

The Bevington porcelains can be very decorative and consequently examples can be costly. It should be noted that several other Bevington firms produced porcelains in the second half of the 19th century.

EDWARD BINGHAM

Manufacturer of pottery (in early style) at Castle Hedingham, Essex, c.1864–1901.

E.B.

Moulded relief mark on early-looking pottery (sometimes with incorrect dates). The signature mark also occurs incised, as do the initials 'E. B.'

A typical specimen with a photograph of Bingham, is included in Godden's *Illustrated Encyclopaedia of British Pottery and Porcelain*. Although these pieces look very old, their appeal is very limited and current values are rather low.

BISHOP & STONIER (LTD)

Manufacturers of porcelain and earthenwares at Hanley, c.1891–1939.

B. & S.

Several different printed marks incorporate the initials B. & S.

Printed trade marks, often with trade-name, 'BISTO', 'ENGLAND' added to these basic marks on most examples.

Other marks of this firm included the name in full, c.1891+.

The desirability of such wares depends on the decorative value of the example, with most prices of a modest nature.

BLAKENEY POTTERY LTD

This firm was founded as the Blakeney Art Pottery, in Stoke-on-Trent, in 1969. Apart from standard products and commemorative earthenwares the company produces a range of decorative articles in the style of collectable 19th-century ceramics such as ironstone or blue-printed wares. Such objects normally bear prominent but perhaps misleading old-style marks, often incorporating versions of the Royal Arms or crowned-garter devices.

Additional Blakeney wording includes: 'VICTORIA', 'VICTORIAN', 'IRONSTONE STAFFORDSHIRE' and 'ENGLAND'. The initials 'M. J. B.' or 'T. M.' can also occur with the Royal Arms or garter devices.

Blakeney pieces are decorative but not antique – although they are sometimes represented as such when sold in the smaller Antique Fairs or markets.

BOOTH(S) (LTD)

Manufacturers of earthenwares at Tunstall, c.1891–1948, producing a good range of mainly useful earthenwares using various name-marks – as the post-1900 samples shown.

'England' or 'Made in England' can appear with these and similar marks. Month and year of potting numbers can also occur impressed into the body, i.e. 7.36, for July 1936.

However, the firm also produced a range of fine quality earthenware copies of mainly 18th-century scale-blue ground Worcester porcelains. Such earthenwares usually bear this crescent-like 'CB' mark. Although such articles are earthenware copies of much earlier porcelains they are decorative and can be quite highly valued.

For further information see *The Earthenwares of Booths*, by W. M. Parkin (Keeling Collection, Matlock, 1997).

CHARLES BOURNE

Manufacturer of porcelain, Fenton, c.1817–30. These porcelains are attractive and collectable, the price range being approximately equal to the rather more plentiful Minton or Spode wares.

His good quality, well-decorated pieces often bear a painted initial mark 'CB'. On repetitive designs these initials are shown over the pattern number in fractional form.

For further information see *Staffordshire Porcelain*, Chapter 16, or the *Encyclopaedia of British Porcelain Manufacturers*.

J. BOURNE (& SON LTD)

Manufacturer of stoneware and earthenwares at Belper and Denby, Derbyshire, c.1812–present day.

Early wares are seldom marked but some mainly utilitarian stonewares bear impressed 'Belper & Denby' or 'Bournes Potteries Derbyshire' marks. Later, mainly 20th-century marks comprise or include the trade-name 'Denby'.

c.1910+

c.1930+   c.1948+

The trade name 'Danesby Ware' also occurs mainly on wares of the 1930s.

The Denby wares can be quite extensive in range, they are not confined to the well-known tablewares. Denby wares, in particular the more unusual items, are collectable but at relatively modest price levels.

For further information see *Denby Stonewares, A Collector's Guide*, by G. & A. Key (Ems & Ens, 1995); *Denby Pottery*, by I. & G. Hopwood (Richard Dennis Publications, 1997); and *Bourne at Denby*, by G. & A. Key (Ems & Ens, 1998).

BOW PORCELAIN FACTORY

This factory, also known as 'New Canton' (a name which occurs on very rare simple inkwells), was established in the 1740s and with the Chelsea and

Limehouse works ranks as one of the earliest British manufactories of porcelain. Specimens, especially the early pre-1760 articles, are rare and desirable, but many pieces do not bear a factory mark. The factory closed c.1776.

Examples of several early incised marks, c.1750–60.

NUMERALS PAINTED IN UNDERGLAZE BLUE

Specimens decorated in underglaze blue often have workmen's numbers painted on the bottom (not on the inside of the footrim as on the similar Lowestoft porcelains).

Painted anchor and dagger mark normally in red and found on post-1760 figures and groups. The marks also sometimes occur on French 'hard-paste' reproductions.

This impressed 'repairer's' mark is found on Bow (as well as other) porcelains (see 'Tebo' Toulouse).

The Bow porcelain body (like that employed at Lowestoft) contains a high proportion of bone ash. Typical specimens can be seen at the Victoria and Albert Museum and at the British Museum in London but relatively few specimens bear a factory mark. For further details and illustrations, see *Bow Porcelain* by E. Adams & D. Redstone (revised edition, Faber & Faber, 1991); *Bow Porcelain, the collection formed by Geoffrey Freeman*, by Anton Gabszewicz (Lund Humphries, 1982); and *Bow Porcelain Figures, 1748–1774*, by P. Bradshaw (Barrie & Jenkins, 1992). Good specimens of Bow porcelain are highly desirable, particularly early specimens. Condition is important.

G. F. BOWERS (& CO.)

Manufacturer of porcelain and pottery at Brownhills, Tunstall, c.1841–71.

Impressed or printed name-mark. The initials 'G. F. B.' were incorporated in other marks, c.1841–71.

For further information see my *Encyclopaedia of British Porcelain Manufacturers*. The marked Bowers porcelains are usually teawares. Although collectable they are not highly valued.

E. BRAIN & CO. LTD

Manufacturers of porcelain at Foley Works, Fenton, 1903–63.

Early printed mark, c.1903+.

Printed mark, c.1905. The word 'FOLEY' was extensively used on many different marks to 1963, with the initials 'E. B. & Co.' or the name in full. Sample later marks are given below relating to good quality porcelains. Value depends on the decorative merits of examples.

1913+ Later 'Made in England' replaces 'England'	1930+	1936+

The 'Foley' trade-name was also used by Wileman & Co. in the 1892–1925 period.

C. H. BRANNAM LTD

Manufacturers of earthenwares at Barnstaple, Devon, c.1879 to present day.

C. H. BRANNAM
BARUM

Incised signature mark in writing letters; many other impressed marks occur, incorporating the name 'BRANNAM' with the place-name 'BARNSTA-PLE' or 'BARUM', c.1879+.

These often individual pieces are decorative and collectable. For further information see *Art Potters of Barnstaple* by A. Edgeler (Nimrod Press, Alton, 1990) and the *Encyclopaedia of British Art Pottery* by Victoria Bergesen (Barrie & Jenkins, 1991).

BRETBY, see Tooth & Co.

BRISTOL

The city of Bristol was one of the earliest centres of the British ceramic industry. Tin-glazed delft-type earthenwares were produced in the first half of the 18th century, but such wares are seldom marked. Various earthenwares were also produced and porcelain as early as c.1749–51. The early porcelains are of a soaprock type porcelain. Very rare examples can be marked BRISTOL or BRISTOLL moulded in relief and are known as 'Lunds Bristol'. Marked specimens are usually decorated in underglaze blue and will be of considerable value.

For further information see my *Encyclopaedia of British Porcelain Manufacturers*, p. 495 and Dr B. Watney's *English Blue & White Porcelain of the 18th Century* (Faber & Faber, revised edition, 1973).

BRISTOL (HARD-PASTE)

This porcelain factory c.1770–81 is related to the earlier Plymouth venture where English hard-paste porcelain was introduced. The Bristol wares made under Richard Champion's management are rare and usually attractive. Not all examples are marked but the factory marks comprise:

A painted cross or letter B, often with a painter's or gilder's number added. Reproductions occur, mainly in a soft-paste body; these reproductions often have a date below the cross mark.

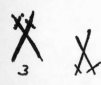

The crossed-swords mark (of the Dresden factory) occurs in underglaze blue on Bristol porcelain of the 1770–81 period, often with painters' or gilders' numerals added in overglaze enamel or in gold. NB. Not all crossed-swords marks relate to Bristol!

This impressed or moulded 'repairer's' mark also occurs on some Bristol porcelain, see under 'Tebo' Toulouse.

Bristol porcelain is highly collectable and can, rightly, be costly especially for rare forms or figures and unusual decoration. Most tablewares bear floral decoration.

For further information and illustrations, see *Bristol Porcelain*, by F. Hurlbutt (1928); *Champion's Bristol Porcelain* by F. Severne Mackenna (F. Lewis, 1947); and my *Encyclopaedia of British Porcelain Manufacturers* (1988). Good examples can be seen in the Bristol City Art Gallery and Museum, and at the Victoria & Albert Museum in London.

WILLIAM BROWNFIELD (& SONS)
Manufacturers of earthenwares and porcelain (the latter from 1871) at Cobridge, c.1850–1892.

W. B.

W. B. & S.

W. B. & Son

Various printed, impressed or moulded marks incorporating these initials were used, with '& S.' or '& Son' added from 1871. The name 'Brownfield' was also used.

The concern was continued by a form of cooperative, the Brownfield Guild Pottery Society, 1892–1900.

The standard book on these wares is *William Brownfield & Sons*, by T. H. Peake (privately published, 1995). The porcelains in particular can be of high quality and are in general undervalued.

BROWN-WESTHEAD, MOORE & CO.

Manufacturers of high-grade earthenwares and porcelain at Cauldon Place, Hanley, c.1862–1904.

Various printed marks incorporating the initials 'BWM' or 'BWM & Co.' used 1862–1904. The name of the firm in full was also used.

The products of this firm are very diverse. The better quality examples are very collectable and important pieces can, rightly, be costly. For further information and illustrations, see my *Staffordshire Porcelain* (1983).

BURGESS & LEIGH (LTD)

This Burslem partnership produced a wide range of earthenwares from c.1862 up to the present day. Ltd was added to the firm's title c.1889.

The earlier marks usually bore the name Burgess and Leigh or initial marks B & L.

Later wares from the 1930s onwards usually bear one of many marks incorporating the trade-name Burleigh Ware.

Whilst by no means all Burgess & Leigh wares can be regarded as collectable, some pieces, especially the Art Deco styled wares of the 1920s and 1930s, are in demand; see *Collecting Burleigh Jugs*, by E. Coupe (Letterbox Publishing, 1998).

BURMANTOFTS

Wilcock & Co, at Burmantofts near Leeds in Yorkshire, produced a range of Art Pottery, mainly decorated with pleasing coloured glazes, from c.1882 into the present century.

BURMANTOFTS
or
BURMANTOFTS
FAIENCE

Standard impressed mark, c.1882–1904.

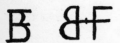

Monogram marks, often with model number added, c.1882–1904.

Burmantofts Art Pottery is collectable and the more important or unusual pieces can be costly. For further information see the *Encyclopaedia of British Art Pottery*, by Victoria Bergesen (Barrie & Jenkins, 1991).

$$C$$

CARLTON WARE

The decorative earthenwares marketed under the trade-name 'Carlton Ware' have become very collectable and popular in recent years. They originated with Messrs Wiltshaw & Robinson (Ltd) of the Carlton Works at Stoke, a partnership founded c.1890. Early printed marks are reproduced below but the now more fashionable products relate to the post-1910 period, indeed some of the later post-1930 products are now highly regarded for their period charm.

c.1890+   c.1894 onwards,   c.1906 onwards
                 variations occur

Typical marks are here reproduced.

c.1925+   c.1925–57

The old title was changed to Carlton Ware Ltd in January 1958 and this became part of the Arthur Wood & Son group in 1967. After various take-overs production ceased in 1969. Some reproductions of popular Carlton lines exist and can bear misleading marks.

A specialist book *Collecting Carlton Ware* by Francis Salman was published in 1993 (K. Francis Publishing). There is a Carlton Ware Collectors' Club, which publishes an informative magazine *The Carlton Times* (Helen & Keith Martin, PO Box 161, Sevenoaks, Kent, TN15 6GA).

CAUGHLEY

Porcelain works, situated near Broseley in Shropshire. Good porcelain in the Worcester style was made by Thomas Turner from c.1775 to 1799, when John Rose of the nearby Coalport factory took over the Caughley concern.

SALOPIAN

Impressed 'Salopian' name-mark on porcelains in upper or lower case letters, c.1775–99.

Blue painted or printed 'S' marks often with a small cross or circle after, found on underglaze-blue decorated wares, c.1775–c.1795.

Printed and painted 'C' marks relating to Caughley but this initial mark is sometimes mistaken for a Worcester crescent mark, c.1775–95.

Numerals disguised as Chinese characters occurring on blue printed porcelains were traditionally attributed to Caughley, but research shows that these are Worcester marks of the 1770–83 period.

ROYAL ARMS

A recessed but relief-moulded version of the Royal Arms is very rarely found under late Caughley jugs of the cabbage-leaf type.

The later 1795–99 wares, often decorated with simple floral motifs, do not appear to have been marked. The overglaze enamelled Caughley porcelains are likewise seldom marked.

Caughley porcelain is highly collectable and rare shapes or patterns, plus of course, inscribed and dated examples are highly regarded. Excavations on the factory site have shed much fresh light on the productions, and the reader is referred to *Caughley and Worcester Porcelains*, by G.A. Godden (revised edition, Antique Collectors' Club, 1981). Good selections of Caughley porcelain are to be seen at the Victoria & Albert Museum and at the Coalport factory which is part of the Ironbridge Gorge Museum in Shropshire.

CHAMBERLAIN (& CO.)

Manufacturers of porcelain at Worcester from c.1788 to 1852.

Chamberlain's

Chamberlain's
Worcester
Warranted

Painted name-mark in writing letters often with place-name 'Worcester' or 'Worcester Warranted' added; the pattern number was sometimes added c.1790–1810. On teapots the mark is inside the cover. Different spellings, even of 'Worcester', occur.

CROWN DEVICE

A crown and/or the word 'Royal' added to name-marks from c.1811 to c.1840.

REGENT CHINA

New 'Regent' body introduced c.1811 and description added to marks. The 'Regent' body was expensive and is rather rare.

Chamberlain's
Worcester
& 63, Piccadilly,
London.

Address of London retail shop added to name-marks from 1814 to mid 1816.

155 NEW BOND STREET

New London address added to marks from July 1816.

CHAMBERLAIN &
CO.

'& Co.' added to style and marks from c.1840; new address 'No. 1. Coventry Street London' also occurs (c.1840–5).

CHAMBERLAINS
WORCESTER

Impressed mark, c.1846–50.

Printed mark, c.1850–2. Factory continued by Kerr & Binns.

For further information and illustrations, see G. A. Godden's *Chamberlain-Worcester Porcelain 1788–1852* (Barrie & Jenkins, 1982). Good marked Chamberlain Worcester is very collectable but the value depends on the decorative merits of the piece, on its rarity and condition. Whilst single standard cups and saucers are not highly priced, a superb marked vase will be costly.

CHELSEA PORCELAIN WORKS

Produced attractive decorative figures, etc., as well as useful wares in porcelain from c.1745 to 1769, when the Chelsea-Derby period commenced. Early Chelsea porcelain is rare and desirable.

Incised (not impressed) triangle mark on early wares, which were sometimes left undecorated. The place-name 'Chelsea' and a date occur on some very rare specimens with an incised triangle mark, c.1745–50. All triangle marked examples are rare.

Very rare underglaze-blue crown and trident mark, c.1748–50.

Rare raised, moulded mark of small size, called the 'raised anchor mark', c.1749–52. Marked examples are rare and desirable. On some examples the anchor is picked out in red.

Photographic reproductions of the above four Chelsea marks are included in the *Illustrated Encyclopaedia of British Pottery and Porcelain*, Plates 115, 116, 122A and 126.

Small anchor painted in red – the 'red anchor mark' used c.1752–6. In some cases numerals occur with the anchor device, as on the example reproduced. Red anchor period Chelsea porcelain is desirable.

Small anchor painted in gold – the 'gold anchor mark' used c.1756–69. Many reproductions of gold anchor period Chelsea porcelain bear this mark, often painted larger than the original; *any anchor mark over a quarter of an inch in height should be treated with great suspicion.*

Most general reference books give at least a brief history of the factory and illustrate some specimens. Specialist books include F. S. Mackenna's *Chelsea Porcelain, the Triangle and Raised Anchor Wares* (F. Lewis, 1948), *Chelsea Porcelain, the Red Anchor Wares* (F. Lewis, 1951), *Chelsea Porcelain, the Gold Anchor Period* (F. Lewis, 1952), and *Chelsea Porcelain* by Elizabeth Adams (Barrie & Jenkins, 1987); also Arthur Lane's *English Porcelain Figures of the 18th Century* (Faber & Faber, 1961), and *English Porcelain 1745–1850* (Benn, 1965) edited by R. J. Charleston. A good selection of illustrations is included in *Godden's Illustrated Encyclopaedia of British Pottery and Porcelain*, Plates 112–46.

Genuine 18th-century Chelsea porcelain is extremely collectable and is usually costly. However, many reproductions have been produced over more than a hundred years. Gold anchor marks should be treated with extreme caution. Chelsea produced soft-paste porcelains, and examples should show some manufacturing faults. Reproductions are usually of a Continental hard-paste body. Good representative collections can be seen in most large museums, particularly in the Victoria & Albert Museum.

CHELSEA-DERBY

William Duesbury, the proprietor of the Derby porcelain factory, purchased the Chelsea works in 1769. Porcelain continued to be made or decorated at the Chelsea factory until 1784 under Duesbury's direction.

The former Chelsea gold anchor mark was continued and two new marks were introduced, incorporating the Chelsea anchor and the Derby crown or initial 'D'. These Chelsea-Derby marks are normally painted in gold. The decoration is tasteful and restrained (see Godden's *Illustrated Encyclopaedia of British Pottery and Porcelain*, Plates 147–52).

The Chelsea-Derby porcelains are always of good quality and are tastefully decorated. In general, however, they seem to be underpriced.

JAMES & RALPH CLEWS

Manufacturers of earthenwares etc. at Cobridge, c.1815–34.

CLEWS
WARRANTED
STAFFORDSHIRE

Several different impressed or printed marks were used by the Clews, each including the name. Good quality blue printed earthenware as well as 'Stone China' was made, much of it for the American market. Porcelain was made in the 1821–5 period, but this does not appear to have been marked.

Clews earthenwares are collectable, especially the rarer or more interesting blue printed designs. For further information on the problematical porcelains see the *Encyclopaedia of British Porcelain Manufacturers*.

CLARICE CLIFF

Clarice Cliff (1899–1972) was a designer rather than a manufacturer. Her jazz-age colourful designs of the 1920s and 1930s are currently very popular and collectable. Some but by no means all examples are costly.

Several different printed marks feature or include her signature, as the sample marks here reproduced.

Numerous articles and specialist books give a good account of her life and work. This handbook can only refer the reader to these sources of detailed information and importantly repeat that not all pieces bearing her signature, as part of standard factory marks, are valuable and that her work has been copied and reused, long after her death in 1972.

The specialist works include *Collecting Clarice Cliff*, by H. Watson (K. Francis, 1988); *Clarice Cliff The Bizarre Affair*, by L. Griffin & L. & S. Meisel (Thames & Hudson, 1988); *Clarice Cliff Price Guide*, by P. & H. Watson (Francis Joseph, 1995); *Rich Designs of Clarice Cliff* by R. Green & D. Jones (Rich Designs, 1995); and *Clarice Cliff and Her Contemporaries*, by Helen C. Cunningham (Schiffer Publishing, 1999).

COALPORT

The Coalport porcelain works near Ironbridge, in Shropshire, were established by John Rose and his partners in the 1790s. The very early examples are unmarked. Name-marks were rarely employed before about 1815 when the standard mix was of the hybrid hard-paste type. Bone china or the Feltspar variety can be expected from c.1820.

The above red painted name-marks are very rare.

Name-marks painted in underglaze blue can occur from c.1820 into the 1840s, mainly on floral encrusted porcelains. 'C. Dale' and the 'CD' marks relate to the place-name Coalbrookdale.

This impressed mark will be found on many examples of Coalport plates, dishes, etc., of the 1815–25 period, other numbers 1 or 6 rarely occur.

The printed Society of Arts marks reproduced below were used for a few years from June 1820. Several slight variations were used.

Several different written or printed name-marks occur in the approximate period 1830–50. The alternative place-name 'Coalbrookdake' can also occur.

Neatly painted CBD (Coalbrookdale) initial mark, c.1851–61.

So-called ampersand mark, neatly painted, c.1861–75.

Mock, popular, Continental marks can also occur on Coalport porcelains in the Sèvres or Dresden style, c.1840–70.

Printed crown marks, c.1881–1939+. 'England' added c.1891. 'Made in England' occurs from c.1920.

Printed marks of the post-war period (above). Variations occur, which give details of the pattern or style.

Revised standard mark, 1960+.

Two post-1970 Coalport China Ltd printed marks.

The Coalport company has passed through several hands from the early John Rose days. In 1926 production was moved from Coalport to the Staffordshire Potteries. Today it is part of the Wedgwood Group. Coalport porcelain is in general of good quality and can be highly decorative. Unusual, early or later signed pieces are likely to be costly but standard designs on tablewares are not necessarily expensive.

Specialist books include *Coalport & Coalbrookdale Porcelains*, by Geoffrey Godden (revised edition, Antique Collectors' Club, 1981) and *Coalport 1795–1926*, by Michael Messenger (Antique Collectors' Club, 1995). The old factory, now part of the Ironbridge Gorge Museum, includes a very good representative collection of Coalport porcelains.

SUSIE COOPER

Susie Cooper OBE (1902–95) was a talented designer who worked under her maiden name and started her ceramic career with A. E. Gray & Co. From c.1930 she traded as Susie Cooper Pottery (Ltd) at Burslem, and later as Susie Cooper China Ltd (1950+) and Susie Cooper Ltd. In 1966 she joined the Wedgwood group. Her design work, renowned for elegant forms and tasteful restrained patterns, won world-wide acclaim. Some later reproductions occur.

Various printed marks occur as the samples here reproduced.

A
SUSIE COOPER
PRODUCTION.
CROWN WORKS,
BURSLEM,
ENGLAND

Susie Cooper
CROWN WORKS
BURSLEM
ENGLAND

Whilst most standard productions are not rare or antique they are typical of their period and are collectable. Numerous articles and general books on 20th-century ceramics feature her work. In 1987 the Victoria & Albert Museum published a specialist book by Ann Eatwell, *Susie Cooper Productions*. Later works include *Susie Cooper Ceramics, a Collectors' Guide* by Andrew Casey (Jazz Publications, 1992); *Susie Cooper*, by A. Woodhouse (Trilby Books, 1992); and *Susie Cooper, an Elegant Affair*, by B.Youds (Thames & Hudson, 1996).

COPELAND & GARRETT

Manufacturers of earthenwares, parian, fine porcelain, etc., at Stoke, 1833–47, succeeding Spode (see under Spode). W. T. Copeland & Sons continued from 1847 (see next entry).

C. & G.

COPELAND & GARRETT

Several printed and impressed marks incorporate the name or initials of this partnership, c.1833–47.

Three typical marks are reproduced.

The Copeland & Garrett wares are usually of high quality and are consequently collectable although they are not as favoured as the earlier Spode pieces. A good selection of pieces are displayed at the Spode factory at Stoke. For further information see my *Encyclopaedia of British Porcelain Manufacturers* or *Staffordshire Porcelain*, Chapter 7.

W. T. COPELAND & SONS

Manufacturers of earthenwares, parian and fine porcelain at Stoke, 1847–1970, then continued under a new title 'Spode Ltd'. Successors to Copeland & Garrett (see preceding entry).

COPELAND

Standard impressed mark found on earthenware, porcelain and especially the parian figures and groups popularized by this firm, c.1847+.

Rare printed mark, c.1847–51.

Standard printed mark, c.1851–85, a fancy version of the rare earlier mark (see above).

Four standard printed marks found on earthenwares, c.1867–90; c.1875–90; c.1894–1910; c.1891 into 20th century.

Printed mark, sometimes in gold on fine porcelains, c.1891 into 20th century.

Example of several post-war printed marks which incorporate the old name 'Spode'.

Impressed month and year initials and numerals will often show the date of potting of post-1870 examples, e.g. J.01 for January 1901. The fine quality Copeland wares, the porcelains in particular, are very collectable and rightly can be costly. A good selection of examples are included in the Works Museum at Stoke. For further information see *Staffordshire Porcelain*, Chapter 8 or my *Encyclopaedia of British Porcelain Manufacturers*.

CROWN DEVON, see S. Fielding & Co. (Ltd)

CROWN STAFFORDSHIRE PORCELAIN

Manufacturers of high-grade porcelain at Fenton, c.1889–1948. In 1948 the firm was retitled Crown Staffordshire China Co. Ltd., and later became a part of the Wedgwood Group. The Crown Staffordshire name has, however, been phased out from the mid 1980s.

Three basic printed marks, c.1889+. The name 'England' often added from 1891, also date of establishment 'A.D. 1801'.

These porcelains can be of very high quality. Some charming figure models and bird groups were produced in the post-1920 period as were floral compositions. In general, I feel, the Crown Staffordshire products are not as highly regarded as they should be. For further information see my *Encyclopaedia of British Porcelain Manufacturers*.

D

HENRY & RICHARD DANIEL (DANIEL & SONS)

Manufacturers of high-grade decorative porcelain and earthenwares at Stoke and Shelton, c.1822–46.

DANIEL & SON Very rare form of mark, c.1822–6.

H. & R. DANIEL Rare form of mark, written or printed, c.1826–9.

 Rare printed mark, c.1826–9.

H. DANIEL & SONS Rare form of mark, c.1829–41.

All Daniel porcelains are of very fine quality and desirable but are seldom marked. The reader is referred to M. Berthoud's excellent book, *H. & R. Daniel 1822–1846* (Micawber, 1980) and to his *The Daniel Tableware Patterns* (Micawber, 1982) plus the 1997 *Daniel Patterns on Porcelain* (Micawber). Helpful general works illustrating typical Daniel porcelains include *Staffordshire Porcelain*, Chapter 19 and *Encyclopaedia of British Porcelain Manufacturers*.

DAVENPORT

Manufacturers (under various styles, W. Davenport & Co., etc.) of earthenwares, porcelain and glass at Longport, c.1793–1887.

Davenport

Standard early impressed marks on earthenwares. The earliest 'Davenport' mark is found in upper and lower case letters, c.1793–1820. The last two numerals of the year of manufacture were sometimes added each side of the anchor, '42' for 1842, etc. on examples of the 1840–60 period.

Standard printed mark found on 'Stone China' wares, c.1815–20.

DAVENPORT

Very many printed wares of the 1815–50 period bear different printed marks incorporating the name 'Davenport' and often the name of the pattern.

Overglaze printed mark on porcelains, c.1815–30. Basic mark used later (c.1840+) but then occurs in underglaze blue.

DAVENPORT
LONGPORT

Rare printed mark on early porcelains, prior to 1820; on some early Davenport porcelains only the name 'LONGPORT' occurs.

DAVENPORT
LONGPORT
STAFFORDSHRE

Standard printed mark, c.1870–87.

Whilst by no means all Davenport wares are of great consequence, the earlier examples and especially the quality porcelains are collectable and can be costly. Some good, typical examples are included in the City Museum, Stoke-on-Trent collection. Examples of Davenport wares are shown in Terence Lockett's and Geoffrey Godden's *Davenport China, Earthenware and Glass, 1794–1887* (Barrie & Jenkins, 1989), Godden's *Illustrated Encyclopaedia of British Pottery and Porcelain*, Plates 190, 200. See also *Staffordshire Porcelain*, Chapter 10.

WILLIAM DE MORGAN

Manufacturer of decorative earthenwares at Chelsea, Fulham, etc., c.1872–1907 (decoration continued to 1911).

W. DE MORGAN

Several different marks incorporate the name 'DE MORGAN', sometimes with addresses; 'Merton Abbey', c.1882–8; 'Sands End', c.1888+. '& Co.' added to most marks after 1888.

Merton Abbey address mark, and other marks incorporating this place-name, all relate to the period 1882–8.

Impressed or painted mark, 1882+.

Sands End address mark. Others were used, all may be dated from 1888 onwards.

Impressed initial mark, with the last two numerals of the year.

The initials of various decorators also occur, 'F. P.' for Frederick Passenger, etc.

The decorative and mainly individually painted, and often lustred, De Morgan earthenwares are very collectable. Good examples can be costly. For further information and illustrations, see *Catalogue of Works by William De Morgan* (Victoria & Albert Museum,

1921); *Victorian Pottery*, by H. Wakefield (H. Jenkins, 1962); *British Pottery*, by G. Godden (Barrie & Jenkins, 1974); and *The Designs of William De Morgan* published by Richard Dennis (1989). Victoria Bergesen's *Encyclopaedia of British Art Pottery* (Barrie & Jenkins, 1991) is also helpful and gives details of assistants with good references to magazine articles on the De Morgan wares.

DENBY, see J. Bourne (& Son Ltd)

DERBY PORCELAIN WORKS

William Duesbury commenced the manufacture of porcelain at Derby, c.1750. The original factory closed in 1848 (a small works continued in the same tradition, see King Street, Derby, in this section). A new company was formed in 1878, which now continues the tradition of Derby fine porcelain.

Duesbury Period

Extremely rare early incised marks, c.1750–5. Most products prior to about 1770 were unmarked.

PAD MARK

Three 'pad marks' or dark patches occur on the bases of Derby figures, groups or vases. These were formed by the wads of clay placed under the bases to prevent the object sticking to the base of the saggar. A photograph of a typical pad-marked base is included in Godden's *Encyclopaedia of British Pottery and Porcelain Marks*, Plate 8, and in the *Encyclopaedia of British Porcelain Manufacturers*, p. 293.

Incised initial, rarely found on flatware – plates, dishes, etc. – not to be confused with abbreviation of 'number' placed before the model number on the base of figures, etc., c.1770–80.

Rather rare painted mark, normally in blue, c.1770–82.

Standard post-1782 mark, *incised* under the bases of figures, groups, vases, etc. *Painted* neatly and of small size, in puce, blue or black, c.1782–1800. *Painted* in red, often carelessly, c.1800–25, into Bloor period.

Impressed printer's type capital letters can occur c.1782–1805 as at Pinxton.

Derby porcelains are in general of very high quality and are very collectable. Special examples can be very costly. Fakes of Duesbury period Derby porcelain exist, including figures and groups which bear copies of standard marks. There is a large selection of specialist reference books which illustrate a wide range of types. The most recent books include *Derby Porcelain, the Golden Years*, by D. G. Rice (David & Charles, 1983); *Derby Porcelain Figures 1750–1848*, by P. Bradshaw (Faber & Faber, 1990); *Derby Porcelain 1750–1798*, by G. Bradley (T. Heneage, 1990); and *Derby Modellers, 1786–1796*, by A. Ledger & C. Roth (Derby Porcelain International Society, 1995). One must not, however, forget older classics such as J. Haslem's 1876 book *The Old Derby China Factory*.

There is a flourishing Derby collectors club, 'The Derby Porcelain International Society', which publishes an interesting newsletter and other publications and organizes seminars and lectures. Most large museums display good representative collections of Derby porcelain. There is also the Derby City Museum collection and the Derby works collection.

Bloor Period

Robert Bloor managed the Derby porcelain factory in 1811 and continued until c.1848. The products made before c.1825 bore the old cross batons, 'D' and crown mark painted in red. Whilst products made in the Bloor period are not as commercially desirable as the earlier Duesbury examples, they can be of good quality and colourful.

Earliest painted or transferred (by the thumb) Bloor Derby mark, in red, c.1825–40.

Painted or printed Bloor Derby marks, c.1825–48.

King Street, Derby

After 1848 a group of six former Derby workmen opened a small factory in King Street. This contin-ued under various owners until absorbed by the Royal Crown Derby company in 1935. The King Street works is often referred to as Stevenson & Hancock Derby as the standard post-1860 marks includes the initials 'SH'. It is probable that the early King Street porcelains bore a close copy of the for-mer Duesbury Derby mark but with crossed swords replacing the old crossed batons. Other early marks include the following but these are rarely found.

1849–59   1859–62   1849–63

 Standard so-called 'Stevenson & Hancock' mark (old Derby mark with new initials 'S' and 'H' at the sides), 1862–1935. This was usually painted in red but can occur in puce, c.1915–35. Initials such as W. P. L. also occur from 1917.

The King Street Derby porcelains can be of very good quality and are certainly collectable. Recent specialist books feature these surprisingly varied pro-ductions. These include *Derby Porcelain. The Factory at*

King Street, 1849–1935, by A. Bambery & R. Blackwood (Derby Museum & Art Gallery, 1993); *In Account with Sampson Hancock, 1860s–1880s*, by J. Twitchett (D. J. C. Books, 1996). There is also a good chapter on the King Street adventure in *Royal Crown Derby*, by J. Twitchett & B. Bailey (Antique Collectors' Club, revised edition, 1988).

Royal Crown Derby

In 1876 a new company was formed with a large factory in Osmaston Road. This was initially termed the Derby Crown Porcelain Company but in 1890 Queen Victoria granted the Royal Warrant and permission to use the trade-name Royal Crown Derby.

Standard painted mark (no words), c.1876–89.

Standard printed mark, from January 1890, note wording 'Royal Crown Derby' added to former mark; the word 'England' was added to mark from 1891, and was replaced by 'Made in England' in about 1921.

Various devices were added below the last two standard marks; these show the year of decoration for any object from 1882 onwards. The key to this dating system is given in Godden's *Encyclopaedia of British Pottery and Porcelain Marks* (1964) and in the *Encyclopaedia of British Porcelain Manufacturers* (1988).

Royal Crown Derby porcelains are always of good quality and enjoy a high reputation. Important examples, especially signed examples by leading artists, can be costly but repetitive standard patterns will obviously be less desirable. Specialist books on the later Derby wares include *Royal Crown Derby*, by J. Twitchett & B. Bailey (Antique Collectors' Club, revised edition, 1988) and *A Case of Fine China*, by H. Gibson (The Royal Crown Derby Porcelain

Company, 1993). Good typical specimens of the later Derby porcelains can be seen in the City Museum and in the Derby works collection.

DOULTON & CO. (LTD)

Manufacturers of stonewares and earthenwares at Lambeth, London, c.1854–1956, and at Burslem, Staffordshire (where porcelains were also made), 1882 to present day.

DOULTON & WATTS
LAMBETH POTTERY
LONDON

Lambeth
Standard impressed mark of Doulton & Watts partnership, c.1820–54.

DOULTON LAMBETH

Standard impressed mark, c.1854+. *Ornamental* wares date from about 1870; about this period an oval impressed mark incorporating these words with the date of production added.

Impressed mark, c.1877–80.

Impressed or printed mark on *earthenware*, c.1872+.

Standard impressed mark, c.1880–1902. The word 'England' added below from 1891.

DOULTON
LAMBETH
ENGLAND

Impressed mark on small pieces, c.1891–1956.

Five marks found on special bodies from c.1881 into the 20th century.

DOULTON
& SLATER'S
PATENT

Sample *incised* decorators' marks found on Doulton stonewares. Monograms of: Arthur B. Barlow, c.1872–9; Hannah Barlow, c.1872–1906; George Tinworth, c.1867–1913. Other decorators' monograms are given in Godden's *Encyclopaedia of British Pottery and Porcelain Marks* and in D. Eyles's *Royal Doulton 1815–1965*.

Standard impressed mark, c.1902–22 and c.1927–36, also used on wares made in Burslem.

Standard impressed mark (without earlier crown), c.1922–56.

The Doulton stonewares made at the Lambeth Pottery are extremely diverse. Different types are collectable and can be costly, especially important individual specimens bearing the signature or monogram of their leading artists and modellers. However, the output was large and by no means all examples are rare or in great demand.

For further information see *Royal Doulton 1815–1965*, by D. Eyles (Hutchinson, 1965); *The Royal Doulton Lambeth Wares*, by D. Eyles (Hutchinson, 1975). There are also very specialist books and price guides, such as J. Lukins's *Doulton Lambeth Advertising Wares* (Venta Books, 1991); Victoria Bergesen's *Encyclopaedia of British Art Pottery* (Barrie & Jenkins, 1991) is also extremely informative. The reader is also referred to the Doulton Burslem section below for details of general books on Royal Doulton wares.

Burslem

In 1877 Henry Doulton purchased an interest in the Staffordshire earthenware firm of Pinder, Bourne & Co. of Nile Street, Burslem. In 1882 Doulton (of Lambeth) took over complete control and commenced to use the Doulton & Co. name. From 1882 onwards good quality earthenwares as well as superb quality porcelains have been produced by Doultons who over the years have taken over many other firms including Mintons. The present Royal Doulton companies are world leaders.

DOULTON

Standard impressed mark on earthenwares (not stonewares) made at the Nile Street, Burslem, factory, c.1882 onwards.

Standard printed or impressed marks, c.1882–1902. 'England' added from 1891.

New 'Royal Doulton' mark c.1902–32.

Revised standard mark, with 'Made in England' added c.1932 onwards.

The words 'Bone China' added on china wares. This was amended to 'English Fine Bone China' in 1959. The description 'ENGLISH TRANSLUCENT CHINA' used from 1960.

Impressed month and year numerals can occur and show the period of manufacture. Other indications of period include the addition of a number added by the standard marks, beginning with '1' in 1928. One therefore adds 27 to that number to discover the year of decoration. The additional wording 'Copyright Doulton & Co. Limited' occurs on most new designs introduced after 1960.

The Doulton Burslem wares, especially the fine porcelains, are very collectable, as are the large range of decorative figures. Numerous price guides have been published giving details on the rarity and desirability of the different models and types.

Specialist reference books include *The Doulton Burslem Wares*, by D. Eyles (Barrie & Jenkins, 1980); *Royal Doulton Figures*, by D. Eyles, R. Dennis & L.

Irvine (Royal Doulton Ltd, revised edition, 1994); *The Doulton Figure Collectors Handbook*, by K. Pearson (K. Francis Publishing, 1986 and later editions); *The Lyle Price Guide to Doulton* (Lyle Publications, 1986 and later editions); *Phillips Collectors Guide to Royal Doulton*, by C. Braithwaite (Boxtree Ltd, 1989); *Doulton for the Collector*, by J. Lukins (Venta Books, 1994); and *Legacy of Sir Henry Doulton: 120 Years of Royal Doulton in Burslem, 1877–1997*, by K. Niblett (Stoke-on-Trent Museum, 1997). There is also a very active Royal Doulton International Collectors' Club which issues an informative magazine and specialist publications. Details of the club from Royal Doulton (UK) Ltd, Minton House, Stoke-on-Trent, Staffordshire.

CHRISTOPHER DRESSER

Dr Christopher Dresser (1834–1904) was an important late Victorian designer. He produced novel ceramic forms for several pottery firms. His reproduced signature, usually impressed or moulded, adds considerably to the interest and value of even massproduced articles.

Victoria Bergesen's *Encyclopaedia of British Art Pottery* (Barrie & Jenkins, 1991) gives basic information and details the many published references to his work.

DUDSON

Various members of the Dudson family potted at Hanley from the 18th century onwards. Marked examples are, however, normally of a post-1850 date. The best known or traditional Dudson wares comprise various coloured fine stoneware type bodies decorated with sprigged relief motifs in the

Wedgwood style. These can be very attractive. Standard impressed marks incorporate the name 'Dudson' with or without 'Hanley'. However, many examples were not marked.

<table>
<tr><td>DUDSON</td><td>c.1850–91</td></tr>
<tr><td>DUDSON
ENGLAND</td><td>c.1891+</td></tr>
<tr><td>DUDSON BROTHERS
ENGLAND</td><td>c.1900+</td></tr>
</table>

Later marks include:

c.1936–45

c.1945+

The Victorian Dudson wares are decorative and collectable but not unduly costly.

The standard reference book is *Dudson. A Family of Potters since 1800*, by Audrey M. Dudson (Dudson Publications, 1985). Typical Wedgwood-type wares are also featured in *British Pottery. An Illustrated Guide*, by G. Godden (Barrie & Jenkins, 1974), Plate 244. The present title is Dudson Brothers Ltd, specialists in durable Hotel wares.

F

FALCON WARE

Like several trade-names 'Falcon' has been used by more than one firm. In this case we have J. H. Weatherby & Sons Ltd of the Falcon Pottery, Hanley (c.1891–present day) and Thomas Laurence Ltd, of the Falcon Pottery at Longton (c.1897–1962) which was continued by Shaw & Copestake (q.v.). The Falcon trade-name, however, probably dates from the 1920s. In 1990 a further complication arose when Ivan Dean established his Falcon China Ltd, at Longton.

In recent years the post-1920s Falcon wares have become collectable. The standard book covering all three above mentioned firms is *The Falcon Ware Story*, by Susan J. Verbeek (Pottery Publications, 1997).

S. FIELDING & CO. (LTD)

Manufacturers of earthenware at Stoke, c.1879–1982. The trade-name 'Crown Devon' was introduced early in the 20th century, in succession to decorative lines termed 'Royal Windsor', 'Crown Chelsea' or 'Louis Ware'. It was initially associated with a decorative range of vellum-coloured fine quality earthenwares very much in the style of the popular Royal Worcester floral decorated wares.

 Post-1891 printed mark, two of several, incorporating initials 'S. F. & Co.' The name 'Fielding' also occurs. Impressed month and year numerals can also occur.

 Early printed 'Crown Devon' mark, c.1905–13.

Standard printed marks, c.1913–30.

Standard printed mark, c.1930–9 and 1945–50s.

The following two marks relate (with variations) to the 1950s up to the closure in 1982.

The second mark can occur with added wording 'Potters for over 200 years'. The impressed name 'FIELDING' also often occurs sometimes with date markings, the last two numerals indicating the year.

The 'Crown Devon' earthenwares have become collectable in recent years but only at a modest price range. The range of products made between about 1900 and 1982 was huge. For further information the reader is referred to *Crown Devon. History of S. Fielding & Co.*, by S. Hall (Jazz Publications, 1993) and to Ray Barker's *The Crown Devon Collectors Handbook* (Francis Joseph, 1997).

G

W. H. GOSS (LTD)
(GOSS CHINA CO. LTD)
Manufacturers of porcelain, parian and earthenwares at Falcon Pottery, Stoke, c.1858–1939.

W. H. GOSS

Early impressed or printed marks incorporate the name or the initials 'W. H. G.', c.1858+.

W.H.COSS.

Printed crest mark, with several slight variations, c.1862–1939.

Whilst the typical mass-produced Goss armorial trinkets featuring the arms or crest of various towns are collectable, the average price is not high. Various special books and price guides have been published. The more modern works include *William Henry Goss,* by L. & N. Pine (Milestone, 1986); *Price Guide to Arms & Decoration of Goss China*, by N. Pine (Milestone, 1990); *The Concise Encyclopaedia & Price Guide to Goss China*, by N. Pine (Milestone, 1992), with later revised editions or updates. A large selection of pieces can be seen at Nicholas Pine's private museum at Horndean, Hampshire. There are also Goss Collectors' Clubs. Doulton now own the Goss trade-name and some of the original pattern books. They have issued modern articles under the Goss name. Some early or special Goss wares and parian wares can be very desirable but by no means all specimens.

GRAINGER-WORCESTER
Factory worked by Grainger, Wood & Co. (c.1801–12), by Grainger, Lee & Co. (c.1812–39) and by George Grainger (& Co.) (c.1839–1902) when the firm was taken over by the Royal Worcester Porcelain Co. Fine porcelains were produced. The name marks of the Grainger-Wood partnership are very rare.

GRAINGER LEE & CO. Printed or painted name-marks in various forms, c.1812–39.

G. GRAINGER Printed or painted name-marks in various forms, c.1839+.

G. GRAINGER & CO. Printed or painted name-marks with '& Co.' added usually found after c.1850.

G. G. W.
G. G. Initial marks in various forms, c.1839+.

  Printed or impressed mark, c.1870–89.

  Printed mark, c.1889–1902. 'England' added from 1891.

From 1891 to 1902 year letters A to L were added under the later shield marks, to indicate the year of production.

The Grainger-Worcester porcelains are of very good quality and the more important specimens are very collectable and may be costly. Typical specimens are on display in the Worcester works collection. The reader is also referred to the specialist work *Grainger's Worcester Porcelain* by Henry & John Sandon (Barrie & Jenkins, 1989). This work includes details of the factory shape and pattern books.

A. E. GRAY & CO. LTD

Albert Edward Gray (1871–1959) established the Globe Pottery in Hanley in 1912. The company was mainly devoted to decorating and employed especially in the 1920s and 1930s a talented team of designers and decorators. The company moved to Stoke in about 1936 and continued to 1961. It was then acquired by Portmeirion Potteries Ltd.

The following printed marks were used.

c.1912–31

c.1931–4

c.1934–61

The Gray wares, both earthenware and porcelains, are typical of their period, they can be very smart and are probably undervalued today. In 1982 the Stoke City Museum mounted a splendid exhibition of Gray's Pottery and issued a helpful exhibition catalogue *Hand-Painted Gray's Pottery*. A revised booklet by P. Niblett was published in 1987. The City (now Potteries) Museum has a good collection of Gray's wares.

H

JAMES HADLEY & SONS (LTD)

Manufacturers of earthenware and porcelain at Worcester, c.1896–1905. James Hadley was formerly modeller to the Royal Worcester Porcelain Company; his signature may be found on some of their finest figures, groups, vases, etc., c.1875–94.

The figures, groups and ornaments modelled by James Hadley for the Royal Worcester Company are of fine quality and are usually very desirable and costly. For this aspect of Hadley's work the reader should consult Henry Sandon's standard work *Royal Worcester Porcelain, from 1862 to the Present Day* (Barrie & Jenkins, 1973 and revisions).

   Printed or impressed mark, 1896–7.

   Printed mark, with variations, c.1897–1902.

   Printed mark, 1902–5.

Early in July 1905 Hadley's private company was taken over and amalgamated with the Royal Worcester Company. Many old Hadley forms were continued and these usually include the name 'Hadley' or 'Hadley Ware'.

The Hadley wares of the 1896–1905 period are interesting and are of good quality. They seem rather neglected by most collectors of Worcester porcelains and consequently prices are in the medium range. Good specimens can be seen in the Worcester Works Museum. The reader is also referred to my *Illustrated Encyclopaedia of British Pottery and Porcelain* (Barrie & Jenkins, 1966) and to the *Encyclopaedia of British Porcelain Manufacturers* (Barrie & Jenkins, 1988).

HERCULANEUM POTTERY

This Liverpool pottery, worked by various owners, produced high-grade earthenware and porcelain, c.1793–1841.

HERCULANEUM

Early impressed name-mark usually found on earthenwares and stonewares, very rarely found on porcelain, c.1793–1820.

Two printed or impressed marks, c.1796–1822.

Printed mark, with Liver-bird device, occurs on porcelains, c.1805–20.

L

A large impressed 'L' can occur on Herculaneum porcelains, c.1805–20.

**HERCULANEUM
LIVERPOOL**

Full name-mark normally impressed, c.1822–33.

The rare and usually unmarked Herculaneum porcelains of the approximate period 1800–20 are very desirable. Unusual specimens will be costly. For further information see my *Encyclopaedia of British Porcelain Manufacturers* (Barrie & Jenkins, 1988). Representative examples of the pottery's varied productions – earthenwares, stonewares and porcelains – are on view in the City Museum & Art Gallery.

ROBERT HERON (& SON)
Manufacturer of earthenwares. Took over the Fife Pottery, Sinclairtown, Scotland, by September 1837.

R. H. F. P.

Printed mark occurs incorporating these initials, c.1837–60.

R. H. & S.

**ROBERT HERON &
SON**

Printed marks incorporating these initials or the name in full occur c.1850–1929.

WEMYSS

Trade name 'Wemyss' or 'Wemyss Ware' on decorative, freely-decorated earthenwares, c.1880 into the 20th century.

Printed mark, c.1920–9. The decorative 'Wemyss' wares often also bear the mark of Goode's, the London retailers.

Whilst the standard Heron earthenwares are not distinguished, the boldly-painted Wemyss wares bearing this trade-name are collectable and can be costly. Specialist books illustrate and discuss these usually

20th-century wares, see *Wemyss Ware 1880–1930*, by R. de Rin (Sotheby's, 1978) or *Wemyss Ware*, by V. de Rin (Scottish Academic Press, 1986). Victoria Bergesen's *Encyclopaedia of British Art Pottery* (Barrie & Jenkins, 1991) also has a helpful entry under 'Fife Pottery'. The reader is warned that later Wemyss-styled wares have been produced and these can bear the Wemyss name.

HICKS & MEIGH (HICKS, MEIGH & JOHNSON)

Manufacturers of earthenwares, 'Stone China', etc., at Shelton in the Staffordshire Potteries, c.1804–22. Subsequently Hicks, Meigh & Johnson, c.1822–35.

Sample printed Royal Arms marks found on fine-quality Hicks & Meigh's 'Stone China', c.1804–22. The pattern number under the basic mark varies.

H. M. J.

H. M. & J.

H. M. & I.

Rare Hicks, Meigh & Johnson marks, 1822–35.

Although these two partnerships are mainly known for their high-quality and colourful 'Stone China' wares, good earthenwares and mainly unmarked porcelains were also produced. These are all collectable and can be costly depending on their decorative merits. For further information see *Staffordshire Porcelain* (1983), Chapter 17; *Encyclopaedia of British Porcelain Manufacturers* (1988); and specialist books on ironstone-type wares.

J

GEORGE JONES (& SONS LTD)

Manufacturers of decorative earthenwares and majolica-style wares at Stoke, c.1861–1951. Porcelain produced from 1872.

Distinguishing monogram found on several relief, impressed or printed marks, c.1861 to late 1873 when '& Sons' was added to marks.

Printed or impressed mark, c.1874–1924. 'England' was added from 1891. 'Crescent China' may occur under mark from c.1893.

Printed or impressed mark, c.1924–51.

George Jones products are usually of good quality and are decorative. Examples are collectable, especially the finer majolica-type colour-glazed earthenwares. Such wares are featured in books on majolica (see Pictorial Glossary). George Jones also produced decorative essays in the Pâte-sur-Pâte technique. The reader is also referred to Godden's *Illustrated Encyclopaedia of British Pottery and Porcelain* or *Staffordshire Porcelain* (1983). The specialist book is *George Jones Ceramics*, by Robert Cluett (Schiffer Publishing, USA, 1998).

L

BERNARD LEACH

The Leach Pottery was established by Bernard
Leach, CBE (1887–1979), at St Ives, Cornwall, in
1921. At this famous pottery a number of talented
studio potters have been trained and have helped to
extend the Leach Pottery tradition for fine crafts-
manship and good design.

 Basic Leach Pottery squared, or circular, impressed
seal, c.1921+. The monogram or sign of individual
potters often occurs with this mark. This is the standard St Ives seal-mark, not that of individual potters.
It occurs on standard tablewares as well as on individual pieces.

Individual painted or incised initial marks used by
Bernard Leach, c.1921–79.

Genuine individual pots by Bernard Leach are very
sought after and will be costly. Hence some copies
have been produced, mainly after the master's death
in 1979.

All books on Studio Pottery will feature Leach's
work and that of his talented team of potters who
worked at the Leach Pottery from time to time. The
reader is referred also to the *Encyclopaedia of British
Porcelain Manufacturers* and to the host of specialist
books which include *The Art of Bernard Leach*, by C.
Hogben (Faber & Faber, 1978); *Bernard Leach.*

Beyond East & West, by B. Leach (Faber & Faber, 1978); *B. Leach, Hamada & Their Circle*, by T. Birks & C. W. Digby (Phaidon/Christie's, 1990); and *The Leach Legacy. St Ives Pottery and its Legacy*, by M. Whybrow (Sansom & Co., 1996).

LEEDS POTTERY

This famous Yorkshire pottery produced a wide range of earthenwares, creamware, basalt, etc., under various proprietorships from c.1758 to c.1878. The early pre–c.1775 wares appear to have been unmarked.

LEEDS POTTERY — Standard impressed mark in upper or lower case letters, c.1775–1800+: this style of mark is sometimes stamped twice, one at right angles to the other. It should be noted that this mark is quite rare on genuine pieces but it appears on a host of later pieces made in the old style.

Readers should consult standard specialist reference books such as *Creamware*, by D. Towner (Faber & Faber, 1978); *The Leeds Pottery*, by D. Towner (Cory, Adams & Mackay, 1963); and the Northern Ceramic Society's 1986 exhibition catalogue *Creamware and Pearlware* (City Museum, Stoke-on-Trent), or buy from knowledgeable sources! The Leeds Pottery is mainly known for its often pierced creamware but various other types of ceramic were produced, see G. Godden's *An Illustrated Encyclopaedia of British Pottery and Porcelain* (1966); typical 20th-century reproductions are shown on Plates 346–8. Genuine, preferably marked, Leeds pottery is very collectable but need not be that costly – especially for standard specimens such as creamware plates. The reader should be aware that a current firm the 'Leedsware Pottery Co. Ltd', of Burslem, produces a wide range of old-style Leeds-type creamware. Such decorative, but non-antique, items are widely available.

WILLIAM LITTLER

William Littler potted at Longton Hall in the Staffordshire Potteries in the 1749–60 period. He subsequently moved to West Pans, near Musselburgh, in Scotland and produced similar types of porcelain, within the approximate period 1764–77, before moving back to Staffordshire.

The often hastily painted blue so-called 'crossed Ls' mark, versions of which are here shown, was formerly believed to relate to Littler's Longton Hall period. Present thinking is that this mark was used at West Pans (c.1764–77), not at Longton Hall.

Littler's porcelains, especially the earlier Longton Hall pieces, are very collectable and can be costly. However, no true Longton Hall mark was used. The reader is referred to G. Godden's *Encyclopaedia of British Porcelain Manufacturers* (1988) and to *Digging for Early Porcelain*, edited by D. Barker and S. Cole (City Museum, Stoke-on-Trent, 1998).

LIVERPOOL

This was one of the centres of the pottery trade in the 18th and early part of the 19th centuries. Tin-glazed delft-type pottery as well as cream-coloured earthenwares and porcelain were produced by several manufacturers but, as a general rule, the Liverpool wares are unmarked.

J. Sadler

Sadler
Liverpool

John Sadler and the firm of Sadler & Green printed earthenwares and porcelain made by other manufacturers from c.1756, and signatures occur on some of these printed motifs.

The early Liverpool pieces are very collectable, at least to specialist collectors, and unusual examples are in demand. As several potters were involved and as the wares were in general unmarked, I can in this Handbook only refer the reader to the now rather outdated *The Illustrated Guide to Liverpool Herculaneum Pottery*, by A. Smith (Barrie & Jenkins, 1970), which contains some information on 18th-century specimens, and Dr Bernard Watney's more recent specialist book *Liverpool Porcelain of the Eighteenth Century* (Richard Dennis, 1997).

LOCKE & CO. (LTD)
Manufacturers of porcelain at Worcester, c.1896–1915.

Early examples of the approximate period 1896–8 may bear written or impressed name marks, such as: Locke & Co. Worcester.

Standard printed mark, c.1896–98. 'Ltd' added below 'Locke & Co.', c.1898–1902.

Standard printed mark, 1902–15.

Whilst Locke-Worcester porcelains are interesting and collectable the general price range is not as high as for Royal Worcester, or for George Grainger pieces. The works were, however, on a small scale and examples are by no means common. Some better than average examples are shown in my 1966 book

An Illustrated Encyclopaedia of British Pottery and Porcelain, Plates 355–6. An interesting booklet by L. H. Harris and T. Willis was issued by the Dyson Perrins Museum at Worcester in connection with an 1989 exhibition of Locke's porcelains.

LOWESTOFT PORCELAIN FACTORY

Charming porcelains painted in underglaze blue were made at this small factory at Lowestoft, Suffolk, c.1757–99. Overglaze enamel colours were used from c.1770 but the blue and white specimens outnumber the coloured pieces. The body is soft paste containing bone ash and similar to that used at the Bow factory. Most products are of a useful nature, tewares, etc., rather than ornamental.

Whilst most Lowestoft is unmarked some underglaze blue examples made before about 1775 can bear a painter's number, usually placed on the inside of a footrim, rather than in the middle of the base. Of these numbers 3 and 5 are the most common. Being individually painted they can vary in their rendering but typical examples are shown.

A copy of the Worcester crescent mark can occur on Lowestoft porcelains decorated in the Worcester style. The crescent may be open (no cross-hatching or shading) or shaded (on printed designs). Copies of the Dresden crossed swords mark can also occur on German-styled designs.

A TRIFLE FROM LOWESTOFT

The inscription 'A Trifle from Lowestoft' can occur on some later pieces – mugs, etc. The Trifles are normally decorated with simple enamelled designs. Many (now old) reproductions of these Trifle inscribed pieces were later made on the Continent. They therefore tend to be of hard-paste porcelain.

Lowestoft porcelains are very collectable. Specimens (other than the more ordinary items) tend to be costly, the inscribed and dated pieces, extremely so!

As the majority of genuine Lowestoft soft-paste porcelain is unmarked, the reader needs to consult specialist well-illustrated reference books. These include *Lowestoft Porcelain in Norwich Castle Museum*, by S. Smith (2 vols, Norwich Museum Service, 1975 & 1985); *Early Lowestoft*, by C. Spencer (Ainsworth & Nelson, 1981); *Lowestoft Porcelains*, by G. Godden (Antique Collectors' Club, 1985); and *Variety in Lowestoft Porcelain*, by M. Corson (Lilac, 1992). In addition various learned papers have been published on different aspects of Lowestoft porcelain, see my *Encyclopaedia of British Porcelain Manufacturers* (1988).

M

JAMES MACINTYRE & CO.

Manufacturers of earthenware at Burslem, c.1860–1928+.

MACINTYRE

Several early impressed or printed marks occur incorporating the name with or without the initial 'J'. '& Co.' was added to name-marks from 1867.

Post-1894 printed mark with word 'Limited' or 'Ltd' added. Since 1928 only electrical wares have been produced.

An 1888 advertisement showing typical wares is reproduced in the *Illustrated Encyclopaedia of British Pottery and Porcelain*, Plate 365. See also Victoria Bergesen's *Encyclopaedia of British Art Pottery* (Barrie & Jenkins, 1991) and books on Moorcroft, see below.

Although the standard Macintyre wares are of good quality and are of interest, the main importance to collectors is that William Moorcroft designed and carried out work for this company before setting up his own factory. Pieces bearing a Macintyre mark or name along with a Moorcroft signature are very desirable.

C. T. MALING & SONS (LTD)

Maling, Newcastle-upon-Tyne earthenwares can date back to the early part of the 19th century but much later specimens have become collectable within recent years, although at modest prices. I reproduce here some of the standard marks, although some patterns or types have their own marks all incorporating the name 'Maling'. Production ceased in 1963.

REG? TRADE MARK

| c.1875–1908 | c.1908–24 | c.1924+ |

With recent interest in these Newcastle earthenwares much research has been carried out and the reader is referred to specialist paperback books, such as *Maling. A Tyneside Pottery*, published without credit to an author by Tyne & Wear Museums (1981); *Maling and other Tyneside Pottery*, by R. C. Bell (Shire Publications, 1986); and *Maling. The Trade Mark of Excellence*, by S. Moore & C. Ross (Tyne & Wear Museums, revised 1992 edition).

MARTIN BROTHERS
The first of the British 'Studio Potters' working together making individually designed stonewares at Fulham and Southall, London, c.1873–1914.

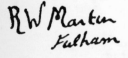

Incised or stamped signature mark with address 'FULHAM', 1873–4.

R. W. MARTIN
LONDON

Incised mark with address 'LONDON', c.1874–8.

SOUTHALL

Various incised or stamped signature marks with address 'SOUTHALL', c.1878–9.

**LONDON &
SOUTHALL**

Signature marks with double address 'LONDON &
SOUTHALL' date from 1879.

**BROS
BROTHERS**

From 1882 'BROS' or 'BROTHERS' added to standard signature 'R. W. MARTIN'.

Most Martin Brothers stoneware bears the incised
date near the signature mark.

Individual 'Martinware' stonewares are very collectable and good specimens will be costly, especially
the famous bird-like pots with loose covers.
However, some fakes occur with mock Martin
Brothers marks. Various books include illustrations of
the brothers at work and their typical pots. See my
Illustrated Encyclopaedia of British Pottery and Porcelain,
Plates 374–8 and more modern specialist works such
as *The Martin Brothers Potters*, by M. Haslam (R.
Dennis, 1978) and Richard Dennis's 1978 exhibition
catalogue. Victoria Bergesen's extremely helpful
Encyclopaedia of British Art Pottery (Barrie and
Jenkins, 1991) is also of value, giving many refer-
ences to articles and papers on the work of the
Martin Brothers.

MASON
A family of potters trading under various styles (see
below) at Lane Delph and Fenton from c.1800 to
c.1854. Charles James Mason patented the famous
'PATENT IRONSTONE CHINA' in 1813.

M. MASON

Standard impressed mark on porcelain made by
Miles Mason, c.1800–13. Specimens are rather rare
and collectable and important pieces can be costly.

MILES

MASON

Printed mark on blue printed porcelain of willow-
pattern type, c.1805–13.

PATENT IRONSTONE CHINA	Impressed mark in various forms with or without the name 'MASON'S', c.1813+.

Standard printed mark on Mason Ironstone wares from c.1815. Very many variations of this mark occur and some have been used by Mason's Ironstone China Ltd, the present owners of many of the original Mason models and patterns.

G. & C. J. M.

Several printed marks were used in the 1813–29 period incorporating the initials 'G. & C. J. Mason'.

C. J. MASON & CO.
C. J. M. & Co.

Many marks were used in the 1829–45 period, incorporating the new style 'C. J. Mason & Co.' or the initials 'C. J. M. & Co'. From 1845 to 1848 and from c.1851 to 1854 Charles Mason traded on his own (without the '& Co.'): the former standard printed 'Mason's Patent Ironstone China' mark was much used.

The Mason patterns, moulds, etc., passed through several firms to G. L. Ashworth & Bros in 1861 and this firm was retitled Mason's Ironstone China Ltd in 1968. It is now part of the Wedgwood group and production continues of traditional old Mason shapes and patterns. Modern versions of the old Mason's Patent Ironstone mark will include 'England' or 'Made in England'. Also a © or ® and probably modern wording relating to the name of the pattern. None of these features occurs on pre-Ashworth products made before the 1850s.

Miles Mason wares and the earlier ironstone wares are highly collectable, especially rare shapes or important specimens.

Several specialist books give good details of the varied Mason products, including *Mason Porcelain & Ironstone 1796–1853*, by R. Haggar & E. Adams

(Faber & Faber, 1977); *Godden's Guide to Mason's China and the Ironstone Wares* (Antique Collectors' Club, 1980); *Mason, a Family of Potters*, by D. Skinner (City Museum & Art Gallery, Stoke-on-Trent, 1982); *Miles Mason Porcelain, a Guide to Patterns and Shapes*, by D. Skinner & V. Young (City Museum & Art Gallery, Stoke-on-Trent, 1992); *Mason's. The First Two Hundred Years*, by G. B. Roberts (Merrell Holperton, 1996); *The Raven Mason Collection at Keele University*, edited by G. B. Roberts and J. Twitchett (Keele University Press, 1997); and *Godden's Guide to Ironstone, Stone and Granite Wares* (Antique Collectors' Club, 1999). Collections of typical Mason wares can be seen at The Potteries Museum in Hanley and at the University of Keele (by prior arrangement). Specialist dealers also stock and exhibit a good range of Mason wares.

JOHN MEIR & SON
Manufacturers of earthenwares at Tunstall, c.1837–97. Formerly John Meir (c.1812–36). The Meir earthenwares are typical of the middle range of Staffordshire earthenwares. They may be decorative but they are not especially valued. Many were exported.

J. MEIR & SON

J. M. & SON

J. M. & S.

Several different impressed or printed marks occur consisting of, or incorporating, these names or initials, c.1837–97. The initial 'I' sometimes replaces the 'J'. A typical printed mark is also reproduced.

W. R. MIDWINTER (LTD)

Although the Midwinter pottery was established at Burslem in 1910, it is the later, post-war, modern-style wares that are most collectable. Various printed marks have been used, all featuring the Midwinter surname. The marks here reproduced are merely samples, as different patterns or forms, such as 'Stylecraft', will have their own individual marks. These can include month and year markings as '5. 62' for May 1962. Since 1970 W. R. Midwinter Ltd has been part of the Wedgwood group, although the Midwinter Pottery was closed in 1987.

c.1930–41

c.1953+

c.1950–87

Whilst Midwinter wares have become popular and collectable, standard patterns will not command high prices. Recent specialist books contain a wealth of information on the contemporary and standard Midwinter forms, patterns and designers. These works include *Midwinter. A Collectors' Guide*, by A. Peat (Cameron & Hollis, 1992) and *Midwinter Pottery. A Revolution in British Tableware*, by S. Jenkins (R. Dennis, 1997).

MINTON

Important manufacturer of porcelain and various types of earthenware at Stoke-on-Trent, under several different partnerships, as listed, 1793 to present day as part of the Doulton Group.

The early earthenwares and pre-1805 porcelains were apparently unmarked. The porcelains may bear pattern numbers that can in some cases be checked with the surviving pattern books.

Painted mark on porcelain, normally in overglaze blue enamel, found with or without pattern number, c.1805–16, mark rather rare.

There was a gap in the production of porcelain between c.1816 and 1824.

Minton porcelains and earthenwares of the approximate period 1824–40 are largely unmarked.

The Dresden crossed-swords mark occurs in underglaze blue on a class of floral-encrusted Minton porcelain of the 1820s. This mock Dresden device can, however, appear on many other types of ceramics.

Several different printed marks of the 1820s and 1830s incorporate the initial 'M'.

Many printed marks of the MINTON & BOYLE period (c.1836–41) incorporate the initials 'M. & B.'

Many different marks of the 1841–73 period incorporate or comprise the initials 'M. & Co.', for MINTON & CO.

M. & H.

Many different printed marks of the MINTON & HOLLINS period (c.1845–68) incorporate the initials 'M. & H.'

B. B.
NEW STONE

Impressed mark on earthenwares, c.1830–60.

Incised mark found on Minton parian figures and groups, c.1845–60.

Painted or printed ermine device found on fine Minton porcelains, c.1850–70. A similar incised mark occurs on parian and other figures from about 1845.

MINTON

MINTONS

The name 'Minton' occurs incorporated in many printed marks from 1851 onwards. The basic impressed mark from 1862 to 1872 was the word 'MINTON', and 'S' was added from 1873 so that the post-1873 basic mark was 'MINTONS'.

Standard printed mark, c.1863–72.

Revised basic printed mark with crown above, c.1873–1912. The word 'England' added from 1891.

Basic printed mark, c.1912–50, often with 'Made in England' added below.

New printed trade-mark introduced in 1951. The words 'Bone China. Made in England', may occur under this mark.

MINTON CHINA Impressed mark on porcelain blanks from c.1951 onwards.

ROYAL DOULTON Since 1968 newly engraved marks usually incorporate the Doulton name with the date of introduction of that pattern and the © copyright device.

Minton porcelains are always of high quality. They are very collectable but values depend on many features, age, rarity, condition, type of body, quality of decoration, etc.

Various specialist books and the better general works illustrate a good range of the very varied Minton products. These include my *Minton Pottery and Porcelain of the First Period 1793–1850* (Barrie & Jenkins, 1978); *The Dictionary of Minton*, by P. Atterbury & M. Batkin (Antique Collectors' Club, 1990); *Minton The First Two Hundred Years of Design and Production,* by Joan Jones (Swan Hill Press, 1993);*Regency Minton Porcelain*, by D. Langford (Canterbury Ceramic Circle, 1997); and *Minton Patterns of the First Period c.1796 to 1816* by R. Cumming & M. Berthoud (Micawber, 1997). More specialist publications are cited in my *Encyclopaedia of British Porcelain Manufacturers* (Barrie & Jenkins, 1988). Other aspects of Minton's wares are represented in books on Majolica and on Pâte-sur-Pâte decoration – see the Pictorial Glossary.

TABLE OF YEAR CYPHERS FOUND IMPRESSED IN THE BODY OF MINTON WARES, SHOWING THE DATE OF PRODUCTION

MINTON'S ART POTTERY STUDIO

This short-lived venture was established by Mintons of Stoke, at Kensington Gore in London, near the Royal Albert Hall, c.1871–5. It aroused great interest at the time as 'educated women, of good social position, were employed (with some male artists) to decorate blanks sent down from Stoke. The experiment was initially under the direction of the well-known artist, designer, and illustrator W. S. Coleman.

This special printed mark was added to the impressed-marked Minton pottery blanks, c.1871–5.

These 'Art Pottery' Minton wares are interesting and collectable. Good, decorative, examples are in demand and may be costly – in Art Pottery terms. An outline of the enterprise was given in my pioneer book *Victorian Porcelain* (1961) but Victoria Bergesen's *Encyclopaedia of British Art Pottery* (Barrie & Jenkins, 1991) gives an excellent and full account with details of the many artists employed by Mintons at their London Art Pottery Studio.

W. MOORCROFT (LTD)

Manufacturers of earthenwares, normally decorated with bold floral designs, at Burslem (Cobridge), c.1913 to present day. Various changes of ownership and title (now Moorcroft Plc) have occurred in post-war years.

William Moorcroft (1872–1945) had earlier designed for and worked for James Macintyre (q.v.). These pre-1913 pieces can also bear his signature mark.

**MOORCROFT
BURSLEM**

Standard impressed mark, c.1915+. Modern wares can have the wording 'Made in England' added.

Signature marks also occur. The initials 'W. M.' occur on some examples. Walter Moorcroft succeeded his father William in 1945. The J. Moorcroft signature dates from c.1990.

Moorcroft wares, particularly the earlier examples, have become very collectable and rare or important specimens can be very costly. Various specialist books have been published including *Moorcroft Pottery*, by P. Atterbury (R. Dennis, 1979); *Moorcroft. A Guide to Moorcroft Pottery 1897–1990*, by P. Atterbury (R. Dennis, revised edition, 1993); *Collecting Moorcroft*, by F. Salmon (K. Francis, 1994); and *Moorcroft, The Phoenix Years*, by F. Street (W. M. Publications, 1997).

MOORE BROS

Manufacturers of decorative porcelains at Longton, c.1870–1905. The firm was continued by Bernard Moore, c.1905–15. In this later period good glaze-effects were produced.

MOORE

MOORE BROS

Standard impressed marks, c.1870–1905. The word 'England' also occurs from 1891.

Standard printed mark, c.1880–1902. With 'England' from 1891.

Rather rare printed mark, c.1902–5.

Painted or stencilled name-mark on Bernard Moore's Chinese-styled glaze-effects, c.1905–15. A BM initial monogram also occurs.

The cactus, hop or lily relief-decorated Moore porcelains are very popular but good examples of Bernard Moore glaze-effects can also be very desirable. The reader is referred to *Bernard Moore, Master Potter 1850–1935*, by A. Dawson (R. Dennis, 1982).

N

NANTGARW PORCELAIN WORKS

Situated at Nantgarw, Glamorgan, Wales, where fine-quality, highly translucent, mellow porcelain was made c.1813–14 and c.1817–22.

NANTGARW

NANT-GARW
C. W.

Standard impressed marks, which are often difficult to see, unless the porcelain is held to a light. The name occurs with, or without, a hyphen.

Painted name-mark in writing letters which should be viewed with great caution, as this overglaze mark is often added to Coalport and other porcelains.

Nantgarw porcelain is rare and highly collectable. Good well-decorated examples, especially when painted by leading decorators, can be costly. The reader is warned that fakes occur and not all porcelain attributed to Nantgarw was necessarily made there! For further information and illustrations, see *The Pottery and Porcelain of Swansea and Nantgarw*, by E. M. Nance (Batsford, 1942); *Nantgarw Porcelain*, by W. D. John (R. H. John, 1948); and *Nantgarw Porcelain 1813–1822*, by R. Williams (Friends of Nantgarw China Works Museum, 1993).

JAMES NEALE & CO.

Manufacturers of high grade, Wedgwood-type earthenware – creamware, basalt, jasper – and rarely porcelain at Hanley, c.1776–92. Robert Wilson (Neale's partner) succeeded from April 1792 but the old Neale marks may have been continued for a few years. Many specimens were, however, unmarked.

NEALE & PALMER   Rare impressed mark used by this early partnership, c.1769–76.

Rare circular impressed or moulded mark on Wedgwood-type black basalt vases, etc., c.1776–80.

NEALE

NEALE & CO.

NEALE & WILSON

Impressed name marks usually found on good quality earthenwares and rare porcelains, c.1776–92.

The attractive and rather rare Neale wares are very collectable, although not excessively expensive. For further information see Diana Edwards's specialist work *Neale Pottery and Porcelain* (Barrie & Jenkins, 1987), and for the porcelains, Chapter 4 of *Staffordshire Porcelain*.

NEW HALL PORCELAIN WORKS

Worked by several partners and changing partnerships at Shelton from c.1781 to 1835. The early pre-1814 products are a type of hybrid hard-paste porcelain; from c.1814 to 1835 the then standard English bone china was made.

The early porcelains do not bear a factory mark, but the pattern number can be painted on teapots, creamers, etc. (not on cups and saucers) from about 1788 onwards. The pattern was usually painted in larger-sized numerals than on other porcelains. Such numbers can occur with a 'No.' or 'N' prefix or without any prefix. Of course, other firms also used similar pattern numbers so these are only helpful when one knows that the number correctly relates to the patterns. A basic list of New Hall numbers is given by David Holgate in his contribution to *Staffordshire Porcelain* (1983); see also *A Guide to New Hall*

N273

Porcelain Patterns, by A. de Saye Hutton (Barrie & Jenkins, 1990).

Painted decorator's (?) sign, found on some otherwise unmarked New Hall porcelain of the 1800–15 period.

**WARBURTON'S
PATENT**

Rare painted mark found on New Hall (hybrid hard-paste) porcelains, printed with gold, c.1810–14.

Printed mark, rather occasionally used on New Hall bone china wares, c.1814–20. Later wares of the 1820–35 period are unmarked, except in some cases for pattern numbers which climbed up into the 3,000 range.

New Hall porcelains are very collectable and rare unrecorded patterns or shapes will be costly. Initially New Hall was popular because it was available and inexpensive. Neither of these conditions now applies and many pieces traditionally attributed to the New Hall partnerships are now believed to have been produced by other firms: New Hall being the market-leader, with many followers – all producing unmarked wares. Consequently these porcelains of the c.1781–1820 period are the subject of learned research and endless debate!

The reader is referred to specialist works such as *New Hall & its Imitators*, by D. Holgate (Faber & Faber, 1971); *Staffordshire Porcelain* (1983); *New Hall*, by D. Holgate (Faber & Faber, 1987), and *A Guide to New Hall Porcelain Patterns*, by A. de Saye Hutton (Barrie & Jenkins, 1990). Details of the various and changing partnerships are given in my *Encyclopaedia of British Porcelain Manufacturers* (Barrie & Jenkins, 1988).

P

PILKINGTON'S POTTERY (ROYAL LANCASTRIAN)

Pilkington's Tile & Pottery Co. Ltd commenced the manufacture of ornamental wares, vases, etc. in about 1897. Until March 1938 decorative lustre effects were produced often with individual motifs designed by leading artists and designers.

Standard impressed mark, c.1904–14. Roman numerals found below this mark show the year of production, e.g. 'VII' for 1907.

Standard impressed mark, c.1914–35. The words 'England' or 'Made in England' also occur.

The stencilled marks of the various designers and artists are also found on Pilkington's wares; the key to these is given in the *Encyclopaedia of British Pottery and Porcelain Marks* (1964).

The 'Royal Lancastrian' wares, especially the lustre-effects, are very collectable and can be costly, but the technique gives rise to very variable results and care should be taken in choosing pleasing top-quality examples. For further information, see *Pilkington's Royal Lancastrian Pottery & Tiles*, by A. J. Cross (R. Dennis, 1980). Victoria Bergesen's *Encyclopaedia of British Art Pottery* (Barrie & Jenkins, 1991) is also extremely helpful.

PINXTON

A porcelain factory was established at Pinxton in Derbyshire by John Coke (a local landowner) and William Billingsley (a talented ex-Derby ceramic decorator) in 1796. Billingsley left for Mansfield in 1799 but the Pinxton factory was continued for a number of years, mainly, I believe, as a decorating establishment. Most Pinxton porcelain is unmarked and bears a close likeness, in body, form and styles of decoration, to the contemporary Derby porcelain.

Pinxton.

Very rare painted or gilt name-mark in writing letters, c.1796–1805.

P/08

The painted initial 'P' rarely occurs, sometimes preceding the pattern number, different numbers occurring on each pattern.

A (etc)

Printer's type letters can occur impressed into the body, as at Derby.

Pinxton porcelain is rare, having been produced for a relatively short period. The best pieces and the rarer, ornamental, shapes will be costly. The attribution of the unmarked Pinxton porcelains is mainly linked to the knowledge of the body and glaze, plus reference to known patterns and pattern numbers and the key shapes. Recent specialist books give a good guide to shapes and typical patterns, in particular *The Patterns and Shapes of the Pinxton China Factory 1796–1813*, by N. D. Gent (privately published, 1996) and *Pinxton Porcelain 1795–1813*, by C. Barry Sheppard (privately published, 1996). Typical specimens can also be seen at the Victoria & Albert Museum, at the Usher Gallery at Lincoln and at the Derby Museum.

PLYMOUTH PORCELAIN FACTORY

Hard-paste porcelain was made under William Cookworthy's proprietorship at Plymouth, Devon, c.1768–70. Hard-paste Plymouth porcelain is rare, desirable and costly. It follows that fakes and reproductions have been produced. Some are antique (but not genuine) in their own right.

MR. WM. COOKWORTHY'S FACTORY. PLYMOUTH.

Very rare or unique inscription mark, in writing letters, on a sauce boat in the Plymouth Museum and Art Gallery. Included in the *Illustrated Encyclopaedia of British Pottery and Porcelain* (1966), Plate 463. Fakes can bear similar inscriptions.

Standard, but rare, painted mark in underglaze blue or overglaze enamel, c.1768–70.

For further information and illustrations, see *Cookworthy's Plymouth and Bristol Porcelain*, by F. Severne Mackenna (F. Lewis, 1946); *English Blue and White Porcelain*, by B. Watney (Faber & Faber, 1963); *English Porcelain 1745–1850*, edited by R. J. Charleston (Benn, 1965); *Illustrated Encyclopaedia of British Pottery and Porcelain* (1966); and my *Encyclopaedia of British Porcelain Manufacturers* (Barrie & Jenkins, 1988). Typical specimens can be seen in the Victoria & Albert Museum and in the Plymouth Museum collection.

POOLE POTTERY

Manufactured originally by Carter, Stabler & Adams (Ltd) at Poole, Dorset, from 1921 to the present day. The Pottery is open to visitors on the Quayside at Poole in Dorset and there is now a Poole Pottery Collectors Club, centred on the factory.

Standard impressed or printed name-mark, with or without border lines, c.1921+. A variation with the firm's name above also occurs, with 'Ltd' after 1925.

POOLE

ENGLAND

Printed trade-mark, c.1950–6.

Poole

English Fine
Bone China

Revised printed mark, c.1956+. Various modern wording such as 'oven tableware' can occur with this and similar Poole marks.

Poole
Studio.

New description introduced c.1963, when new title Poole Pottery Ltd was adopted.

Poole
English Fine
Bone China.

Various printed 'Fine Bone China' marks introduced in 1983.

Poole pottery is very fashionable and collectable but desirability and therefore value varies greatly. Readers are recommended to consult up-to-date specialist works such as *The Poole Potteries*, by J. Hawkins (Barrie & Jenkins, 1980); *Poole Pottery, Carter & Co. and their Successors 1873–1995*, by L. Hayward (R. Dennis, 1995); and *Poole Pottery. Poole in the 1950s*, by P. Atterbury (R. Dennis, 1997).

F. & R. PRATT

Manufacturers of earthenwares at Fenton, c.1818, continued into 20th century. This Staffordshire firm is best known for its high-quality Victorian multi-colour printing from sets of copper-plates, engraved by Jesse Austin. This technique, perfected by 1851, is widely known from the long series of pot-lid designs. However, the firm produced many other types of ceramics including good terra-cotta.

F. & R. P.
F. & R. P. & Co.

Several different printed marks occur, incorporating these initials, c.1818–50. '& Co.' added c.1840. These initial marks mainly occur on single-colour printed wares.

PRATT
FENTON.

F.& R. PRATT &
FENTON Co.

Printed marks occurring, rather rarely, on the colour-printed earthenwares of pot-lid type, for which this firm is famous. These marks generally appear only on later examples, often of 20th-century date. Most multicolour printed wares were unmarked and by no means all pot-lids and related pieces were made by Pratts.

Pot-lids and other multicolour printed wares are very collectable and later reproductions or reissues abound. Rare subjects and uncommon shapes can be costly. Several general and specialist books give information and illustrate typical specimens. To date, the most helpful is the late A. Ball's *The Price Guide to Pot-Lids and other Underglaze Multicolour Prints on Ware* (Antique Collectors' Club, 2nd edition, 1980). The Potteries Museum at Hanley houses an interesting collection. There is also a 'Pot Lid Circle' which publishes newsletters and holds meetings. Specialist sales are conducted by various auctioneers featuring Pratt-type wares.

R

SAMUEL & JOHN RATHBONE

Manufacturers of porcelains and probably earthen-wares at Tunstall, c.1812–35.

Printed mark, usually in underglaze blue, c.1812–35.

S. & J. R.
               Initials incorporated in various marks, c.1812–35.

S. J. R.

For details of these reattributed marks the reader is referred to *Staffordshire Porcelain* (1983) and the *Encyclopaedia of British Porcelain Manufacturers* (Barrie & Jenkins, 1988). The Rathbone porcelains are interesting but not especially valuable.

RIDGWAY

The various Ridgway partnerships centred on the Cauldon Place Pottery at Shelton (Hanley) in the Staffordshire Potteries are of interest and importance. The various periods from c.1802 onwards are here treated separately. For further information and illustrations of typical wares the reader is referred to G. Godden's standard work *Ridgway Porcelains* (Antique Collectors' Club, 1985) or to *Staffordshire Porcelain*.

Job Ridgway (& Sons)

I. RIDGWAY

Very rare impressed mark, c.1802–8.

RIDGWAY & SONS

Rare impressed mark found on some early porcelains, c.1808–13.

J. & W. Ridgway
From 1813 to 1830 Job's two sons John and William Ridgway traded together at Cauldon Place, producing a wide variety of earthenwares and porcelains.

J. & W. RIDGWAY.
J.& W. R.
J. W. R.
I. & W. R.
I. W. R.

Various printed or rarely impressed name or initial marks as used in the 1813–30 period. Note the 'J' was often rendered as an 'I' at this period.

In 1830 the two brothers separated, John continued the Cauldon Place Works to 1855 and William Ridgway worked the Bell Works (and other factories) at Shelton (see below).

John Ridgway (& Co.)
Manufacturer of fine porcelain and earthenwares at Cauldon Place, Shelton, c.1830–55, in succession to J. & W. Ridgway.

J. R.
I. R.
JOHN RIDGWAY

Several printed marks occur incorporating the initials 'J. R.' (or 'I. R.') or the name 'John Ridgway', c.1830–41. The basic mark is the Royal Arms with the initials worked in the ribbon under; two specimen marks are reproduced.

J. R. & Co

Similar initial or name-marks with the addition of '& Co.' occur, c.1841–55.

John Ridgway & Co. was succeeded by JOHN RIDGWAY, BATES & CO., c.1856–58, then BATES, BROWN-WESTHEAD, MOORE & CO., c.1859–61, then BROWN-WESTHEAD, MOORE & CO., c.1862–1904 (q.v.); initial and name-marks were used by these different firms.

The Ridgway wares, particularly the J. & W. Ridgway and the John Ridgway wares, are collectable and of a general high quality. Commercial value depends on the object or on the quality of the decoration, the porcelains being in higher regard than the earthenwares.

William Ridgway (& Co.)

Manufacturers of earthenwares of various types at Bell Works, Shelton, and Church Works, Hanley, c.1830–54. Also traded under other styles.

W. R.
W. RIDGWAY

Several printed or impressed marks, incorporating these initials or the name, c.1830–4.

W. R. & Co.
W. RIDGWAY & CO.

Several printed or impressed marks occur from c.1834 to 1854; note the addition of '& Co.'

W. R. S. & Co.

From c.1838 to 1848 the firm of WILLIAM RIDGWAY, SON & CO. worked the Church Works and the Cobden Works (c.1841–6); the initials were incorporated in several printed marks.

RIDGWAY, MORLEY, WEAR & CO.

Manufacturers of earthenwares at Shelton, c.1836–42. Partnership succeeded Hicks, Meigh & Johnson and was followed by Ridgway & Morley, c.1842–5.

R. M. W. & Co.

Several different printed marks occur incorporating these initials or the name in full, c.1836–42.

Several different printed marks occur incorporating the initials 'R. & M.' or the name of the firm in full, c.1842–5.

ROBINSON & LEADBEATER (LTD)

Manufacturers of parian figures, etc., at Stoke, c.1864–1924.

Impressed initial mark, found on the back of the base of parian and china figures and groups, c.1885+.

A selection of Robinson & Leadbeater's figures are featured in the *Illustrated Guide to Victorian Parian China*, by C. and D. Shinn (Barrie & Jenkins, 1971) and in *The Parian Phenomenon*, edited by Paul Atterbury (R. Dennis, 1989). This partnership specialized in the production of parian wares. Much is of average quality but some very fine examples were produced, some of which were tinted. As with all parian, the desirability is mainly dependent on the attractiveness of the composition, the quality and condition!

ROCKINGHAM WORKS

Situated on the Earl Fitzwilliam's Rockingham estate, near Swinton in Yorkshire. From 1806 to 1842 the works were managed by the Bramelds. A wide range of earthenwares were produced; also decorative porcelain from 1826.

**B
BRAMELD
BRAMELD & CO.**

Several printed, impressed and moulded marks were used on earthenwares from 1806, incorporating the initial 'B' or the name 'Brameld' (often with crosses or numerals, after the name).

Cl. CL6. CCL.

Painted, printed or gilt 'class marks' of small size, found on otherwise unmarked Rockingham porcelains, c.1826–40.

Printed griffin mark (the crest of Earl Fitzwilliam) in *red* (or rarely in underglaze blue), c.1826–30. The mark occurs *impressed* on some figures. After 1830 the basic mark occurs printed in puce; different wording appears under the crest: 'Royal Rock(ingham) Works' and/or 'China Manufacturers to the King'. The wording 'Manufacturers to the Queen' probably denotes wares decorated by Alfred Baguley after the closure of the factory in 1842.

Rockingham porcelain has always enjoyed a high reputation. It is certainly very decorative and collectable. Rare or especially fine quality examples will be costly. Fakes have been produced and these bear copies of the Griffin crest mark. However, genuine examples are seldom marked – in a teaset only the saucers were marked. Many unmarked porcelains produced by other makers of the 1820–40 period tend to be attributed to Rockingham in error.

The reader is recommended to consult the several specialist books, which include *Rockingham Ornamental Porcelain*, by D. G. Rice (Adam Publishing, 1965); *The Illustrated Guide to Rockingham Pottery & Porcelain*, by D. G. Rice (Barrie & Jenkins, 1971); *The Rockingham Pottery*, by A. E. Eaglestone & T. A. Lockett (revised edition, David & Charles, 1973); *Rockingham Pottery & Porcelain 1745–1842*, by A. & A. Cox (Faber & Faber, 1983); or the more modern general books such as my *Encyclopaedia of British Porcelain Manufacturers* (Barrie & Jenkins, 1988). The Rotherham Museum in Yorkshire has a good collection of their local wares.

It should be noted that the description 'Rockingham Glaze' is a generic term, which relates to a brownish treacle-like glaze effect found on domestic wares, mainly teapots of many makes and periods.

RUSKIN POTTERY
Manufacturers of earthenwares under the proprietorship of W. Howson Taylor, at Smethwick, near Birmingham, from 1898 to July 1935.

TAYLOR   Early impressed name-mark, c.1898+.

   Painted or incised marks, c.1898+.

RUSKIN
RUSKIN POTTERY   Several impressed or printed marks incorporating the name 'RUSKIN', in various forms; the name 'W. HOWSON TAYLOR' also occurs. The wording 'Made in England' added to most marks from c.1920.

Ruskin pottery is very collectable and good examples can be very costly, especially the high temperature Oriental-style glaze-effect examples. Victoria Bergesen's *Encyclopaedia of British Art Pottery* (Barrie & Jenkins, 1991) gives a good account (under William Howson Taylor) and lists the more important specialist papers and articles that have featured these decorative wares. The reader is also referred to *Ruskin Pottery*, by P. Atterbury & J. Henson (R. Dennis, 1993).

S

SHAW & COPESTAKE (LTD)

This Longton partnership rose from small beginnings in about 1901 to become large producers of mainly inexpensive 'Vases and Fancy Wares', at firstly the Drury Pottery and then the Sylvan Works at Longton. Production ceased in 1982.

The early earthenwares were seemingly unmarked but in the 1930s trade names such as 'Scello' and 'SylvaC', 'SylvaC Ware' or 'SylvaC Ceramics' were employed. The first so-called Daisy-mark was perhaps introduced before 1920, without the name.

'SylvaC' marks date from c.1935. Typical examples, one pre-war, one post-war, are here reproduced.

The 'SylvaC' earthenwares are currently very popular and at a modest price level and a 'SylvaC Collectors Circle' is active. For further information the reader should consult *The SylvaC Companion*, by S. Verbeek (Pottery Publications, 1991); *Shaw & Copestake. The Collectors Guide to Early SylvaC 1894–1939*, by A. Van Der Woerd (Pottery Publications, 1992); or *SylvaC Collectors Handbook* by the same authority (Georgian Publications, 1997). Fakes of popular 1950s 'SylvaC' wares have been reported recently.

SHELLEY POTTERIES LTD

This company at Foley, Fenton was established in 1929 although the Shelley trade-name was used previously by Wileman & Co. (q.v.) and by Shelley's, c.1925–9. Shelley China Ltd since 1966.

The main post-1929 Shelley printed marks as found on bone china wares are shown below, although some other versions may be found.

c.1925–40

c.1940–66   c.1940–66

The Shelley porcelains are of very high quality and are tasteful and typical of their period c.1929–1965.

The pre-war products, in particular, are now collectable and prices have risen as interest grows in quality porcelains of the 1930s. The standard works on these porcelains are *Shelley Potteries. The History and Production of a Staffordshire Family of Potters*, by C. Watkins, W. Harvey & R. Senft (Barrie & Jenkins, 1980); *Wileman. A Collectors' Guide*, by R. Knight & S. Hill (Jazz Publications, 1995); and *Shelley Pottery. The Later Years*, by C. Davenport (Heather Publications, 1997). There is also 'The Shelley Group' of collectors with its quarterly magazine and The Shelley Group's annual Fair. Doultons now own the 'Shelley' trade-name.

JOSIAH SPODE

Manufacturer, with his sons, of fine-quality earthenwares and porcelains, at Stoke, c.1770 to April 1833, when Copeland & Garrett succeeded (see p. 67). Josiah Spode is credited with introducing English bone china in about 1800, but perhaps earlier essays can bear the impressed mark STOKE CHINA.

Spode	Rare early impressed mark in upper and lower case letters, c.1780–1810.
SPODE or Spode	Standard name-marks, impressed, printed or written, c.1790–1833.

Typical hand-painted name and pattern number marks, normally found on porcelains, from about 1810 onwards. The pattern number naturally changes with each design.

One of several printed marks found on Spode's high-quality 'Stone China', c.1813–33.

One of several large printed marks commemorating the new 'Felspar' body. Some early examples incorporate the date 1821. This and related marks usually appear on high quality products, c.1821–30.

Two typical printed marks, incorporating the names of special bodies, c.1820–33.

It should be noted that several later Copeland marks can incorporate the old name 'Spode'. Also, the Copeland firm reverted to the 'Spode' name in 1970.

Spode earthenwares and porcelains are highly collectable although the commercial value will vary considerably depending on period, type of ware, decoration, quality, rarity and condition. Spode wares are not in general rare and not all examples are of great value.

The standard specialist book is still L. Whiter's *Spode* (Barrie & Jenkins, revised edition, 1989). The reader should also consult Robert Copeland's Chapter 8 in *Staffordshire Porcelain* and my *Encyclopaedia of British Porcelain Manufacturers* (Barrie & Jenkins, 1988). Good details of the various marks and pattern numbers will be found in Robert Copeland's *Spode & Copeland Marks* (Studio Vista, revised edition, 1998).

STOCKTON POTTERY (or 'STAFFORD POTTERY')
A wide range of earthenwares was made at this Yorkshire pottery under various managements (as listed below), from c.1825.

William Smith (& Co.), c.1825–55

W. S. & Co.

W. SMITH & CO.

W. S. & Co.
QUEEN'S WARE
STOCKTON

Many printed or impressed marks incorporating the initials 'W. S. & Co.', often with the place-name 'STOCKTON'. The word 'WEDGWOOD' or 'WEDGEWOOD' was also incorporated before 1848 and sometimes the description 'Queen's Ware'.

George Skinner & Co., c.1855–70

G. S. & Co.

Several printed or impressed marks incorporate these initials, c.1855–70.

Skinner & Walker, c.1870–80

S. & W.

Several printed or impressed marks incorporate these initials, often with the place-name 'STOCK-TON' and the description of the body, 'PEARL WARE', etc., c.1870–80.

Stockton pottery is collectable, especially some of the interesting multicoloured printed wares produced by William Smith in the 1840s. Prices, however, should be modest.

SUNDERLAND POTTERIES

The potteries at Sunderland are associated with a type of 'splash-lustre'. Several different potteries were working in the Sunderland area, and many pieces are unmarked. The marks met with include:

'DAWSON'; 'I. DAWSON'; 'J. DAWSON'; 'DAWSON & CO.'

These name-marks relate to the Ford and South Hylton Potteries, c.1799–1864.

'J. PHILLIPS'; 'PHILLIPS & CO.'; 'DIXON, AUSTIN & CO.'; 'DIXON & CO.'; 'DIXON, PHILLIPS & CO.'

These name-marks, sometimes incorporated in printed designs, relate to the 'Sunderland' or 'Garrison' Pottery, c.1807–65.

'MOORE & CO.'; 'S. MOORE & CO.': 'S. M. & CO.'

These marks relate to Moore's Wear Pottery.

'A. SCOTT'; 'A. SCOTT & CO.'; 'SCOTT & SONS'; 'SCOTT BROS.'

These name-marks (and the relevant initials) relate to Scott's Southwick Pottery, c.1800–97.

The Sunderland earthenwares are in general of interest and unusual specimens may be costly. This centre is particularly noted for a type of splash-lustre or 'Sunderland-lustre'. This aspect of the output of various factories in or around Sunderland is featured in *Collecting Lustrewares*, by G. Godden & M. Gibson (Barrie & Jenkins, 1991). The reader is also referred to *Sunderland Ware. The Potteries of Wearside*, by J. C. Baker (County Borough of Sunderland, revised edition, 1984).

SWANSEA

Pottery as well as fine porcelain (c.1814–22) was produced at Swansea in Wales under the management of various firms. Swansea earthenwares before the 1780s were not marked.

SWANSEA

CAMBRIAN

CAMBRIAN POTTERY

Three early impressed or painted marks found on earthenwares; the 'Cambrian Pottery' mark is rare, c.1783–c.1810.

DILLWYN & CO.

DILLWYN SWANSEA

IMPROVED STONE WARE DILLWYN

Three basic 'DILLWYN' marks (on pottery) incorporating the name of this proprietor. Several different printed marks incorporate this name or the initial 'D' or 'D. & Co.', c.1811–17 and 1824–50.

SWANSEA

Basic name-mark on fine translucent *porcelain*, impressed, printed over the glaze, or painted, c.1814–22. Reproductions also bear this name-mark. A variation has crossed tridents below the word 'Swansea'; this mark is normally impressed into the porcelain.

BEVINGTON & CO. SWANSEA

Rare impressed or painted mark, c.1817–24.

EVANS & GLASSON SWANSEA

Several different printed or impressed marks of the 1850–62 period incorporate the names 'Evans & Glasson', found on earthenwares only.

D. J. EVANS & CO.   Many different printed or impressed marks of the 1862–70 period incorporate or comprise the name 'D. J. Evans & Co.', found on earthenwares only.

The varied Swansea wares, especially the finer porcelains, are very collectable, particularly in Wales, but not all specimens are marked. The reader is recommended to consult the standard reference books, which include E. Morton Nance's *The Pottery and Porcelain of Swansea and Nantgarw* (Batsford, 1942); W. D. John's *Swansea Porcelain* (Ceramic Book Co., 1957); the *Illustrated Encyclopaedia of British Pottery and Porcelain* (1966); *Swansea Porcelain, Shapes and Decoration*, by A. E. Jones and Sir L. Joseph (D. Brown & Sons, 1988); and *The Glamorgan Pottery, Swansea 1814–38*, by H. Hallesy (Gower Press, 1995). The National Museum of Wales in Cardiff and the Glynn Vivian Art Gallery at Swansea have particularly fine and interesting collections.

SylvaC, see Shaw & Copestake

T

'TEBO' TOULOUSE

The name given to a modeller or 'repairer' who used the impressed mark 'To' or, rarely, 'T'.

This impressed (or relief moulded) mark is found on various 18th-century English porcelains; Bow porcelain, c.1750–60; Worcester porcelain, c.1760–9; Plymouth porcelain, c.1769–70; Bristol porcelain, c.1770–3. The mark is also found (very rarely) on Caughley porcelain, c.1775–80 and on Chamberlain Worcester porcelains of the 1790s. Recent research suggests that this mark may relate to a modeller named John Toulouse. See *Chamberlain-Worcester Porcelain 1788–1852* by G. A. Godden (Barrie & Jenkins, 1982).

TOOTH & CO. (LTD)

This company succeeded Tooth & Ault (c.1883–6), in 1887 at the Bretby Art Pottery, Woodville, Derbyshire.

The Bretby sun-burst trade-mark was registered in 1884. The word 'England' was added c.1891; this gave way to 'Made in England' after about 1914.

The initials of Henry Tooth can also occur on Bretby earthenwares. Various trade-names, such as 'Clanta Ware' (c.1914+), also occur in different types or bodies.

The Bretby art wares can be decorative and collectable. Values vary greatly depending on the importance of the specimen. Victoria Bergesen's

Encyclopaedia of British Art Pottery (Barrie & Jenkins, 1991) gives a good account of the Tooth earthenwares and lists many magazine articles dealing with the Bretby wares. The firm is still in production but the items currently of interest to collectors can be said to be restricted to the earlier products, c.1887–c.1920.

JOHN TURNER

Manufacturer of earthenwares – creamwares, basalt, jasper, porcelain, etc. – at Lane End, c.1762–c.1806.

Very early wares are apparently unmarked.

TURNER Standard impressed mark, c.1770+. Very rarely found on porcelain.

TURNER & CO. Standard impressed mark, c.1780–6 and 1803–6, but the single name 'TURNER' is also used at these periods. From 1784 the Prince of Wales's feather plumes may appear with the standard name-mark.

TURNER'S PATENT Rather rare written mark on special bodies patented in January 1800; used to c.1805.

The Turner wares are of a uniformly high quality and are very collectable by the discerning! They are, however, not of high value. All but very exceptional examples should be available for less than £250.

The standard book is *The Turners of Lane End*, by B. Hillier (Cory, Adams & Mackay, 1965). Other aspects of Turner's output are featured in *Black Basalt*, by D. Edwards (Antique Collectors' Club, 1994), *Staffordshire Porcelain*, edited by G. Godden (1983); and *English Dry-Bodied Stoneware. Wedgwood and Contemporary Manufacturers 1774 to 1830*, by D. Edwards & R. Hampson (Antique Collectors' Club, 1998).

VEDGWOOD

Misleading mock-Wedgwood mark found impressed on earthenwares of the 1830–60 period. Mark probably used by several manufacturers, including Carr & Patton (Newcastle-on-Tyne) c.1838–47, and William Smith & Co. (Stockton-on-Tees) c.1825–55. The earthenwares bearing this misleading name-mark are of ordinary quality and have little commercial value.

'**VICTORIA**' ironstone or stoneware, see Blakeney Pottery Ltd

CHARLES VYSE

Modeller of earthenware figures and groups 1920s and 1930s and Chinese glaze-effect wares to 1963.

C. V.

Painted or incised initials, c.1919–63, often with place-name 'CHELSEA'.

VYSE
or
C. VYSE
or
CHARLES VYSE

Several different name-marks occur with the place-name 'CHELSEA' and often the year of production.

The Vyse figures and groups are decorative and scarce. They are collectable and of higher than average value. The glaze-effect and studio pottery is also collectable and of value, depending on the importance of the specimen.

Typical Vyse figures are shown in my *British Pottery* (1974), Plate 548. The reader is also directed to Richard Dennis's 1974 exhibition catalogue *Charles Vyse 1882–1971*.

W(★★★)

An interesting grouping of English ceramics, earthenwares as well as porcelain, bears this unhelpful impressed mark. These wares of the approximate period c.1790–1815 are collectable and being researched by specialists seeking to attribute these wares. For further information see *Staffordshire Porcelain* (1983), Appendix V1 or my *Encyclopaedia of British Porcelain Manufacturers* (Barrie & Jenkins, 1988), p. 743.

GEORGE WADE (& SON LTD)

George Wade commenced potting at the Manchester Pottery, Burslem c.1899. In June 1919 the firm's title was amended to George Wade & Son Ltd. This continued to 1958 when the new name The Wade Group of Potteries was adopted to embrace A. J. Wade, George Wade & Son Ltd, and Wade (Ulster) Ltd. The present title is Wade Ceramics Ltd.

The three marks given below are standard marks used by George Wade & Sons Ltd, from the mid-1930s. Earlier wares were seldom marked.

c.1936+

c.1936+

c.1947+

The following basic marks relate to a separate but linked company, Wade Heath & Co. (Ltd) of Burslem, c.1927–69. Many different marks were used relating to individual styles and types.

c.1927+

c.1934+

c.1939+
with or with out the
word FLAXMAN

c.1953+

In general the Wade wares and novelties were of an inexpensive nature. They are, however, now collectable on an international scale and several books feature these articles. Such well-illustrated works include *The World of Wade*, by I. Warner & M. Posgay (USA, 1988 and 1994); *Wade Whimsical Collectables. The Charlton Price Guide*, by P. Murray (USA, 3rd edition, 1996); *Wade Collectors' Handbook. Complete Listing and Prices to Wade Collectables*, by F. Salmon (F. Joseph, 1996); *Wade Price Trends. The World of Wade and the World of Wade Book*, by I. Warner & M. Posgay (USA, 1996); and the *Charlton Standard Catalogue of Wade Tableware* (USA, 1997). There is also a Wade Collectors' Club.

JOHN WALTON

Manufacturer of earthenware figures and groups at Burslem, c.1818–35.

WALTON

Moulded or impressed name-mark found on the back of figures, etc., c.1818–35.

The Walton Staffordshire earthenware figures are one of the very few groups that bear a maker's mark. They are in general above average quality and are collectable. Their value is above that of the unmarked types but many later copies have been produced, with the 'Walton' name-mark. Typical examples are shown in my *Illustrated Encyclopaedia of British Pottery and Porcelain*, Plates 591–2, also in most books on Staffordshire figures, notably P. A. Halfpenny's *English Earthenware Figures 1740–1840* (Antique Collectors' Club, 1991).

WATCOMBE POTTERY CO.

Manufacturers of ornamental terra-cotta wares at Watcombe, South Devon, c.1867–1901, continued as ROYAL ALLER VALE & WATCOMBE POTTERY CO., c.1901–62.

WATCOMBE

Basic impressed marks incorporate the word 'Watcombe' with or without the place-name 'TORQUAY', c.1867–1901.

Printed mark, c.1875–1901.

The Watcombe earthenwares are usually of good quality and of interest. They are collectable, mainly in the West Country, but prices are reasonable. Victoria Bergesen's *Encyclopaedia of British Art Pottery* (Barrie & Jenkins, 1991) gives a good account of the Watcombe wares and artists.

JOSIAH WEDGWOOD (& SONS LTD)

Celebrated manufacturers of earthenwares and porcelain at Burslem, Etruria and Barlaston, Staffordshire, c.1759 to present day.

wedgwood

WEDGWOOD

Basic impressed name-mark on earthenwares, c.1759+. Early specimens show individually impressed upper and lower case letters; subsequently all letters are of the same style, sans serif type from c.1929. The word 'ENGLAND' should be added from 1891 or 'MADE IN ENGLAND' from c.1910.

Four impressed 'WEDGWOOD & BENTLEY' marks found on ornamental basalt, jasper and marbled wares, c.1769–80. Examples are rare. The desirable circular mark has in recent years been added to unmarked objects; these fake marks are relatively soft and can consequently be marked by a pin, knife, etc.

WEDGWOOD & BENTLEY  W. & B.

WEDGWOOD *Printed* name-mark on rare *porcelains*, c.1812–22.

WEDGWOOD ETRURIA Impressed mark with place-name 'ETRURIA', c.1840–5.

From 1860 Wedgwood creamwares, etc., bear impressed letters which show the month and year that a specimen was potted. The table opposite shows the year letters and relevant dates. The year letter is normally the last of the set of three.

 Typical signature mark found on the Wedgwood earthenwares painted by the celebrated French artist Emile Lessore, c.1858–76. Examples of this artist's work are shown in Colour Plate XV of the *Illustrated Encyclopaedia of British Pottery and Porcelain*.

WEDGWOOD Basic printed mark on *porcelain*, c.1878+. The word 'ENGLAND' was added after 1891 and 'MADE IN ENGLAND' after about 1910. The description 'BONE CHINA' also appears.

WEDGWOOD Basic impressed name-mark in *sans serif* type, from 1929.

WEDGWOOD'S IMPRESSED YEAR LETTERS

Occurring in sets of three (from 1860), the *last* date letter shows the year of manufacture

O = 1860	U = 1866	Z = 1871	E = 1876	J = 1881
P = 1861	V = 1867	A = 1872	F = 1877	K = 1882
Q = 1862	W= 1868	B = 1873	G = 1878	L = 1883
R = 1863	X = 1869	C = 1874	H = 1879	M = 1884
S = 1864	Y = 1870	D = 1875	I = 1880	N = 1885
T = 1865				

O = 1886			
P = 1887		A = 1898	From 1898 to
Q = 1888		B = 1899	1906 the letters
R = 1889	From 1886 to 1897	C = 1900	used from
S = 1890	the earlier (1860–71)	D = 1901	1872 to 1880
T = 1891★	letters are repeated	E = 1902	re-occur, but
U = 1892		F = 1903	'ENGLAND'
V = 1893	★ From 1891 'ENGLAND	G = 1904	should also
W= 1894	should occur on specimens.	H = 1905	appear
X = 1895		I = 1906	
Y = 1896			
Z = 1897			

From 1907 the sequence was continued, but a '3' replaces the first letter. From 1924 a '4' replaces the '3'. After 1930 the month is numbered in sequence and the last two numbers of the year are given, i.e. 1A 32 = January 1932, 'A' being the workman's mark.

Standard printed mark from c.1940. Note the then new Barlaston address.

Several different versions of the standard Portland vase mark have been employed since the early 1970s. These usually occur printed in two colours – the vase device being in black. Various pattern names and reference numbers also appear on different designs.

The trade mark registration letter ® was added from 1973.

WEDGWOOD®
Bone China
MADE IN ENGLAND

Black & gold
c.1973–80

WEDGWOOD®
Bone China
MADE IN ENGLAND

Black & sepia
c.1980–91

WEDGWOOD®
Bone China
MADE IN ENGLAND

Black & sepia
c.1991–7

New trade mark introduced in November 1997.

The Wedgwood wares are of uniformly high quality and are of course collectable. The earlier examples, particularly marked examples of the Wedgwood & Bentley period, are rightly costly. The reader should remember, however, that the output of this large factory working for more than 200 years has been huge and not all specimens are rare or valuable.

Many books give good information on this famous firm: examples include The Story of Wedgwood, by A. Kelly (Faber & Faber, 1975); Wedgwood Portrait Medallions, by R. Reilly and G. Savage (Barrie & Jenkins, 1973); The Dictionary of Wedgwood, by R. Reilly and G. Savage (Antique Collectors' Club, 1980); 18th Century Wedgwood, by D. Buten (Buten Museum of Wedgwood, USA, 1980); Wedgwood Ceramics 1846–1959), by M. Batkin (R.

Dennis, 1982); Wedgwood, by R. Reilly (2 vols, Macmillan, 1989); Josiah Wedgwood 1730–1795, by R. Reilly (Macmillan, 1992); Wedgwood Jasper, by R. Reilly (Thames & Hudson, 1994); The Green Frog Service, by M. Raeburn (Cacklegoose Press, 1995); and English Dry-Bodied Stoneware. Wedgwood and Contemporary Manufacturers 1774 to 1830, by D. Edwards & R. Hampson (Antique Collectors' Club, 1998).

There are also Wedgwood Societies in England and in the USA. The Wedgwood factory site at Barlaston in Staffordshire includes a fine museum and collection of old Wedgwood as well as an interesting Visitors' Centre.

WEDGWOOD & CO. (LTD)

Manufacturers of earthenwares at Tunstall, c.1860–1965, then retitled 'Enoch Wedgwood (Tunstall) Ltd', it subsequently became part of the Wedgwood group but the old name was discontinued. The 'Wedgwood & Co.' earthenwares are not of special value.

WEDGWOOD & CO.

Standard name-mark, found incorporated in several printed marks, or used alone impressed, c.1860–1900; 'Ltd' added from about 1900. Impressed mark also rarely found on wares of the 1790–1801 period, produced at the Ferrybridge Pottery in Yorkshire or in Staffordshire by Ralph Wedgwood.

Printed mark, one of several incorporating the name Wedgwood & Co., c.1860+.

The marks and wares of this firm are often mistaken for those of Josiah Wedgwood & Sons who used the simple word 'Wedgwood', not 'Wedgwood & Co.' or 'Wedgwood & Co. Ltd'.

WILEMAN & CO.

Manufacturers of china and earthenware at Foley Works, Fenton, c.1890–1925.

Printed mark, c.1890, note trade name 'FOLEY'.

Printed trade marks, two of several incorporating the trade name 'Shelley', c.1911+.

The Wileman porcelains are collectable but generally in the lower price ranges. The reader is also referred to the Shelley section, and to *Wileman, A Collectors' Guide*, by R. Knight & S. Hill (Jazz Publications, 1995).

WILTSHAW & ROBINSON (LTD)

Manufacturers of earthenware and china at Carlton Works, Stoke, c.1890–1957, retitled Carlton Ware Ltd in January 1958.

Three sample printed marks, of which several occur incorporating the initials 'W. & R.' or the trade-name 'Carlton Ware', c.1890+.

Carlton ware has become collectable, within modest price levels. The reader is referred to *Collecting Carlton Ware*, by Francis Salmon (Kevin Francis Publishing, 1993). See also under Carlton Ware.

ENOCH WOOD (& SONS)

Celebrated modeller and manufacturer of earthenwares at Burslem, c.1784–90. In partnership under the style 'Wood & Caldwell' from c.1790 to 1818. Traded as Enoch Wood & Sons from July 1818 to 1846.

E. W.

E. WOOD

Rather rare impressed initial or name-marks found on fine creamwares, basalt, jasper, etc., c.1790–1818.

WOOD & CALDWELL

Standard impressed mark, c.1790–1818, rather rare.

Standard impressed mark of the 1818–46 period with the new-style 'Enoch [or 'E'] Wood & Sons'. Fine blue-printed earthenwares were made especially for the American market.

E. W. & S.

E. & E. W.

E. WOOD & SONS

Several printed marks of the 1818–46 period incorporate these initials, as on the sample printed mark reproduced below, or the name in full.

Enoch Wood's products are varied and interesting. A large assortment of blue-printed tablewares were produced, much for our export markets. Most examples are of modest price but rare or special items are obviously in demand. Good examples are in The Potteries Museum at Hanley. For further information and illustrations, see *The Wood Family of Burslem*, by F. Falkner (1912). Typical examples are also shown in the *Illustrated Encyclopaedia of British Pottery and Porcelain*, Plates 639–43. For a review of his rare porcelains see my *Encyclopaedia of British Porcelain Manufacturers* (Barrie & Jenkins, 1988).

WORCESTER PORCELAIN FACTORY

Established in 1751 by Dr John Wall and partners, after acquiring the Bristol works of Benjamin Lund. Worcester porcelain is justly celebrated for its charm and quality. The glaze is perfect, not discoloured or crazed; some early wares were decorated with overglaze prints and with attractive underglaze-blue designs.

Dr Wall Period

Many early specimens decorated in underglaze-blue bear various workmen's signs on the base or under the handle: four typical marks are reproduced, see also the *Encyclopaedia of British Porcelain Manufacturers*, p. 797. Porcelains bearing these devices would date c.1752–65.

The first standard Worcester mark is the blue crescent device, filled in (or with cross-hatching) on printed designs, open (outlines only) crescent on hand-painted examples, c.1758–83.

Blue painted or printed examples sometimes bear the rather rare 'W' mark, which occurs in various differing forms, c.1760–80.

Many different factory Oriental-style marks also occur painted in underglaze-blue, often on colourful Japanese-type patterns, c.1760–75. Such mock oriental marks are not confined to Worcester.

Two typical examples of the 'square' or 'seal' mark found painted by hand in underglaze-blue on Worcester porcelains, often in conjunction with colourful 'scale blue' patterns. Many variations occur, c.1760–75. Reproductions often bear such 'square' marks.

  Two examples of the Worcester version of the Dresden crossed-swords mark found on overglaze printed specimens as well as ornate and colourful designs.

  Printed Worcester numeral marks, disguised with Oriental-styled flourishes, formerly attributed to the Caughley factory in error, c.1770–83.

The first or 'Dr Wall' period of Worcester porcelain came to an end in September 1783. The factory, moulds, etc., were purchased by Thomas Flight and the works were continued under various partnerships, using different marks, as listed.

Flight Period
 Early standard crescent mark continued but now very small, c.1783–92.

 Rather rare blue mark, c.1783–8.

 Rather rare blue mark with crown, c.1788–92.

 FLIGHT'S Other rare marks comprise or incorporate the name 'Flight' or 'Flight's', c.1788–92.

Barr, also Flight & Barr Period
 Standard incised 'B' marks, often with a small cross, c.1792–1807.

F. & B.
FLIGHT & BARR

Other rather rare marks incorporate or comprise the name 'Flight & Barr', or the initials 'F. & B.'

Barr, Flight & Barr Period
Standard impressed or incised BFB marks (with or without crown), c.1807–13.

BARR FLIGHT
& BARR
ROYAL PORCELAIN
WORKS
WORCESTER

One of several printed or written marks incorporating the name 'Barr, Flight & Barr', c.1807–13.

Flight, Barr & Barr Period
Standard impressed mark, the initials 'FBB' under a crown, c.1813–40.

FLIGHT, BARR & BARR

Several different printed or written marks occur with the title in full, c.1813–40.

Messrs Chamberlains (q.v.) continued the works from 1840 to 1852.

Kerr & Binns Period
Standard impressed or printed mark, *without* crown above, c.1852–62.

Rare printed shield-mark on fine-quality specimens: the last two numerals of the year occur in the central bar, 57 for 1857, etc.

W. H. KERR & CO

Some rare marks incorporate the title 'W. H. Kerr & Co.', c.1856–62.

Royal Worcester
Standard printed or impressed mark, with crown above, c.1862–75 (numerals under the main mark are the last two of the year of decoration, 73 for 1873, etc.).

Amended printed or impressed mark, note crescent instead of 'C' in centre and filled-in crown settling on circle, c.1876–91.

Post-1891 standard printed mark, note wording around, not found on earlier versions. The dots each side of the crown are year markings starting with one in 1892.

Revised printed mark, c.1944–55; from 1956 the words are placed below the main device.

Version with words 'Bone China' below 'Royal Worcester', c.1956+

Revised version, c.1959+. Year-marks occur with these marks up to the early 1970s, when the year-marks were discontinued

Standard mark c.1970 onwards but special marks can relate to special issues or projects.

Methods of dating Royal Worcester porcelain to the year are given by G. A. Godden in the *Encyclopaedia of British Pottery and Porcelain Marks* (1964) and in Henry Sandon's specialist book *Royal Worcester Porcelain from 1862 to the Present Day* (Barrie & Jenkins, 3rd edition, 1978).

Worcester porcelains are of an uniformly high quality. All periods are collectable but the price varies greatly – ranging up to over £10,000 for very special pieces. The reader is warned that fakes exist, mainly but not exclusively relating to copies of 18th-century types.

Many specialist books have been written on the various aspects of Worcester porcelain. The following will be found helpful: *Worcester Porcelain* by F. A. Barrett (1953, revised edition, 1966); *Coloured Worcester Porcelain of the First Period*, by H. Rissik Marshall (Ceramic Book Co., 1954); *Victorian Porcelain*, by G. A. Godden (H. Jenkins, 1961); *English Blue and White Porcelain of the 18th Century*, by B. Watney (Faber & Faber, 1963, revised edition 1973); *Illustrated Encyclopaedia of British Pottery and Porcelain*, by G. A. Godden (1966); *Caughley and Worcester Porcelains, 1775–1800*, by G. A. Godden (Antique Collectors' Club, 1981); *The Illustrated Guide to Worcester Porcelain*, by H. Sandon (Barrie & Jenkins, 1969); the same author's *Flight and Barr Worcester Porcelain 1783–1840* (Antique Collectors' Club, 1978); his *Royal Worcester Porcelain from 1862 to the Present Day* (Barrie & Jenkins, 1978); *Worcester Blue & White Porcelain 1751–1790*, by L. Branyan, N. French & J. Sandon (Barrie & Jenkins, 1989); *The Dictionary of Worcester Porcelain*, Vol 1, *1751–1851*, by John Sandon (1993); and *Worcester Porcelain 1751–1790. The Zorensky Collection*, by Simon Spero & John Sandon (Antique Collectors' Club, 1997).

Most major museum collections feature a representative selection of Worcester porcelain but the splendid, comprehensive, collection on display at the Worcester Porcelain Works, Severn Street, Worcester is a must!

Potters' Initial Marks

This helpful section lists the initials used as a mark, or part of a mark, by various 19th-century potters or partnerships, with their approximate working period. An asterisk indicates an entry in the main marks section.

A. Bros	*G. L. Ashworth & Bros, Hanley	1861–1968
A. & Co.	Edward Asbury & Co., Longton	c.1875–1925
A. B.	Adams & Bromley, Hanley	c.1873–86
A. B. & C.	Allman, Broughton & Co., Burslem	c.1861–8
A. B. & Co.	Allman, Broughton & Co., Burslem	c.1861–8
A. B. & Co.	A. Bullock & Co., Hanley	c.1895–1902
A. & B.	Adams & Bromley, Hanley	c.1873–86
A. B. J.	A. B. Jones, Longton	c.1900
A. B. J. & S.	A. B. Jones & Sons, Longton	c.1900 +
A. B. J. & Sons	A. B. Jones & Sons, Longton	c.1900 +
A. & C.	Adams & Cooper, Longton	c.1850–77
A. F. & S.	A. Fenton & Son, Hanley	c.1887–1901
A. G.	A. Godfrey, Hanley	c.1829–37
A. G. H. J.	A. G. Harley Jones, Fenton	c.1907–34
A. G. R.	A. G. Richardson, Cobridge	c.1920–1
A. G. R. & Co. Ltd	A. G. Richardson & Co. Ltd, Tunstall	c.1915 +
A. J. M.	A. J. Mountford, Burslem	c.1897–1901
A. J. W.	A. J. Wilkinson, Burslem	c.1885 +
A. M. L.	A. Mackee, Longton	c.1892–1906
A. P. Co.	Anchor Porcelain Co., Longton	c.1901–18
A. P. Co. L.	Anchor Porcelain Co. Ltd, Longton	c.1901–18
A. S.	A. Shaw, Tunstall	c.1853–85
A. & S.	Arkinstall & Sons, Stoke	c.1904–24
A. S. B.	A. Stanyer, Burslem	c.1916–41
A. S. & Co.	Ambrose Smith & Co., Burslem	c.1784–6
A. S. W.	Rye Pottery, Sussex	c.1920–3
A. W. L.	Arthur Wood, Longport	c.1904–28
B. (incised)	*Worcester, Barr period	c.1792–1807
B. (impressed)	J. & E. Baddeley, Shelton	c.1784–1806
	Thomas Barlow, Longton	c.1849–82
	T. W. Barlow & Son Ltd, Longton	c.1882–1940
B. (painted)	*Bow, London	c.1747–76
	*Bristol (porcelains)	c.1770–81
B. (printed)	*Rockingham (earthenwares)	c.1810–42
B. & Co.	Barrow & Co., Fenton	c.1853–4
	L. A. Birks & Co., Stoke	c.1896–1900
	Bodley & Co., Burslem	c.1865
	Boulton & Co., Longton	c.1892–1902
B. Ltd	Barlows (Longton) Ltd, Longton	c.1920–52
B. & Son	Bodley & Son, Burslem	c.1874–5
B. A. & B.	Bradbury, Anderson & Betteney, Longton	c.1844–52
B. A. J.	A. B. Jones, Longton	c.1900 +

B. A. J. & S(ons)	A. B. Jones, Longton	c.1900 +
B. B.	★Minton, Stoke	c.1830–60
B. B. B.	Booths Ltd, Tunstall	c.1891–1948
B. B. B.	Bridgett, Bates & Beech, Longton	c.1875–82
B. B. C.	J. Shaw & Sons Ltd, Longton	c.1931–63
B. B. & Co.	★Baker, Bevans & Irwin, Swansea	c.1813–38
B. & B.	Baggerley & Ball, Longton	c.1822–36
	Bailey Ball, Longton	c.1843–9
	Bailey & Batkin, Lane End	c.1814–27
	Bates & Bennett, Cobridge	c.1868–95
	Blackhurst & Bourne, Burslem	c.1880–92
	L. A. Birks, Stoke	c.1896–1900
	Bridgett & Bates, Longton	c.1882–1915
B. B. Ltd	Barker Bros Ltd, Longton	c.1876 +
B. B. & I.	★Baker, Bevans & Irwin, Swansea	c.1813–38
B. B. W. & M.	Bates, Brown-Westhead & Moore, Shelton	c.1859–61
B. & C.	Bridgwood & Clarke, Burslem	c.1857–64
B. C. Co.	Britannia China Co., Longton	c.1895–1906
B. C. G.	B. C. Godwin, Burslem	c.1851
B. & E.	Beardmore & Edwards, Longton	c.1856–8
B. E. & Co.	Bates, Elliott & Co., Burslem	c.1870–5
B. F.	B. Floyd, Lane End	c.1843
B. F. (monogram)	★Burmantofts, Leeds	c.1882–1904
B. F. B.	★Worcester, Barr, Flight & Barr	c.1807–13
B. G.	B. Godwin, Cobridge	c.1834–41
B. G. P. Co.	Brownfield's Guild Pottery Society Ltd, Cobridge	c.1891–1900
B. G. & W.	Bates, Gildea & Walker, Burslem	c.1878–81
B. H. & Co.	Beech Hancock & Co., Tunstall	c.1851–5
B. & H.	Bednall & Heath, Hanley	c.1879–99
	Beech & Hancock, Tunstall	c.1855–76
	Blackhurst & Hulme, Longton	c.1890–1932
	Bodley & Harrold, Burslem	c.1863–5
B. & K.	Barkers & Kent, Fenton	c.1889–1941
B. & K. L.	Barkers & Kent, Longton	c.1889–1941
B. & L.	Bourne & Leigh, Burslem	c.1892–1941
B. & L.	★Burgess & Leigh, Burslem	c.1862 +
B. & L. Ltd	★Burgess & Leigh, Burslem	c.1889 +
B. M. & Co.	Bayley Murray, Glasgow	c.1875–84
B. M. & T.	Boulton, Machin & Tennant, Tunstall	c.1889–99
B. N. & Co.	Bourne, Nixon & Co., Tunstall	c.1828–30
B. P.	Bovey Pottery & Co. Ltd, Devon	c.1894–1957
B. P. Co.	Blyth Porcelain Co. Ltd, Longton	c.1905–35
	Bovey Tracey Pottery Co., Devon	c.1894–1957
	Bridge Products Co., Somerset	c.1954–63
	Brownhills Pottery Co., Tunstall	c.1872–96
B. P. Co. Ltd	Blyth Porcelain Co. Ltd, Longton	c.1905–35
	Britannia Pottery Co. Ltd, Glasgow	c.1920–35
B. R. & Co.	Birks, Rawlins & Co., Stoke	c.1900–33
B. R. & T.	Baxter, Rowley & Tams, Longton	c.1882–5
B. & S.	Barker & Son, Burslem	c.1850–60
	Beswick & Son, Longton	c.1916–30

	*Bishop & Stonier, Hanley	c.1891–1939
	Brown & Stevenson, Burslem	c.1900–23
B. S. & T.	Barker, Sutton & Till, Burslem	c.1834–43
B. & T.	Barker & Till, Burslem	c.1843–50
	Blackhurst & Tunnicliffe, Burslem	c.1879
B. T. P. Co.	Bovey Tracey Pottery Co., Devon	c.1894–1957
B. T. & S. F. B.	B. Taylor & Sons, Ferrybridge Pottery, Yorks	c.1852–6
B. & W.	Birch & Whitehead, Shelton	c.1796
	Boughley & Wiltshire, Longton	c.1892–5
B. W. & B.	Batkin, Walker & Broadhurst, Lane End	c.1840–5
B. W. & Co.	Bates Walker & Co., Burslem	c.1875–8
	Buckley, Wood & Co., Burslem	c.1875–85
B. W. M.	*Brown-Westhead, Moore & Co., Hanley	c.1862–1904
B. W. M. & Co.	*Brown-Westhead, Moore & Co., Hanley	c.1862–1904
C.	*Caughley, Shropshire	c.1775–99
C. & Co.	Calland & Co., Swansea	c.1852–6
	Clokie & Co., Castleford, Yorks.	c.1888–1961
	Colclough & Co., Longton	c.1887–1928
	J. H. Cope & Co., Longton	c.1887–1947
C. A. L.	C. Amison, Longton	c.1889–1962
C. A. & Co. Ltd	Ceramic Art Co. Ltd, Hanley	c.1892–1903
C. A. & Sons	*C. Allerton & Sons, Longton	c.1859–1942
C. B.	*Charles Bourne, Fenton	c.1807–30
	Christie & Beardmore, Fenton	c.1807–30
	Collingwood Bros, Longton	c.1887–1957
C. B. D.	*Coalport, Shropshire	c.1851 +
C. & B.	Carter & Barker, Hanley	c.1834–41
	Christie & Beardmore, Fenton	c.1902–3
	Cotton & Barlow, Longton	c.1850–5
C. B. & C.	Cyples, Barlow & Cyples, Lane End	c.1841–4
	C. Collinson & Co., Burselm	c.1867–75
	Cockson and Chetwyn, Colridge	c.1867–75
C. D.	*Coalport, Shropshire	c.1815–30
C. & D.	Cooper & Dethick, Longton	c.1876–88
C. & E.	Cartwright & Edwards, Longton	c.1857 +
	Cope & Edwards, Longton	c.1844–57
C. & E. Ltd	Cartwright & Edwards, Longton	1857 +
C. E. & M.	Cork, Edge & Malkin, Burslem	c.1860–71
C. F.	Charles Ford, Hanley	c.1874–1904
C. & F.	Cockran & Fleming, Glasgow	c.1896–1920
C. & F. G.	Cockran & Fleming, Glasgow	c.1896–1920
C. & G.	Collingwood & Greatbatch	c.1870–87
	*Copeland & Garrett, Stoke	c.1833–47
C. H.	Charles Hobson, Burslem	c.1865–73
C. H. Co.	Hanley China Co., Hanley	c.1899–1901
C. H. & G.	Copestake, Hazzall & Gerard	c.1828–30
C. H. & S.	C. Hobson & Son, Burslem	c.1873–80
C. & H.	Cockson & Harding, Shelton	c.1856–62
	Coggins & Hill, Longton	c.1892–8
	Coombs & Holland, Wales	c.1855–8

	Cumberlidge & Humphreys, Tunstall	c.1886–95
C. J. M. & Co.	★C. J. Mason, Fenton	c.1829–45
C. J. W.	Wileman & Co., Fenton	c.1892–1925
C. K.	Charles Keeling, Shelton	c.1922–5
C. M.	Carlo Manzoni, Hanley	c.1895–8
	Charles Meigh, Hanley	c.1835–49
C. & M.	Clokie & Masterman, Castleford, Yorks.	c.1888–1961
C. M. & S.	Charles Meigh & Son, Hanley	1851–61
C. M. S. & P.	Meigh & Pankhurst, Hanley	1850–1
C. & P.	Carr & Patton, North Shields	c.1838–47
C. P. Co.	Campbellfield Pottery, Glasgow	c.1850–1905
	Clyde Pottery, Greenock	c.1850–1903
C. P. P. Co.	Crystal Porcelain Pottery Co., Cobridge	c.1882–6
C. & R.	Chesworth & Robinson, Lane End	c.1825–40
	Chetham & Robinson, Longton	c.1822–37
C. T. M.	★C. T. Maling, Newcastle	c.1859–90
C. T. M. & Sons	★C. T. Maling & Sons, Newcastle	1890–1963
C. V.	★Charles Vyse, London	c.1919–63
C. W.	C. Waine, Longton	c.1891–1920
C. & W.	Capper & Wood, Longton	c.1895–1904
C. & W. K. H.	C. & W. K. Harvey, Longton	c.1835–53
C. Y. & J.	Clementson, Young & Jameson	c.1844
C. & Y.	Clementson & Young, Shelton	c.1845–47
D.	★Derby	c.1750–1848
	T. J. Dimmock & Co., Shelton	c.1828–59
	Dillwyn & Co., Swansea	c.1811–17
D. & B.	Deakin & Bailey, Lane End	c.1828–32
	Deaville & Badderley, Hanley	c.1853–4
D. B. & Co.	Davenport Banks & Co., Hanley	c.1860–73
	Davenport Beck & Co., Hanley	c.1873–80
	Dunn Bennett & Co., Burslem	c.1875 +
D. & C. L.	Dewes & Copestake, Longton	c.1894–1915
D. D. & Co.	D. Dunderdale & Co., Castleford, Yorks.	c.1790–1820
D. L. & Co.	D. Lockhart & Co., Glasgow	c.1865–98
D. L. & S.	D. Lockhart & Sons, Glasgow	c.1898–1953
D. M.	★W. De Morgan, London	c.1872–1907
D. M. & S.	D. Methven & Sons, Kirkcaldy	c.1875–1930
D. P. Co.	Diamond Pottery Co., Hanley	c.1908–35
	Dresden Porcelain Co., Longton	c.1896–1904
D. R.	Della Robbia Co., Birkenhead	c.1894–1901
D. & S.	Dimmock & Smith, Hanley	c.1826–59
E. & Co.	Edgerton & Co., Lane End	c.1823–7
E. B.	E. Bailey, Lane	c.1827–30
	★E. Bingham, Castle Hedingham, Essex	c.1864–1901
E. & C.	Edgerton & Co., Lane End	c.1823–7
E. B. & B.	Edge, Barker & Barker, Fenton	c.1836–40
E. B. & Co.	★E. Brain & Co., Fenton	c.1903–63
	Edge, Barker & Co., Fenton	c.1835–6
E. & B.	Evans & Booth, Burslem	c.1856–69
E. & B. L.	Edwards & Brown, Longton	c.1882–1933

E. B. & S.	E. Booth & Son, Stoke	c.1791–1802
E. B. & J. E. L.	Bourne & Leigh, Burslem	c.1892–1941
E. C.	E. Challinor, Tunstall	c.1842–67
E. & C. C.	E. & C. Challinor, Fenton	c.1862–91
E. & E. W.	★Enoch Wood & Sons, Burslem	c.1818–46
E. & F.	Elsmore & Forster, Tunstall	c.1853–71
	Evans & Foulkes, Hanley	c.1876
E. F. B.	E. F. Bodley & Co., Burslem	c.1862–5
E. F. B. & Co.	F. Bodley & Co., Burslem	c.1862–5
E. F. B. & Son	E. F. Bodley & Son, Longport	c.1881–98
E. G. & C.	Everard Glover & Colclough, Lane End	c.1847
E. & G. P.	E. & G. Phillips, Longport	c.1822–34
E. & H.	Eardley & Hammersley, Tunstall	c.1862–6
E. I. B.	E. J. Birch, Shelton	c.1796–1814
E. J.	Elijah Jones, Cobridge	c.1831–40
E. J. D. B.	E. J. D. Bodley, Burslem	c.1875–92
E. K. B.	Elkin, Knight & Bridgwood, Fenton	c.1827–40
E. K. & Co.	Elkin Knight & Co., Fenton	c.1822–6
E. M. & Co.	Edge, Malkin & Co., Burslem	c.1871–1903
E. & N.	Elkin & Newton, Longton	c.1844–5
E. P. Co.	Empire Porcelain Co., Stoke	c.1896–1967
E. S. & Co.	Eardley, Spear & Co., Tunstall	c.1873
E. W.	Edward Walley, Cobridge	c.1845–60
	★Enoch Wood, Burslem	c.1790–1818
E. W. & M.	Ellis, Unwin & Mountford, Hanley	c.1860–1
E. W. & S.	★Enoch Wood & Sons, Burslem	1818–46
F. & Co.	T. Fell & Co., Newcastle	c.1817–90
F. & Sons	Ford & Sons, Burslem	c.1893–1938
F. & Sons Ltd	Ford & Sons Ltd, Burslem	c.1908–38
F. B.	Frederick Booth, Bradford, Yorks.	c.1881
	Ferrybridge Pottery, Yorks.	19th–20th century
F. B. & Co.	★F. Beardmore & Co., Fenton	c.1903–14
F. & B.	★Worcester, Flight & Barr	c.1792–1807
F. B. B.	★Worcester, Flight, Barr & Barr	c.1813–40
F. C.	F. Cartlidge & Co., Longton	c.1889–1904
F. C. & Co.	Ford Challinor & Co., Tunstall	c.1865–80
F. & C.	Ford, Challinor & Co., Tunstall	c.1865–80
F. G. B.	G. F. Bowers, Tunstall	c.1842–68
F. & H.	Forester & Hulme, Fenton	c.1887–93
F. M.	F. Malcolm, Stoke	c.1859–60
	F. Mills, Hanley	c.1884–92
	Francis Morley, Hanley	c.1845–9
F. M. & Co.	F. Morley & Co., Hanley	c.1849–58
F. & P.	Ford & Pointon, Hanley	c.1917–36
F. & R.	Ford & Riley, Burslem	c.1882–93
F. & R. P.	★F. & R. Pratt & Co., Fenton	1818 +
F. & R. P. & Co.	F. & R. Pratt & Co., Fenton	1818 +
F. & S.	Ford & Son, Burslem	c.1893–1964
F. T. & R.	Flacket, Toft & Robinson, Longton	c.1858
F. W. & Co.	F. Winkle & Co., Stoke	c.1890–1931

G. & Co.	Gallimore & Co., Longton	c.1906–34
	★Grainger & Co., Worcester	c.1839–1902
	Grove & Co., Stoke	c.1867–9
G. & A.	Galloway & Atkinson, Newcastle	c.1870
G. Bros	J. & R. Godwin, Cobridge	c.1834–66
	Grimwade Bros, Hanley and Stoke	c.1886–1900
	Gelson Brothers	c.1868–75
G. B.	George Baguley, Hanley	c.1850–4
	Grimwades Ltd, Stoke	c.1900 +
G. B. & Co.	G. Bennett & Co., Stoke	c.1894–1902
G. & B.	Goodwin & Bullock, Longton	c.1852–6
G. B. H.	Goodwin, Bridgwood & Harris, Lane End	c.1829–31
G. B. & H.	Goodwin, Bridgwood & Harris, Lane End	c.1829–31
G. B. O.	Goodwin, Bridgwood & Orton, Lane End	c.1827–9
G. B. & O.	Goodwin, Bridgwood & Orton, Lane End	c.1827–9
G. & C. J. M.	★Mason, Lane Delph	c.1813–29
G. C. P. Co.	Clyde Pottery Co., Greenock	c.1850–1903
G. & D.	Guest & Dewsbury, Llanelly	c.1877–1927
G. &. E.	Goodwin & Ellis, Lane End	c.1839–40
G. F. B.	★G. F. Bowers, Tunstall	c.1842–68
G. F. B. B. T.	★G. F. Bowers, Tunstall	c.1842–68
G. F. S.	G. F. Smith, Stockton	c.1855–60
G. G.	George Guest, Tunstall	c.1875–92
G. G. & Co.	★G. Grainger, Worcester	c.1839–1902
G. G. W./S. P.	★G. Grainger, Worcester	c.1848–65
G. H. & Co.	Gater Hall & Co., Tunstall and Burslem	c.1895–1943
G. & H. H.	Godwin & Hewitt, Hereford	c.1889–1910
G. J.	★George Jones, Stoke	c.1861–73
G. J. & S(ons)	★George Jones & Sons, Stoke	c.1874–1951
G. L. A.	★G. L. Ashworth & Bros, Hanley	c.1862 +
G. L. A. & Bros	★G. L. Ashworth & Bros, Hanley	c.1862 +
G. L. B. & Co.	G. L. Bentley & Co., Longton	c.1898–1912
G. M. C.	Creyke & Sons Ltd, Hanley	c.1920–48
G. P.	George Phillip, Longport	c.1834–47
	George Procter, Longton	c.1840–2
G. P. Co.	★Baker, Bevans & Irwin, Swansea	c.1813–38
	George Proctor & Co., Longton	c.1892–1940
G. R.	George Ray, Longton	c.1846–52
	G. Rogers, Hanley	c.1829–32
G. P. Co.	★Baker, Bevans & Irwin, Swansea	c.1813–38
G. P. & Co.	George Proctor & Co., Longton	c.1891–1940
G. R. & Co.	Godwin Rowley & Co., Burslem	c.1828–31
G. S. & Co.	George Skinner & Co., Stockton	c.1855–70
G. S. & S.	George Shaw & Sons, Rotherham	c.1887–85
G. & S.	Grove & Stark, Longton	c.1871–85
G. & S. Ltd	Gibson & Sons, Burslem	c.1885 +
G. T. M.	G. T. Mountford, Stoke	c.1888–98
G. T. & S.	G. W. Turner & Sons, Tunstall	c.1873–95
G. W.	★George Grainger, Worcester	c.1839–1902
	George Weston, Lane End	c.1807–30
	G. Wooliscroft, Tunstall	c.1851–54
G. W. & Co.	G. Wood & Co., Shelton	c.1853

G. W. & S.	G. Warrilow & Sons, Longton	c.1887–1940
G. W. & Sons Ltd	G. Warrilow & Sons, Longton	c.1887–1940
G. W. T. S.	G. W. Turner & Sons, Tunstall	c.1873–
G. W. T. & S.	G. W. Turner & Sons, Tunstall	c.1873–95
G. & W.	Gildea & Walker, Burslem	c.1881–5
G. & W. S. & Co.	G. & W. Smith & Co., Stockton	c.1860
H.	Hackwood, Hanley	19th century
	W. & J. Harding, Shelton	c.1862–72
	F. Hughes & Co., Fenton	c.1889–1953
	W. Hulme, Burslem	c.1891–1941
H. & Co.	Hackwood & Co., Hanley	c.1807–27
	Hammersley & Co., Longton	c.1887–1932
	Hill & Co., Longton	c.1898–1920
H. A. & Co.	H. Alcock & Co., Cobridge	c.1861–1910
	H. Adams & Co., Longton	c.1870–85
	H. Aynsley & Co., Longton	c.1873 +
H. & A.	Hammersley & Astbury, Longton	c.1872–5
	Hulse & Adderley, Longton	c.1869–75
H. B.	H. Burgess, Burslem	c.1864–92
	Hawley Bros, Rotherham, Yorks.	c.1868–1903
	Hines Bros, Fenton	c.1886–1907
H. B. & Co.	Harvey, Bailey & Co., Lane End	c.1833–5
	Heath, Blackhurst & Co., Burslem	c.1859–77
H. & B.	Hampson & Broadhurst, Longton	c.1847–53
	Harrap & Burgess, Hanley	c.1894–1903
	Heath & Blackhurst, Burslem	c.1859–77
	Hibbert & Boughey, Longton	c.1889
H. & C.	Harding & Cockson, Cobridge	c.1834–60
	Hope & Carter, Burslem	c.1862–80
	Hulme & Christie, Fenton	c.1893–1902
H. C. Co.	Hanley China Co., Hanley	c.1899–1901
H. & D.	Hallam & Day, Longton	c.1880–5
H. F.	F. Hughes & Co., Fenton	c.1889–1953
H. F. W. & Co. Ltd	H. F. Wedgwood & Co. Ltd, Longton	c.1954–9
H. & G.	Heath & Greatbatch, Burslem	c.1891–3
	Holland & Green, Longton	c.1853–82
	Hollinshead & Griffiths, Burslem	c.1890–1909
	Hulse & Ginder, Fenton	c.1827–33
H. & H.	Hilditch & Hopwood, Lane End	c.1835–59
H. H. & M.	Holdcraft, Hill & Mellor, Burslem	c.1860–70
H. J.	A. G. Harley Jones, Fenton	c.1907–34
H. J. C.	H. J. Colclough, Longton	c.1897–1937
H. J. W.	H. J. Wood, Burslem	c.1884 +
H. & K.	Hackwood & Keeling, Hanley	c.1835–6
	Hollinshead & Kirkham, Tunstall	c.1870–1956
H. L. & Co.	Hancock, Leigh & Co., Tunstall	c.1860–2
H. & M.	Hamilton & Moore, Longton	c.1840–58
	★Hicks & Meigh, Shelton	c.1806–22
	Hilditch & Martin	c.1815–32
H. M. I.	★Hicks, Meigh & Johnson, Shelton	c.1822–35
H. M. & I.	★Hicks, Meigh & Johnson, Shelton	c.1822–35

H. M. J.	*Hicks, Meigh & Johnson, Shelton	c.1822–35
H. M. & J.	*Hicks, Meigh & Johnson, Shelton	c.1822–35
H. M. W. & Sons	H. M. Williamson & Sons, Longton	c.1879–1941
H. N. & A.	Hulse, Nixon & Adderley, Longton	c.1853–68
H. P.	H. Palmer, Hanley	c.1760–80
H. P. Co.	Hanley Porcelain Co., Hanley	c.1892–9
H. & P.	Harrison & Phillips, Burslem	c.1914–15
H. P. & M.	Holmes, Plant & Maydew, Burslem	c.1876–85
H. & R.	Hall & Read, Burslem	c.1882–8
	Hughes & Robinson	
H. & R. J.	H. & R. Johnson, Cobridge and Tunstall	c.1902 +
H. & S.	Hart & Son (Retailers), London	c.1826–69
	Hilditch & Sons, Lane End	c.1819–35
	Holmes & Son, Longton	c.1898–1903
H. T.	Tooth & Co., Derbyshire	c.1887–1900
H. W. & Co.	Hancock, Whittington & Co., Burslem	c.1863–72
	Hawley, Webberley & Co., Longton	c.1895–1902
H. & W.	Hancock & Whittingham, Stoke	c.1873–9
	Holdcroft & Wood, Tunstall	c.1864–71
I. D. B.	J. D. Baxter, Hanley	c.1823–7
I. E. B.	J. & E. Baddeley, Shelton	c.1784–1806
I. H.	J. Heath, Hanley	c.1770–1800
I. H. & Co.	J. Heath & Co., Tunstall	c.1828–41
I. K.	J. Kishere, London	c.1800–43
I. M.	*J. Meir, Tunstall	c.1812–36
I. M. & Co.	J. Miller & Co., Glasgow	c.1869–75
I. M. & S.	*J. Meir & Sons, Tunstall	c.1837–97
I. R.	J. Ridgway, Shelton	c.1830–41
I. R. & Co.	*Coalport, Shropshire	c.1820–50
I. T.	J. Twigg, Kilnhurst	c.1822–81
I. W. & Co.	I. Wilson & Co., Yorks.	c.1852–87
I. W. R.	*Ridgway, Hanley	c.1813–30
I. W. & R.	*Ridgway, Hanley	c.1813–30
J. & Co.	Jackson & Co., Yorks	c.1870–87
J. A.	J. Alcock, Colridge	c.1848–60
	J. Amison, Longton	c.1882–99
	J. Aynsley, Longton	c.1864–73
J. B.	J. Beech, Burslem	c.1877–89
	J. & M. P. Bell & Co., Glasgow	c.1842–1928
	J. Bevington, Hanley	c.1872–92
	J. Broadhurst & Sons, Fenton	c.1862 +
J. B. & Co.	J. Bennett & Co., Hanley	c.1896–1900
	Bennett & Shenton, Hanley	c.1900–3
	J. Bevington & Co., Hanley	c.1869–7
J. B. & S.	J. Beech & Son, Longton	c.1860–98
	J. Broadhurst & Sons, Fenton	c.1862 +
J. B. W.	J. B. Wathen, Fenton	c.1864–9
J. C.	J. Clementson, Shelton	c.1839–64
J. C. L.	J. Chew, Longton	c.1903–4
J. C. & Co.	J. Carr & Co., North Shields	c.1845–1900

	J. Cartlidge & Co., Longton	c.1864–7
	J. Chetham & Co., Stoke	c.1870–2
J. & C. W.	J. & C. Wileman, Fenton	c.1864–9
J. D.	J. Deaville, Hanley	c.1854
	J. Drewry, Lane End	c.1812–25
	J. Dudson, Hanley	c.1838–88
J. D. & Co.	J. Dimmock & Co., Hanley	c.1862–1904
J. D. B.	J. D. Baxter, Hanley	c.1823–7
J. E.	Jones Edwards, Burslem	c.1842–51
	John Edwards, Longton	c.1847–53
J. E. B.	J. & E. Baddeley, Shelton	c.1784–1806
J. E. & Co.	J. Edwards & Co., Fenton	c.1847–1900
J. E. & S.	J. Edwards & Son, Burslem	c.1851–82
J. F. A.	J. F. Adderley, Longton	c.1901–5
J. F. & Co.	J. Furnival & Co., Cobridge	c.1845–70
J. F. & C. W.	J. & C. Wileman, Fenton	c.1864–7
J. F. E.	J. F. Elton & Co. Ltd, Burslem	c.1901–10
J. F. E. & Co. Ltd	J. F. Elton & Co. Ltd, Burslem	c.1901–10
J. F. W.	J. F. Wileman, Fenton	c.1869–92
J. G.	J. Gerrard, Hanley	c.1846–53
	John Goodwin, Longton	c.1845–51
	J. Gosling, Burslem	c.1896–8
	J. Grove, Hanley	c.1852–61
	★George Jones, Stoke	c.1861–1951
J. & G. L.	Jackson & Gosling, Longton	c.1866 +
J. & G. A.	J. & G. Alcock, Cobridge	c.1839–46
J. G. S. & Co.	J. Goodwin, Stoddard & Co., Longton	c.1898–1940
J. & G. V.	J. & G. Vernon, Burslem	c.1880–9
J. H.	J. Holdcroft, Longton	c.1865–1939
	J. Holland, Turnstall	c.1852–4
J. H. & Co.	J. Heath & Co., Tunstall	c.1828–41
	J. Hollins & Co., Hanley	c.1888–92
J. H. B.	J. H. Baddeley, Hanley	c.1841–53
J. H. C. & Co.	J. H. Cope & Co., Longton	c.1887–1947
J. H. W.	J. H. Walton, Longton	c.1912–21
J. H. W. & Sons	J. H. Weatherby & Sons, Hanley	c.1891 +
J. J. & Co.	J. Jackson & Co., Rotherham	c.1870–87
J. K.	J. Kent, Longton	c.1897 +
J. K. L.	J. Kent, Longton	c.1897 +
J. K. K.	J. K. Knight, Longton	c.1846–55
J. L. C.	J. L. Chetham, Longton	c.1841–62
J. M.	★J. Meir, Tunstall	c.1812–36
	J. Miller, Glasgow	c.1869–75
J. M. & Co.	★James Macintyre & Co., Burslem	c.1860
	John Marshall & Co., Bo'ness	c.1860–99
	J. Maudesley & Co., Tunstall	c.1862–4
	J. Miller & Co., Glasgow	c.1869–75
J. M. & S.	★J. Meir & Son, Tunstall	c.1837–97
J. & M. P. B. & Co.	J. & M. P. Bell & Co., Glasgow	c.1842–1928
J. P.	J. Proctor, Longton	1843–6
J. P. & Co.	J. Pankhurst & Co., Hanley	c.1852–83
J. P. & Co. (contd)	J. Plant & Co., Stoke	c.1891–1902

	J. Pratt & Co., Lane Delph	c.1851–72
J. P. & Co. (L)	J. Pratt & Co. Ltd, Fenton	c.1872–8
J. P. Ltd	J. Pearson Ltd, Brampton	c.1907 +
J. & P.	Jackson & Patterson, Newcastle	1830–45
J. R.	James Reeves, Fenton	c.1870–1948
	★J. Ridgway, Shelton	c.1830–55
	J. Robinson, Burslem	c.1876–98
J. R. & Co.	J. Ridgway & Co., Shelton	c.1830–55
	★Coalport, Shropshire	c.1820–60
J. R. B. & Co.	J. Ridgway, Bates & Co., Shelton	c.1856–58
J. R. & F. C.	J. R. & F. Chetham, Longton	c.1846–69
J. & R. G.	J. & R. Godwin, Cobridge	c.1834–66
J. R. H.	J. & R. Hammersley, Hanley	c.1877–1917
J. R. & S.	J. Robinson & Son, Castleford	c.1905–33
J. S. & Co.	Jones, Shepherd & Co., Longton	c.1867–8
	J. Shore & Co., Longton	c.1887–1905
J. S. H.	Hill Pottery & Co., Burslem	c.1861–7
J. S. S. B.	J. Sadler & Sons, Burslem	c.1899 +
J. S. W.	J. S. Wild, Longton	c.1904–27
J. & S. A.	J. & S. Alcock, Colridge	c.1848–9
J. T.	J. Tams (& Sons Ltd), Longton	c.1875 +
	J. Twenlow, Shelton	c.1795–7
	J. Twigg, Kilnhurst, Yorks.	c.1822–81
J. T. Ltd	J. Tams Ltd, Longton	c.1912 +
J. T. & S(ons)	J. Tams & Sons, Longton	c.1903–12
	J. Thompson & Sons, Glasgow	c.1816–84
J. & T. B.	J. & T. Bevington, Hanley	c.1865–78
J. & T. E.	J. & T. Edwards, Burslem	c.1839–41
J. & T. F.	J. & T. Furnival, Shelton	c.1843
J. & T. L.	J. & T. Lockett, Longton	c.1836–49
J. T. H.	J. T. Hudden, Longton	c.1859–85
J. V.	James Vernon, Burslem	c.1860–80
J. V. junr	James Vernon, Burslem	c.1860–80
J. V. & S.	James Vernon, Burslem	c.1860–80
J. W.	J. Woodward, Swadlincote	c.1859–88
J. & W.	Jones & Walley, Cobridge	c.1841–3
J. W. D.	Ashby Potters Guild, Woodville, Derbys.	c.1909–22
J. W. P. & Co.	J. W. Pankhurst & Co., Hanley	c.1850–82
J. W. R.	★Ridgway, Shelton	c.1814–30
J. & W. R.	★Ridgway, Shelton	c.1814–30
J. W. & S.	J. Wilson & Sons, Fenton	c.1898–1926
J. Y.	J. Yates, Hanley	c.1784–1835
K. & Co.	Keeling & Co., Burslem	c.1886–1936
	W. Kirby & Co., Fenton	c.1879–85
	Kirkland & Co., Etruria	c.1892 +
K. & B.	★Worcester, Kerr & Binns	1852–62
	King & Barratt, Burslem	c.1898–1940
	Knapper & Blackhurst, Tunstall	c.1867–88
K. & Co. B.	Keeling & Co., Burslem	c.1886–1936
K. E. & Co.	Knight, Elkin & Co., Fenton	c.1826–46
K. E. B.	King, Edge & Barratt, Burslem	c.1896–7

	Knight, Elkin & Bridgwood, Fenton	c.1829–40
K. & E.	Knight & Elkin, Fenton	c.1826–47
K. F. A. P. Co.	Kensington Fine Art Pottery Co., Hanley	c.1892–9
K. & M.	Keys & Mountford, Stoke	c.1850–7
K. P. B.	Kensington Pottery Ltd, Hanley	1922 +
K. P H.	Kensington Pottery Ltd, Hanley	1922 +
L.	Herculaneum Pottery, Liverpool	c.1793–1841
L. & Sons	Lancaster & Sons, Hanley	c.1900–44
L. & A.	Lockhart & Arthur, Glasgow	c.1855–64
L. B. & C.	Lockett, Baguley & Cooper, Hanley	c.1855–61
L. E. & S.	Liddle, Elliot & Son, Burslem	c.1862–70
L. H.	Lockett & Hulme, Lane End	c.1822–6
L. & L.	Lovatt & Lovatt, Langley Mill, Notts.	c.1895 +
L. & M.	Ynysmedw Pottery, Swansea	c.1860–70
L. & P.	Lakin & Poole, Burslem	c.1791–5
L. P. & Co.	Livesley, Powell & Co., Hanley	c.1851–66
L. P. Co. Ltd	Longton Pottery Co. Ltd, Longton	c.1946–55
L. S.	Lancaster & Sons, Hanley	c.1900–44
L. W.	Lewis Woolf & Sons, Ferrybridge, Yorks.	c.1856–83
L. W. & S.	Lewis Woolf & Sons, Ferrybridge, Yorks.	c.1856–83
M.	J. Maddock, Burslem	c.1842–55
	*Maling, Newcastle	c.1817–30
	*Minton, Stoke	c.1793 +
	Royal Albion China Co., Longton	c.1921–48
M. & Co.	*Minton, Stoke	c.1841–73
	Moore & Co., Hanley	c.1898–1903
	Moore & Co., Fenton	c.1872–92
M. & A.	Morley & Ashworth, Hanley	c.1859–61
M. & B.	*Minton, Stoke	c.1836–41
M. & C. L.	Matthews & Clark, Longton	c.1902–6
M. & E.	Mayer & Elliott, Longport	c.1856–61
M. E. & Co.	*Middlesbrough Earthenware Co., Yorks.	c.1844–52
M. F. & Co.	Morley, Fox & Co., Fenton	c.1906–44
M. H. & Co.	Mason, Holt & Co., Longton	c.1857–84
	Minton, Hollins & Co., Stoke	c.1845 +
M. & H.	Marsh & Heywood, Tunstall	c.1818–36
	Mason & Holt, Longton	c.1857–84
	Middleton & Hudson, Longton	c.1877–88
	*Minton, Stoke	c.1845–68
M. J. B.	*Blakeney Pottery Ltd., Stoke	c.1969 +
M. L. & Co.	Moore, Leason & Co., Fenton	c.1892–6
M. & M.	Mayer & Maudesley, Tunstall	c.1837–8
	Price Bros, Burslem	c.1896–1903
M. & N.	Mayer & Newbold, Lane End	c.1817–33
M. P. & Co.	Middlesbrough Pottery Co., Yorks.	c.1834–44
M. & P.	Meigh & Pankhurst, Hanley	c.1850–1
M. & S.	Maddock & Seddon, Burslem	c.1839–42
	Mayer & Sherratt, Longton	c.1906–41
	*C. Meigh & Son, Hanley	c.1851–61
M. S. & Co.	Myott Son & Co., Stoke, Cobridge	c.1898 +

M. T. & Co.	Marple, Turner & Co., Hanley	c.1851–3
M. & T.	Machin & Thomas, Burslem	c.1831–2
M. & U.	Mogridge & Underhay (retailers) Ltd	c.1912 +
M. V. & Co.	Mellor, Venables & Co., Burslem	c.1834–51
M. W. & Co.	Massey & Wildblood & Co., Longton	c.1887–9
	Morgan, Wood & Co., Burslem	c.1860–70
M. W. H.	Malkin, Walker & Hulse, Longton	c.1858–64
N. H.	*New Hall, Shelton	c.1820–35
N. H. & Co.	Neale, Harrison & Co., Hanley	c.1875–85
N. S.	*Spode (on 'New Stone' wares), Stoke	c.1805–25
N. W. P. Co.	New Wharf Pottery Co., Burslem	c.1878–94
O. H. E. C.	Old Hall Earthenware Co., Hanley	c.1861–86
O. P.	Ollivant Potteries Ltd, Stoke	1948–54
O. P. L.	Ollivant Potteries Ltd, Stoke	1948–54
P.	Pennington, Liverpool	c.1770–85
	*Pilkingtons, nr Manchester	c.1897–1957
	*Pinxton Porcelain Works, Derbys.	c.1796–1813
	J. H. Proctor, Longton	c.1857–84
P. & Co.	Pearson & Co., Chesterfield	c.1805 +
	Pountney & Co., Bristol	c.1849–89
P. & Co. Ltd	Pountney & Co. Ltd, Bristol	c.1889 +
P. & A.	Pountney & Allies, Bristol	c.1815–35
P. A. B. P.	Pountney & Allies, Bristol	c.1815–35
P. B.	Poulson Bros, Ferrybridge, Yorks.	c.1884–1927
P. & B.	Powell & Bishop, Hanley	c.1876–8
P. B. & Co.	Pinder Bourne & Co., Burslem	c.1862–82
P. B. & H.	Pinder, Bourne & Hope, Burslem	1851–62
P. B. L.	Plant Bros, Longton	c.1898–1906
P. B. & S.	Powell, Bishop & Stonier, Hanley	c.1878–91
P. & C.	Physick & Cooper, Hanley	c.1899–1900
P. & F. W.	P. & F. Warburton, Cobridge	c.1795–1802
P. G.	Sampson Bridgwood & Son, Longton	c.1870 +
P. H. Co.	Hanley Porcelain Co., Hanley	c.1892–9
P. H. & Co.	P. Holdcroft & Co., Burslem	c.1846–52
P. H. G.	Pratt, Hassall & Gerrard, Fenton	c.1822–34
P. L.	R. H. & S. L. Plant (Ltd), Longton	c.1898 +
P. P.	Pearl Pottery Co. Ltd, Hanley	c.1894–1912
P. P. Co. Ltd	Pearl Pottery Co. Ltd, Hanley	c.1912–36
	Plymouth Pottery Co. Ltd	c.1856–63
P. & S.	Pratt & Simpson, Fenton	c.1878–83
P. & S. L.	R. Plant & Sons, Longton	c.1895–1901
P. & U.	Poole & Unwin, Longton	c.1871–6
P. W.	P. Warburton, Cobridge	c.1802–12
P. W. & Co.	Podmore, Walker & Co., Tunstall	c.1834–59
P. W. & W.	Podmore, Walker & Co., Tunstall	c.1834–59
R.	S. & J. Rathbone, Tunstall	c.1812–35
	*J. Ridgway, Hanley	c.1830–55
R. & Co.	Reid & Co., Longton	c.1913–46

R. & A.	Ridgway & Abington, Hanley	c.1847–60
R. B.	Robinson Bros, Castleford	c.1897–1904
R. B. & Co.	R. Britton & Co., Leeds	c.1850–3
R. B. & S.	R. Britton & Son, Leeds	c.1872–8
R. C. & A.	Read, Clementson & Anderson, Hanley	c.1836
R. C. & Co.	R. Cockran & Co., Glasgow	c.1846–1918
R. & C.	Read & Clementson, Hanley	c.1833–5
R. (C) Ltd	A. G. Richardson, Cobridge	c.1920–1
R. C. R.	S. & E. Collier, Reading	c.1870–1957
R. & D.	Redfern & Drakeford, Longton	c.1892–1933
R. F. & S.	R. Floyd & Sons, Stoke	c.1907–30
R. G.	R. Gallimore, Longton	c.1906–34
	R. Garner, Fenton	18th century
R. G. S.	R. G. Scrivener & Co., Hanley	c.1870–83
R. G. S. & Co .	R. G. Scrivener & Co., Hanley	c.1870–83
R. H.	R. Hammersley, Burslem	c.1860–83
R. H. & Co.	R. Hall & Co., Tunstall	c.1841–9
R. H. F. P.	*R. Heron (& Son) Scotland	c.1837–60
R. H. & S.	R. Hammersley & Son, Burslem	c.1884–1905
	*R. Heron & Son, Scotland	c.1850–60
R. H. P. & Co.	R. H. Plant & Co., Longton	c.1881–98
R. H. & S. L. P.	R. H. & S. L. Plant, Longton	c.1898 +
R. & L.	*Robinson & Leadbeater, Stoke	c.1864–1924
R. & M.	*Ridgway & Morley, Hanley	c.1842–5
R. & M.	Roper & Meredith, Longton	c.1913–24
R. M. A.	R. M. Astbury, Lane End	c.1790
R. M. & S.	R. Malkin & Sons, Fenton	c.1882–92
R. M. W. & Co.	*Ridgway, Morley, Wear & Co., Hanley	c.1836–42
R. & N.	Rowley & Newton Ltd, Longton	c.1896–1901
R. & P.	Rhodes & Proctor, Burslem	c.1883–5
R. S.	S. Radford, Fenton	c.1879–1957
	R. Stevenson & Son, Cobridge	c.1810–32
R. & S.	Rigby & Stevenson, Hanley	c.1894–1954
	Robinson & Son, Longton	c.1881–1903
R. S. & Co.	Rathbone, Smith & Co., Tunstall	c.1883–97
R. S. R.	Ridgway, Sparkes & Ridgway, Hanley	c.1873–9
R. S. & S.	R. Stevenson & Son, Cobridge	c.1832–5
R. S. W.	Stevenson & William, Cobridge	c.1825
	Rye Pottery, Sussex	c.1869–1920
R. & T.	Reed & Taylor, Ferrybridge Pottery, Yorks.	c.1843–50
R. T. & Co.	Reed & Taylor, Ferrybridge Pottery, Yorks.	c.1843–50
R. V. W.	R. V. Wildblood, Longton	c.1887–8
R. & W.	Ray & Wynne, Lane End	c.1837–46
	Robinson & Wood, Hanley	c.1832–6
R. W. & B.	Robinson, Wood & Brownfield, Cobridge	c.1838–41
R. W. M.	*Martin Brothers, London	c.1873–1914
S. (printed)	*Caughley, Shropshire	c.1775–99
S. (impressed)	*Spode, Stoke	c.1777–1805
S. Bros	Stubbs Bros, Fenton	c.1899–1904
S. & C.	Shore & Coggins, Longton	c.1911 +
S. Ltd	Swinnertons Ltd, Hanley	c.1906 +

S. & Sons	Southwick Pottery, Sunderland	c.1829–38
S. A. & Co.	★S. Alcock & Co., Burslem	c.1830–59
S. B. & S.	S. Barker & Son, Swinton, Yorks.	c.1834–93
	S. Bevington & Son, Hanley	c.1851–63
	S. Boyle & Sons, Hanley	c.1850–2
	S. Bridgwood & Son, Longton	c.1853 +
S. & B.	Sefton & Brown, Ferrybridge	c.1897–1919
	Shorter & Boulton, Stoke	c.1878–1905
S. & B. T.	Smith & Binnall, Tunstall	c.1897–1900
S. C.	S. Clive, Tunstall	c.1875–80
S. & C.	Shore & Coggins, Longton	c.1911 +
S. C. C.	Star China Co., Longton	c.1900–19
S. C. & Co.	S. Clive, Tunstall	c.1875–80
S. C. H. L.	Shore, Coggins & Holt, Longton	c.1905–10
S. E.	S. Elkin, Longton	c.1856–64
S. & E.	Swift & Elkin, Longton	c.1840–3
S. & F.	Smith & Ford, Burslem	c.1895–8
S. F. & Co.	★S. Fielding & Co., Stoke	c.1879 +
S. H.	S. Hallen, Burslem	c.1851–4
	S. Hancock, Tunstall and Stoke	1858–90
	★Derby, King Street	c.1861–1935
S. H. & S.	S. Hancock & Sons, Stoke	c.1891–35
	S. Hughes & Son, Burslem	c.1853–5
S. J.	S. Johnson, Burslem	c.1887–1912
S. J. B.	S. Johnson, Burslem	c.1887–1912
S. & J. B.	S. & J. Burton, Hanley	c.1832–45
S. J. R.	★S. & J. Rathbone, Tunstall	c.1812–35
S. & J. R.	S. & J. Rathbone, Tunstall	c.1812–35
S. K. & Co.	S. Keeling & Co., Hanley	c.1840–50
S. L.	S. Longbottom, Nafferton, Yorks.	Late 19th cent.
S. & L.	Stanley & Lambert, Longton	c.1850–4
S. M. & Co.	★Sunderland Potteries	c.1803–74
S. & N. L.	Salt & Nixon, Longton	c.1897–1904
So. (printed)	★Caughley, Shropshire	c.1775–99
S. P. Ltd	Sylvan Pottery Ltd, Hanley	c.1946 +
S. S.	S. Smith Ltd, Longton	c.1846–1963
	Southwick Pottery, Sunderland	c.1872–82
S. & S.	D. Sutherland & Sons, Longton	c.1865–75
S. & S. S.	Shaw & Sons, Tunstall	c.1892–1910
S. & V.	Sant & Vodrey, Cobridge	c.1887–93
S. & W.	Stockton Pottery	c.1870–80
S. W. P.	South Wales Pottery, Llanelly	c.1839–58
Sx. (printed)	★Caughley, Shropshire	c.1775–99
T.	See mark list under 'Tebo' Toulouse	c.1750–90
T. A.	T. Ainsworth, Stockton	c.1858–67
T. A. & S. G.	T. A. & S. Green, Fenton	c.1876–89
T. B.	T. Bevington, Hanley	c.1877–91
T. & B.	Tomkinson & Billington, Longton	c.1868–70
T. B. & Co.	T. Booth & Co., Burslem	c.1868–72
T. B. & S.	T. Boote & Son, Burslem	c.1842 +
T. B. & S. (contd)	T. Brown & Sons, Ferrybridge	c.1919 +

T. B. G.	T. & B. Godwin, Burslem	c.1809–34
T. & B. G.	T. & B. Godwin, Burslem	c.1809–34
T. C.	T. Cone, Longton	c.1892 +
T. & C. F.	T. & C. Ford, Hanley	c.1854–71
T. C. W.	T. Wild & Co., Longton	c.1896–1904
T. D. & Co.	T. Dimmock & Co, Shelton	c.1828–67
T. E.	T. Edwards, Burslem	c.1844–8
T. F.	T. Ford, Hanley	c.1853–74
	T. Forester, Longton	c.1880–3
	T. Fradley, Stoke	c.1875–85
T. F. & Co.	T. Fell & Co., Newcastle	c.1830–90
	T. Forester & Co., Longton	c.1888
	T. Furnival & Co., Hanley	c.1844–6
T. F. & S.	T. Forester & Sons, Longton	c.1883–1959
T. F. & Sons	T. Furnival & Sons, Cobridge	c.1871–90
T. F. & S. Ltd	T. Forester & Sons Ltd, Longton	c.1891–1959
T. G.	T. Godwin, Burslem	c.1834–54
	T. Goodfellow, Tunstall	c.1828–60
	T. Green, Fenton	c.1848–58
T. G. B.	T. G. Booth, Tunstall	c.1876–83
T. G. & F. B.	T. G. & F. Booth, Tunstall	c.1883–91
T. G. G. & Co.	T. G. Green & Co. Ltd, Church Gresley, Derbys.	c.1864 +
T. I. & Co.	T. Ingleby & Co., Tunstall	c.1834–5
T. I. & J. E.	T. I. & J. Emberton, Tunstall	c.1869–82
T. J. & J. M.	T. J. & J. Mayer, Burslem	c.1843–55
T. & K. L.	Taylor & Kent, Longton	c.1867 +
T. & L.	Tams & Lowe, Longton	c.1865–74
T. L. K.	Taylor & Kent Ltd, Longton	c.1867 +
T. M.	*Blakeney Pottery, Stoke	c.1969 +
	T. Mayer, Stoke	c.1956 +
	T. Morris, Longton	c.1897–1901
T. M. R.	T. M. Randall (decorator), Madeley	c.1825–40
T. N. & Co.	T. Nicholson & Co., Castleford	c.1854–71
To.	See mark list under 'Tebo' Toulouse	c.1750–90
T. P.	T. Peake, Tunstall	c.1830–51
	T. Pinder, Burslem	c.1848–51
	T. Plant, Lane End	c.1825–50
T. P. L.	T. P. Ledgar, Longton	c.1900–5
T. P. & S.	T. Phillips & Son, Burslem	c.1845–6
T. R. & Co.	T. Rathbone & Co., Tunstall	c.1898–1923
	T. Rathbone & Co., Portobello	c.1810–45
T. & R. B.	T. & R. Boote, Burslem	c.1842 +
T. R. & P.	Tundley, Rhodes & Proctor, Burslem	c.1873–83
T. S. & C(oy)	T. Shirley & Co., Greenock	c.1840–57
T. T.	Taylor, Tunnicliffe & Co., Hanley	c.1868 +
	T. Till, Burslem	c.1850
T. T. & Co.	Taylor, Tunnicliffe & Co., Hanley	c.1868 +
T. & T.	Turner & Tomkinson, Tunstall	c.1860–72
T. T. & S.	Thomas Till & Sons, Burslem	c.1850–1929
T. U. & Co.	U. Thomas & Co., Hanley	c.1888–1905
T. W. & Co.	T. Wood & Co., Burslem	c.1885–96

T. W. & S.	T. Wood & Sons, Burslem	c.1896–7
U. C. & N.	U. Clark & Nephews, Dicker, Sussex	c.1900–20
U. H. P. Co.	Upper Hanley Pottery Co., Hanley	c.1895–1910
U. H. & W.	Unwin, Holmes & Worthington, Hanley	c.1865–8
U. M. & T.	Unwin, Mountford & Taylor, Hanley	c.1864
U. T. & Co.	U. Thomas & Co., Hanley	c.1888–1905
V. & B.	Venables & Baines, Burslem	c.1851–2
V. M. & Co.	Venables, Mann & Co.	c.1853–6
W.	E. Walley, Cobridge	c.1845–56
	Wardle & Co., Hanley	c.1871–1935
	T. Wolfe, Stoke	c.1784–1818
	*E. Wood, Burslem	c.1784–92
	*Worcester porcelains`	c.1760–75 ·
W(★★★)	See mark list	c.1790–1815
W. & C.	Wade & Co., Burslem	c.1887–1927
	Whittaker & Co., Hanley	c.1886–92
	*Wileman & Co., Longton	c.1892–1925
W. & Sons	H. M. Williamson & Son, Longton	c.1874–1941
W. & A.	Wardle & Ash, Hanley	c.1859–62
	Warren & Adams, Longton	c.1853–64
	Wild & Adams, Longton	c.1909–27
W. A. & Co.	*William Adams, Tunstall and Stoke	c.1893–1917
W. A. & S.	*William Adams, Tunstall and Stoke	c.1819–64
W. A. A.	W. A. Adderley (& Co.), Longton	c.1876–1905
W. A. A. & Co.	W. A. Adderley & Co., Longton	c.1876–1905
W. B.	W. Baker (& Cò.), Fenton	c.1839–68
	W. Beech, Burslem	
	W. Bennett, Hanley	c.1882–1937
W. & B.	Wagstaff & Brunt, Longton	c.1880–1927
	*J. Wedgwood (& Sons Ltd)	c.1769–80
	Wood & Baggaley, Burslem	c.1870–80
	Wood & Bowers, Burslem	c.1839
	Wood & Brownfield, Cobridge	c.1838–50
W. & B. Ltd	Wood & Barker Ltd, Burslem	c.1897–1903
W. B. & S.	*W. Brownfield & Sons, Cobridge	c.1871–91
W. B. & Sons	*W. Brownfield & Sons, Cobridge	c.1871–91
W. & C.	Walker & Carter, Longton	c.1872–89
	Wood & Challinor, Tunstall	c.1828–43
	Wood & Clarke (& Co.), Burslem	c.1871–2
W. C. & Co.	*Chamberlain & Co., Worcester	c.1845–52
	Wood, Challinor & Co., Tunstall	c.1860–4
W. & Co.	Wardle & Co., Hanley	c.1882–1909
W. D. M.	*W. De Morgan, London	c.1872–1907
W. E.	W. Emberton, Tunstall	c.1851–69
W. & E. C.	W. & E. Corn, Longport	c.1864–1904
W. E. W.	W. E. Withinshaw, Burslem	c.1873–8
W. F.	W. Fifield (decorator), Bristol	c.1810–55
W. F. & Co.	Whittingham, Ford & Co., Burslem	c.1868–73
W. F. & R.	Whittingham, Ford & Riley, Burslem	c.1876–82
W. & G.	W. & G. Harding, Burslem	c.1851–5

W. H.	W. Hackwood, Hanley	c.1827–43
	W. Hudson, Longton	c.1889–1941
W. & H.	Wildblood & Heath, Longton	c.1889–99
	Wood & Hulme, Burslem	c.1882–1905
	Worthington & Harrop, Hanley	c.1856–73
W. H. & Co.	Whittaker, Heath & Co., Hanley	c.1892–8
W. H. & S.	W. Hackwood & Sons, Hanley	c.1846–9
	Wildblood, Heath & Sons, Longton	c.1899–1927
W. H. G.	*W. H. Goss, Stoke	c.1858–1944
W. H. L.	W. H. Lockitt, Hanley	c.1901–19
W. H. & W.	Wood, Hulse & Winkle, Hanley	c.1882–5
W. & J. B.	W. & J. Butterfield, Tunstall	c.1854–61
W. & J. H.	W. & J. Harding, Hanley	c.1862–72
W. K. & Co.	W. Kirkby & Co., Fenton	c.1879–85
W. L. L.	W. Lowe, Longton	c.1874–1930
W. & L.	Wildblood & Ledgar, Longton	c.1896–1900
W. & L. L.	Wathen & Lichfield, Fenton	c.1862–4
W. & P.	Wood & Piggott, Tunstall	c.1869–71
W. P. Co.	Wellington Pottery Co., Hanley	c.1899–1901
W. R.	*W. Ridgway, Hanley	1830–54
W. & R.	*Carlton Ware, Stoke	c.1958 +
	Wilkinson & Richhuss, Hanley	c.1856–62
	Wiltshaw & Robinson, Stoke	c.1890–1957
	Wittman & Roth, London	c.1880 +
	Wright & Rigby, Cobridge	c.1882–4
W. R. & Co.	*W. Ridgway & Co., Hanley	c.1834–54
W. R. S. & Co.	*W. Ridgway, Son & Co., Hanley	c.1838–48
W. S.	W. Smith & Co., Stockton, Yorks	c.1845–84
W. S. & Co.	*Stockton Pottery	c.1825–55
W. S. Junr & Co.	W. Smith & Co., Stockton, Yorks	c.1845–55
W. S. K.	W. S. Kennedy, Burslem	c.1844–55
W. & Sons	H. M. Williamson & Sons, Longton	c.1879–1941
W. & S. E.	W. & S. Edge, Lane Delph	c.1841–8
W. & T. A.	W. & T. Adams, Tunstall	c.1860–90
W. T. H.	W. T. Holland, South Wales Pottery	c.1860s
W. W.	J. Wedg-Wood, Burslem	c.1841–60
	Wilkinson & Wardle, Denby, Yorks	c.1864–6
W. & W. B.	Wooldridge & Walley, Burslem	c.1898–1901
W. & W. Co.	W. Wood & Co., Burslem	c.1873–1932
Y.	Yale & Barker, Longton	c.1841–53
Y. M. P.	Ynysmendw Pottery, Swansea	c.1850
Y. P.	Ynysmendw Pottery, Swansea	c.1850
Z. B.	Z. Boyle, Hanley	c.1823–8
Z. B. & S.	Z. Boyle & Son, Hanley	c.1828–50

Further details of many of the marks listed in this section will be found in the *Encyclopaedia of British Pottery and Porcelain Marks* (Herbert Jenkins Ltd, 1964). The reader is also referred, in the case of initials found on porcelains, to my *Encyclopaedia of British Porcelain Manufacturers* (Barrie & Jenkins, 1988), Section V, pages 817–29.

Registered Designs 1839–1883 and Registration Numbers 1884–1999

The British Government passed various Acts to give copyright protection to new designs. The Sculpture Copyright Act of 1797 and the updated 1814 version gave protection to modelled forms provided that the proprietor marked his productions with the words 'Published by', followed by his name, a simple address and the date of first issue. Obviously such clear markings are self-explanatory but few ceramic objects, apart from jugs, bear this form of marking.

From 1839 to 1842 new designs were required to be registered at the Board of Trade in London, under Acts 2 & 3 Victoria c. 17. Again the name, address and date of the initial publication had to be given on the copies. A relatively few ceramic designs were registered, see following list.

1839

Nov 19	no. 106	John Ridgway

1840

Mar 5	273	John Ridgway
Mar 5	274	John Ridgway
Oct 28	444	John Ridgway

1841

May 10	692	John Ridgway & Co.
Sept 2	808–9	J. & T. Edwards
Sept 10	832	J. & T. Edwards
Sept 27	849	John Ridgway & Co.
Dec 31	1002–5	Kidston & Co. (Glasgow)

1842

Mar 17	1141–2	Charles Meigh
May 30	1266–8	James Edwards

The dates of these registrations, together with the allocated number, can occur as part of the printed mark on these 1839–42 designs.

In 1842 a system was introduced whereby a new design or form could be registered at the Design Office, in London. To secure the copyright protection a rendering of the new unique form, or pattern, had to be sent to the office in Whitehall, together with the required registration fee. The relevant facts were then entered in ledgers, under various 'classes'. There were thirteen classes, of which class IV covered ceramic objects (glass wares were class III).

Each day several designs would have been received for registration. These were entered in the first register under the date of receipt and allocated a reference number and a 'parcel number'. This parcel number indicated the entry number for that day but each entry could cover several objects registered by any one firm. The drawings or other representation of the article were filed in separate books.

Once entered, a special coded device was issued by the Registrar and sent to the manufacturer. Exact copies of this device had to be affixed to the protected product. This British Registered Design mark took the basic diamond shape shown opposite.

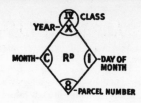

The class number IV appears at the top. The initials R^D appear in the centre, standing for registered. The inner angles showed the coded letter for the year, at twelve o'clock; the day of the month, given in clear numbers, at three o'clock; the parcel number at six o'clock; and the code letter for the month at nine o'clock.

The above placing applies to the period 1842 to 1867. From 1868 to 1883 the order was amended, so that the year letter appears in the three o'clock position; the coded month letter at six o'clock; the parcel number at nine o'clock; and the day number at twelve o'clock. I here show this amended device as used from 1868.

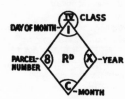

Below are given the year and month letters for the two periods.

YEARS

1842–67		1868–83	
Year Letter at Top		*Year Letter at Right*	

A = 1845	N = 1864	A = 1871	L = 1882
B = 1858	O = 1862	C = 1870	P = 1877
C = 1844	P = 1851	D = 1878	S = 1875
D = 1852	Q = 1866	E = 1881	U = 1874
E = 1855	R = 1861	F = 1873	V = 1876
F = 1847	S = 1849	H = 1869	W = March 1–6 1878
G = 1863	T = 1867	I = 1872	X = 1868
H = 1843	U = 1848	J = 1880	Y = 1879
I = 1846	V = 1850	K = 1883	
J = 1854	W = 1865		
K = 1857	X = 1842		
L = 1856	Y = 1853		
M = 1859	Z = 1860		

MONTHS (BOTH PERIODS)

A = December	E = May	K = November (and December 1860)
B = October	G = February	M = June
C or O = January	H = April	R = August (and September 1–19 1857)
D = September	I = July	W = March

Once decoded, the present-day owner can discover the date, month and year of registration. This of course only represents the earliest possible date of the piece. The initial fee gave protection for a three-year period but in practice the mark can occur on pieces made after this period had lapsed.

Having discovered the date of registration, the reader can further ascertain the name of the person or firm concerned in the registration, with the assistance of the following list. In most cases this will be the manufacturer but in a few instances the registration was made by other persons or firms, such as the designer or a retailer. I have marked such non-ceramic names with an asterisk. In a very few cases a design was registered by two firms and, of course, there was nothing to stop the copyright owner selling on the rights to another manufacturer. Such provisions are, however, very rare and in most cases the name given in this listing will relate to the manufacturer. It is, of course, vital to read and decode the mark correctly!

As some registrations relate to the form of the piece (or part of a piece, such as a moulded-edged design) and other entries relate to the added decoration it is possible to have two separate registration marks on a single piece. In general terms an impressed or moulded mark will relate to the basic shape of the piece, whilst a printed mark will relate to the decoration.

I have in this unique listing been at pains to give some helpful basic indication of the subject of the registration: the form or added pattern. As the listing exceeds 4,000 entries each description has to be brief. For this reason also I have not quoted the official entry number as this does not normally appear on the piece. I have also needed to abbreviate the place-name of the manufacturer's town or city.

By far the largest number of firms were situated in the group of Staffordshire towns which make up the district we know as The Potteries, now embraced by the City of Stoke-on-Trent. These Staffordshire townships were Burslem (B); Cobridge (C); Fenton (F); Hanley (H); Lane End (LE); Longport (Lpt); Longton (L); Shelton (Sh), part of Hanley; Stoke (S); and Tunstall (T). To these Staffordshire place-names one can add Etruria (E), the name of the Wedgwood factory, and Newcastle-under-Lyme (N). Other place-names and my abbreviations included in this comprehensive list are: Belleek (Bel); Birmingham (Bir); Broseley (Br); Burton-on-Trent (BT); Cambridge (Cam); Cardiff (Cf); Coalport (Cpt); Derby (D); Devon (De); Dublin (Du); France (Fr); Germany (Ger); Glasgow (G); Great Yarmouth (GY); Hastings (Hgs); Ireland (Ire); Jackfield (J); Leeds (Lds); Liverpool (Liv); Llanelly (Ll); London (Ln); Manchester (M); New York (NY); Newcastle-upon-Tyne (NT); Norwich (No); Prescot (P); Scotland (Sc); Sheffield (Sd); Shropshire (Shrop); Sunderland (Su); Swadlincote (Sw); Swinton (Sn); Tamworth (Tam); Wales (Ws); Wareham (Wm); Watcombe (Wat); Weston-super-Mare (WsM); Winchester (Win); Worcester (W); Wordsley (Wy); and Yorkshire (Y).

The original files covering the 1839–42 and the 1842–83 systems are held at the Public Record Office at Kew. The general references are BT43 for the representations of the designs or shapes and BT44 for the registers of names and addresses with the reference number. It should be noted that some of these records are in a very bad state and some are not available for public study.

The Potteries Museum (at Bethesda Street, Hanley) has a good selection of British ceramics of registered forms or bearing registered patterns and marks.

The copyright in the following unique listing is twofold. The basic list of names and dates has been extracted from the original official documents retained at the Public Record Office at Kew. These are covered by Crown Copyright and have been published here by kind permission of the authorities. The additional information on the manufacturers and their registered products plus the format of the listing is covered by my copyright. This listing must not therefore be copied without written permission from both parties.

As mentioned earlier, an asterisk in the list below refers to non-manufacturing persons or firms, mainly situated away from pottery producing areas.

Date	Parcel	Manufacturer	Town	Object
1842 (X at top)				
Sep 22	1	James Dixon & Son★	Sd	Jug, for mounting
Nov 2	1	Joseph Wolstenholme★	Sd	Tray
Nov 3	1	Joseph Wolstenholme★	Sd	Covered jug
Nov 26	3	Henry Hunt★	Ln	Flower pot
Nov 26	3	Henry Hunt★	Ln	Flower pot
Dec 2	3	Joseph Clementson	Sh	Lucerne design
Dec 2	3	Joseph Clementson	Sh	Rustic scenery design
Dec 30	2	James Edwards	B	Toiletwares
1843 (H at top)				
Jan 24	2	John Ridgway & Co.	Sh	Candlestick
Jan 24	2	John Ridgway & Co.	Sh	Candlestick
Feb 3	4	T. Woodfield★	Ln	Water closet
Feb 21	1	Samuel Alcock & Co.	B	Vase form
Feb 21	1	Samuel Alcock & Co.	B	Flared vase
Feb 21	1	Samuel Alcock & Co.	B	Two-handled vase
Feb 21	1	Samuel Alcock & Co.	B	Celery vase
Feb 21	1	Samuel Alcock & Co.	B	Inkstand
Mar 21	5	Josiah Wedgwood & Sons	E	Fluted ewer
Mar 21	5	Josiah Wedgwood & Sons	E	Moulded ewer
Mar 31	6	Samuel Alcock & Co.	B	Pierced vase
May 2	4	Josiah Wedgwood & Sons	E	Printed design
May 5	1	W. S. Kennedy	B	Bell pull
May 11	2	W. S. Kennedy	B	Door knob
May 13	4	Jones & Wolley	C	Moulded jug
Jun 14	5	Samuel Alcock & Co.	B	Teawares
Aug 30	8	James Edwards	B	Dinnerwares
Oct 6	2	James Edwards	B	Dinner ware
Nov 10	3	Minton & Co.	S	Plate form
Nov 28	5	Thomas Dimmock & Co.	Sh	Indian festoon print
Dec 14	10	G. F. Bowers & Co.	T	Teawares
1844 (C at top)				
Feb 15	9	Samuel Alcock & Co.	B	Vases
Feb 20	4	Samuel Alcock & Co.	B	Vases
Mar 1	6	Hamilton & Moore	L	Teawares
Mar 5	3	Mellor, Venables & Co.	B	Teawares
Mar 7	4	J. & T. Lockett	LE	Teawares
April 3	3	Thomas Edwards	B	Dinnerwares
April 11	4	Hilditch & Hopwood	LE	Teawares
May 7	4	T. Dimmock, jnr & Co.	Sh	Rhine pattern
Jun 29	3	T. Dimmock, jnr & Co.	Sh	Lily pattern
July 20	5	John Ridgway & Co.	Sh	Tureen form and printed patterns
July 30	2	Herbert Minton & Co.	S	Cup forms
Aug 15	3	Knight & Elkin	S	Baronial Halls pattern

Aug 21	7	Herbert Minton & Co.	S	Figures & ewer
Sept 9	7	Cyples, Barlow & Cyples	LE	Teawares
Sept 19	4	John Ridgway & Co.	Sh	Dinnerwares
Sept 21	2	Henry Hunt★	Ln	Hyacinth pot
Sept 30	7	Charles Meigh	H	Moulded jug
Oct 14	4	Copeland & Garrett	S	Floral design
Oct 17	3	Clementson, Young & Jameson	Sh	Aleppo pattern
Oct 23	4	Thomas Davenport	Bir	Button
Oct 30	4	Herbert Minton & Co.	S	Dinnerwares & figure
Nov 6	4	Herbert Minton & Co.	S	Toiletwares
Nov 11	5	James Edwards	B	Printed design
Nov 13	4	John Ridgway & Co.	Sh	Dinnerwares
Nov 22	4	Thomas Dimmock, junr & Co.	Sh	Bohemia pattern
Nov 26	3	Ray & Wynne	LE	Teawares
Dec 2	3	Copeland & Garrett	S	Printed patterns
Dec 7	4	Thomas Edwards	B	Fluted tea wares
Dec 16	6	W. Ridgway, Son & Co.	H	Catshill moss pattern
Dec 24	2	John Meir & Son	T	Mazara pattern

1845 (A at top)

Jan 11	6	George Phillips	Lpt	Corinth pattern
Jan 15	2	Clementson, Young & Jameson	Sh	Jug form
Jan 21	6	T. J. & J. Mayer	Lpt	Moulded jug
Jan 27	5	John Rose & Co.	Cpt	Moulded edging
Feb 26	5	W. S. Kennedy	B	Forms
Feb 27	3	George Phillips	Lpt	Dinnerwares
Mar 5	1	Copeland & Garrett	S	Moulded edging
Mar 6	5	H. Minton & Co.	S	Figure
Mar 17	10	H. Minton & Co.	S	Printed design
Mar 20	1	H. Minton & Co.	S	Moulded jug
Mar 31	4	Thomas Pearce★	Ln	Figure – Wesley
April 10	1	Thomas Pearce★	Ln	Figure – Fletcher
April 25	2	Copeland & Garrett	S	Printed pattern
April 26	1	George Pearce★	Ln	Figure – J. Wesley
April 26	3	T. & R. Boote with Edward Walley and E. Jones	B C H	Dinnerwares
April 30	2	Jacob Furnival	C	Printed design
May 8	2	Herbert Minton & Co.	S	Moulded jug
May 10	3	E. Walley and T. & R. Boote	C	Moulded jug
May 31	1	Francis Morley	Sh	Dinnerwares
Jun 19	1	George Phillips	Lpt	Lobelia pattern
Jun 26	3	Minton & Co.	S	Moulded cup
July 5	1	George Phillips	Lpt	Six forms
July 5	2	Enoch Wood	B	Lucerne pattern
July 26	1	William Adams & Sons	S	Habrana pattern
Aug 28	3	Joseph Clementson	Sh	Printed design
Sept 4	3	Copeland & Garrett	S	Tartan designs
Sept 11	2	Thomas Phillips & Son	B	Floral pattern
Sept 19	1	Minton & Co.	S	Moulded font
Oct 6	1	H. Minton & Co.	S	Open work border & printed pattern

Oct 21	1	Copeland & Garrett	S	Printed design
Oct 22	2	Clementson & Young	Sh	Dinnerwares
Nov 15	2	Bayley & Ball	L	Printed jug
Nov 22	2	Minton & Co.	S	Moulded jug
Dec 4	4	John Ridgway	Sh	Dinnerwares
Dec 24	2	W. Pigott★	Ln	Button
Dec 27	3	James Edwards	B	Jug shape
Dec 29	2	Joseph Clementson	Sh	Dinnerwares
Dec 30	3	Furnival & Clark	H	Falstaff jug

1846 (I at top)

Jan 7	2	Joseph Clementson	Sh	Tessino pattern
Jan 24	2	Jacob Furnival & Co.	C	Printed design
Feb 26	5	T. J. & J. Mayer	Lpt	Covered bowl
Mar 2	4	Minton & Co.	S	Moulded jug
Mar 11	2	W. S. Kennedy	B	Finger plates
April 7	1	W. S. Kennedy	B	Finger plates
April 17	3	Copeland & Garrett	S	Finger plate
May 21	3	H. Minton & Co.	S	Ewer & basin
May 26	2	H. Minton & Co.	S	Moulded jugs
Jun 6	1	W. Chamberlain & Co.	W	Moulded edge
Jun 26	2	H. Minton & Co.	S	Moulded edge
Jun 30	3	John Goodwin	L	Printed design
July 11	1	J. K. Knight	L	Printed design
July 16	1	W. Ridgway Son & Co.	H	Moulded jug
July 17	1	John Ridgway & Co.	H	Aladdin design
July 21	1	Francis Morley & Co.	Sh	Printed design
Aug 1	2	Josiah Wedgwood & Sons	E	Toiletwares
Aug 3	1	Josiah Wedgwood & Sons	E	Floral design
Aug 3	2	H. Minton & Co.	S	Toiletwares
Sept 3	2	George Phillips	Lpt	Printed design
Sept 3	3	Francis Morley & Co.	Sh	Printed design
Sept 14	4	Copeland & Garrett	S	Printed design
Sept 26	2	John Ridgway & Co.	Sh	Forms
Sept 29	3	T. J. & J. Mayer	B	Moulded jug
Sept 30	2	Copeland & Garrett	S	Finger plate
Oct 26	1	Francis Morley & Co.	Sh	Dinnerwares
Oct 26	5	James Edwards	B	Jug form
Nov 3	1	Ridgway & Abington	H	Rustic teapot
Nov 5	2	George Phillips	Lpt	Friburg pattern
Nov 12	3	Charles Meigh	H	Gothic jug
Nov 16	2	H. Minton & Co.	S	Floral design
Nov 16	2	H. Minton & Co.	S	Moulded edge
Nov 21	2	Thomas Furnival & Co.	H	Printed pattern
Nov 21	2	Thomas Furnival & Co.	H	Jug form
Dec 3	4	Ridgway & Abington	H	Moulded jug
Dec 4	2	H. Minton & Co.	S	Printed design
Dec 4	4	T. R. Swaine	P	Chimney top
Dec 10	3	Joseph Clementson	SL	Toiletwares
Dec 14	3	James Edwards	B	Coffee pot
Dec 14	4	Minton & Co.	S	Floral pattern
Dec 16	1	John Goodwin	L	Printed design

Dec 17	2	Copeland & Garrett	S	Border designs
Dec 29	2	Edward Challiner	T	Printed design
Dec 31	3	Josiah Wedgwood & Sons	E	Printed design

1847 (F at top)

Jan 9	4	John Ridgway & Co.	Sh	Dinnerwares
Jan 9	7	Copeland & Garrett	S	Dinnerwares
Feb 2	7	T. & R. Boote	B	Jug form
Feb 8	5	T. J. & J. Mayer	B	Pot & cruet
Feb 12	5	George Greatback	E	Hearth stone
Feb 15	4	Copeland & Garrett	S	Border design
Feb 15	4	Copeland & Garrett	S	Nightlightholder
Mar 11	4	Stock & Sharp★	Bir	Pump case
Mar 17	3	John Wedge Wood	T	Printed design
Mar 17	6	John Ridgway & Co.	Sh	Printed designs
Mar 19	4	Batty & Co.★	Ln	Cruet
Mar 22	2	Bailey & Ball	L	Moulded plate
Mar 23	7	H. Minton & Co.	S	Inkstand
Mar 30	1	James Edwards	B	Jug form
April 3	6	S. Alcock & Co.	B	Rustic jug
April 27	1	S. Alcock & Co.	B	Jug –Maomi
May 12	4	Copeland & Garrett	S	Garden border
May 14	1	H. Minton & Co.	S	Dolphin ornament
May 14	1	H. Minton & Co.	S	Moulded jug
May 19	1	C. Heaton & Co.★	Ln	Anchovey pot
Jun 5	2	Joseph Mappin★	Sd	Knife handle
Jun 11	4	James Edwards	B	Dinnerwares
Jun 11	6	Joseph Alexander★	No	Plate design
Jun 21	5	J. Rose & Co.	Cpt	Moulded jug
Jun 25	2	James Edwards	B	Dinnerwares
Jun 25	5	Edmund Sharpe	Dshire	Spittoon
July 5	5	Mellor, Venables & Co.	B	Dinnerwares
July 5	5	Mellor, Venables & Co.	B	Medici design
July 15	1	Mellor, Venables & Co.	B	Dinnerwares
July 16	5	James Edwards	B	Shapes (4)
July 27	3	T. J. & J. Mayer	B	Dinnerwares
Aug 3	3	J. Rose & Co.	Cpt	Jug form
Aug 16	2	James Edwards	B	Covered dish
Aug 17	2	W. T. Copeland	S	Plate form
Aug 17	2	W. T. Copeland	S	Portland vase jug
Aug 19	3	H. Minton & Co.	S	Una & lion
Aug 26	2	James Edwards	B	Plate form
Sept 9	3	W. T. Copeland	S	Floral print
Sept 16	3	W. T. Copeland	S	Floral print
Sept 25	5	John Wedge Wood	T	Fluted teapot
Oct 1	4	Thomas Peake	T	Tile
Oct 2	5	John Ridgway & Co.	Sh	Dinnerwares
Oct 4	3	H. Minton & Co.	S	Dorathea figure
Oct 8	4	John Wedge Wood	T	Dinnerwares
Oct 13	1	W. T. Copeland	S	Toiletwares
Oct 23	2	H. Minton & Co.	S	Jug form
Oct 23	2	H. Minton & Co.	S	Vandyke pattern

Oct 27	1	John Ridgway & Co.	Sh	Dinnerwares
Nov 11	4	H. Minton & Co.	S	Border form
Nov 23	2	E. P. Willock & Co.	M	Wall bracket
Nov 23	4	Josiah Wedgwood & Co.	E	Printed design
Dec 1	2	J. Rose & Co.	Cpt	Moulded borders
Dec 1	2	J. Rose & Co.	Cpt	Teaware forms
Dec 10	3	H. Minton & Co.	S	Children figures
Dec 15	4	H. Minton & Co.	S	Printed design
Dec 23	2	E. P. Willock & Co.	M	Wall bracket

1848 (U at top)

Jan 1	4	Barker & Till	B	Dinnerwares
Jan 6	4	G. Grainger	W	Plate form
Jan 18	2	W. T. Copeland	S	Floral design
Feb 11	3	H. Minton & Co.	S	Garden seat?
Feb 11	3	H. Minton & Co.	S	Jardinere
Feb 17	2	E. P. Willock	M	Wall bracket
Feb 18	3	E. P. Willock	M	Wall bracket
Feb 29	12	H. Minton & Co.	S	Knife handle
Mar 4	4	H. Minton & Co.	S	Bread dish
Mar 7	1	Ridgway & Abington	H	Moulded jugs
Mar 14	2	W. T. Copeland	S	Printed design
Mar 15	2	W. T. Copeland	S	Covered dish
Mar 20	7	Wood & Brownfield	C	Plate form
Mar 27	8	J. & S. Alcock, junr	C	Dinnerwares
April 15	4	J. Ridgway & Co.	Sh	Dinnerwares
April 22	3	Josiah Wedgwood & Sons	E	Cheese dish
April 27	4	Josiah Wedgwood & Sons	E	Tureen form
May 30	3	Thomas Peake	T	Ridge tile
Jun 20	4	G.F. Bowers & Co.	T	Teawares
Jun 30	2	W.T. Copeland	S	Printed designs
Jun 30	3	Ridgway & Abington	H	Moulded design
July 26	5	F. Hands★	Bir	Frame
July 27	2	Thomas Peake	T	Tile
Aug 10	3	G. Grainger	W	Tureen form
Aug 14	3	John Campbell★	G	Bear design
Aug 16	8	Thomas Pinder	B	Printed design
Aug 23	2	John Wedge Wood	T	Printed design
Aug 26	2	John Meir & Son	T	Roselle design
Sept 12	1	Hart & Sons★	Ln	Finger plate
Sept 15	3	W.T. Copeland	S	Printed design
Sept 18	4	Charles Meigh	H	Moulded jug
Sept 20	1	Hart & Sons★	Ln	Finger plate
Sept 30	7	John Ridgway & Co.	Sh	Dinnerwares
Oct 17	3	T. & R. Boote	B	Moulded jug
Nov 4	2	W.T. Copeland	S	Moulded jug
Nov 13	4	W.T. Copeland	S	Moulded jug
Nov 15	3	Henry Meadows★	Ln	Moulded jug
Nov 21	5	H. Minton & Co.	W	Moulded jug
Nov 21	5	H. Minton & Co.	W	Printed design
Nov 27	2	John Ridgway & Co.	Sh	Printed design
Dec 16	3	James Edwards	B	Dinnerwares
Dec 28	2	John Ridgway	Sh	Teaware forms

1849 (S at top)

Jan 3	2	W. Adams & Sons	T	Athens design
Jan 20	2	W. Davenport & Co.	Lgt	Teaware forms
Feb 2	4	Mellor, Venables & Co.	B	Dinnerwares
Feb 16	5	Minton & Co.	S	Printed design
Feb 16	11	Ridgway & Abington	H	Moulded design
Feb 26	2	J. Rose & Co.	Cpt	Moulded jug
Mar 13	2	Joseph Clementson	Sh	Printed design
Mar 26	5	Minton & Co.	S	Moulded bowl
Mar 27	2	Cope & Edwards	L	Moulded teapot
Mar 31	2	J. Ridgway & Co.	Sh	Moulded teawares
April 2	5	Podmore, Walker & Co.	T	California pattern
April 10	4	W. T. Copeland	S	Moulded edge
April 16	6	C. J. Mason	L	Plate form
May 24	1	Mr Wedge Wood	T	Printed design
Jun 7	3	T. J. & J. Mayer	Lpt	Printed design
July 5	3	Hart & Son★	Ln	Finger plate
July 16	2	Ridgway & Abington	H	Moulded design
Aug 11	4	W. T. Copeland	S	Moulded pot
Aug 15	2	H. Minton & Co.	S	Moulded jug
Aug 17	2	W. T. Copeland	S	Printed design
Aug 27	5	Mellor, Venables & Co.	B	Windsor design
Sept 14	6	F. & R. Pratt & Co.	F	Moulded jar
Sept 28	6	J. Ridgway	Sh	Moulded forms
Oct10	2	J. Ridgway	Sh	Printed design
Oct 12	4	Minton & Co.	S	Plate form
Oct 26	5	J. Hollinshead	Sh	Wesley design
Nov 9	4	W. T. Copeland	S	Moulded jug
Nov 17	2	Minton & Co.	S	Moulded jug
Nov 22	2	W. T. Copeland	S	Printed design
Nov 30	5	J. Rose & Co.	Cpt	Moulded edge
Dec 6	3	W. T. Copeland	S	Printed holly design
Dec 15	4	T. J. & J. Mayer	Lpt	Moulded jar

1850 (V at top)

Jan 3	1	W. Davenport & Co.	Lpt	Dinnerwares
Jan 14	4	J. Ridgway	Sh	Hand basins
Jan 26	6	George Grainger	W	Printed design
Feb 13	1	George Grainger	W	Printed design
Feb 13	3	J. & M. P. Bell & Co.	G	Ionia print
Feb 27	4	George Grainger	W	Moulded edge
Mar 9	3	W. T. Copeland	S	Printed design
Mar 12	5	John Isaac★	Liv	Ink bottle
Mar 30	9	J. Rose & Co.	Cpt	Teaware forms
April 2	11	William Pierce★	L	Fireplace
April 3	5	James King★	L	Pomatuim pot
April 4	4	T. J. & J. Mayer	B	Printed design
April 8	1	J. Clementson	Sh	Siam design
April 13	7	Minton & Co.	S	Fluted teawares
April 18	11	J. Rose & Co.	Cpt	Teaware forms
April 25	3	Minton & Co.	S	Floral design
May 25	8	James Moon	M	Smoke conductor

Jun 4	1	J. & M. P. Bell & Co.	G	Vase print
Jun 5	3	Barker & Son	B	Missouri print
Jun 21	4	Edward Walley	C	Moulded jug
July 2	2	T. J. & J. Mayer	B	Moulded jug
July 16	5	C. & W. K. Harvey	L	Dinnerwares
July 30	3	Charles Young	Ln	Loaf casket
Aug 16	3	E. P. Willock & Co.	M	Wall bracket
Aug 23	2	J. Wedge Wood	T	Printed design
Sept 9	5	Thomas Till	B	Moulded jug
Sept 16	8	J. & M. P. Bell & Co.	G	Fluted teawares
Sept 16	9	J. Ridgway	Sh	Printed design
Sept 19	2	W. T. Copeland	S	Printed design
Sept 21	1	Mellor, Venables & Co.	B	Dinnerwares
Sept 28	2	E. P. Willock & Co.	M	Wall bracket
Oct 9	2	Minton & Co.	S	Toiletwares
Oct 17	6	W. T. Copeland	S	Moulded bracket
Oct 23	6	Crosse & Blackwell★	L	1851 Exh. meat pot
Oct 31	5	Gabriel Benda★	L	Tobacco jar
Nov 4	4	Josiah Wedgwood & Sons	E	Cambridge ale jug
Nov 20	7	Francis Morley & Co.	Sh	Dinnerwares
Nov 22	3	J. Rose & Co.	Cpt	Moulded border
Dec 5	3	Francis Morley & Co.	Sh	Dinnerwares
Dec 19	5	J. Rose & Co.	Cpt	Moulded edge
Dec 19	6	T. J. & J. Mayer	Lpt	Moulded jug
Dec 20	6	W. T. Copeland	S	Floral design

1851 (P at top)

Jan 7	4	James Green★	Ln	1851 exhibition print
Feb 10	9	William Brownfield	C	Moulded border
Feb 26	8	J.C. Quince★	Ln	1851 exhibition print
Mar 14	4	J.C. Quince★	Ln	Houses of Parliament
Mar 17	13	John Ridgway & Co.	Sh	Teawares
Mar 17	13	John Ridgway & Co.	Sh	Dinnerwares
Mar 17	13	John Ridgway & Co.	Sh	Fountains
Mar 17	13	John Ridgway & Co.	Sh	Wash basins
Mar 31	4	J. & M. P. Bell & Co.	G	Jug form
April 8	5	J. Gardner★	Ln	Punch inkstand
April 9	2	T. Till & Son	B	Moulded jar
April 11	4	J. & M. P. Bell & Co.	G	Toiletwares
April 11	6	W. S. Kennedy	B	Finger plate
April 14	7	J. & M. P. Bell & Co.	G	Dinnerwares
April 14	7	J. & M. P. Bell & Co.	G	Teapot
April 26	3	Edward Walley	Co	Ceres jug
April 29	2	T. S. Bale	Sh	Marble designs
May 30	4	W. S. Copeland	S	Printed designs
Jun 7	4	J. Ridgway & Co.	Sh	Staircase
Jun 11	2	W. T. Copeland	S	Printed design
Jun 11	3	Ralph Scragg (modeller)	H	Dinnerwares
Jun 19	5	W. T. Copeland	S	Printed design
July 10	3	R. Britton & Co.	Lds	Printed design
July 14	3	W. T. Copeland	S	Moulded floral pot
July 21	7	T. & R. Boote	B	Teawares

July 24	2	T. Till & Son	B	Teapot form
July 26	3	C. Collinson & Co.	B	Floral design
Aug 5	4	J. H. Maw	W	Tile
Aug 16	2	Ridgway & Abington	H	Moulded jug
Sept 2	4	T. J. & J. Mayer	B	Dinnerwares
Sept 19	3	T. & R. Boote	B	Dinnerwares
Sept 29	4	James Edwards	Lpt	Dinnerwares
Sept 30	3	James Edwards	Lpt	Dinnerwares
Oct 1	1	W. T. Copeland	S	Floral print
Oct 7	3	Chamberlain & Co.	W	Moulded borders
Oct 10	4	William Brownfield	C	Toiletwares
Oct 10	6	T. & R. Boote	B	Plate form
Oct 14	4	T. Till & Son	B	Woodbine print
Oct 16	4	William Brownfield	C	Moulded jug
Oct 17	3	George Bowden Sander★	Ln	Moulded jug
Oct 21	3	William Ridgway	Sh	Moulded jug
Nov 1	5	George Bowden Sander★	Ln	Printed designs
Nov 10	4	Ralph Scragg (modeller)	H	Teapot form
Nov 12	6	Minton & Co.	S	Printed designs
Nov 12	6	Minton & Co.	S	Jug form
Nov 13	2	Charles Meigh & Son	H	Moulded jug
Nov 14	4	George Bowden Sander★	Ln	Dinnerwares
Nov 17	8	Thomas Jackson★	M	Pot lid print
Dec 2	2	Messrs. Mayer	B	Moulded jug
Dec 4	3	Minton & Co.	S	Jardinere
Dec 4	3	Minton & Co.	S	Garden seat
Dec 5	5	John Ridgway & Co.	Sh	Dinnerwares
Dec 8	8	W. T. Copeland	S	Printed design
Dec 15	6	George Bowden Sander★	Ln	Printed border
Dec 16	1	T. Till & Son	B	Printed design

1852 (D at top)

Jan 27	1	W. & G. Harding	B	Printed design
Jan 30	6	Thomas Jackson★	M	Covered pot
Feb 17	1	Venables & Baines	B	Union print
Mar 4	2	William Brownfield	C	Toiletwares
Mar 13	3	William Ridgway	Sh	Printed design
Mar 22	7	Ralph Scragg (modeller)	H	Moulded jug
Mar 24	3	James Edwards	B	Anchor crest
Mar 24	4	Minton & Co.	S	Moulded pot
Mar 25	1	John Milner★	C	Jug cover
Mar 26	3	J. & M. P. Bell & Co.	G	Moulded jug
Mar 29	3	Thomas Jackson★	M	Printed pot lid designs
April 1	1	T. Till & Son	B	Moulded jug
April 8	4	T. Till & Son	B	Moulded candlestick
April 21	4	George Ray (modeller)	L	Polka jug
May 5	5	J. M. Blashfield	Ln	Vase forms
May 6	5	George Bowden Sander★	Ln	Teawares
May 7	2	J. M. Blashfield	Ln	Garden vases
May 7	2	J. M. Blashfield	Ln	Flower troughs
May 14	5	W. T. Copeland	S	Moulded designs
May 18	1	Minton & Co.	S	Moulded bowl

Jun 1	2	J. M. Blashfield	Ln	Tazza & bowl
Jun 5	5	Minton & Co.	S	Fluted jug
Jun 14	4	W. T. Copeland	S	Printed design
Jun 21	2	J. & T. Lockett	L	Moulded jug
July 1	2	Thomas Jackson★	M	Printed pot lid
July 5	3	J. Parkhurst & Co.	H	Moulded jug
July 23	3	Minton & Co.	S	Moulded jugs
Aug 4	3	W. T. Copeland	S	Printed designs
Aug 13	5	T. Till & Co.	B	Moulded jug
Aug 25	4	C. Meigh & Son	H	Moulded design
Aug 25	5	George Bowden Sander★	Ln	Floral printed design
Sept 3	7	Minton & Co.	S	Moulded designs
Sept 15	5	T. Till & Co.	B	Moulded jug
Sept 16	1	Minton & Co.	S	Moulded jug
Sept 24	1	Minton & Co.	S	Moulded edge
Sept 27	3	Warburton & Britton	Lds	Moulded jug
Oct 1	6	W. T. Copeland	S	Printed design
Oct 7	5	Ralph Scragg (modeller)	H	Tureen form
Oct 23	4	Davenports & Co.	Lpt	Dinnerwares
Oct 25	2	William Brownfield	C	Moulded jug
Oct 30	3	Marple, Turner & Co.	H	Printed design
Nov 4	5	John Holland	T	Printed design
Nov 11	3	Minton & Co.	S	Printed design
Nov 22	3	J. Parkhurst & Co.	H	Moulded teapot
Nov 22	3	J. Dimmock	H	Moulded teapot
Nov 25	4	Keys & Mountford	S	Parian model
Dec 16	4	J. Rose & Co.	Cpt	Moulded edge
Dec 27	1	Warburton & Britton	Lds	Moulded jug

1853 (Y at top)

Jan 3	3	W. T. Copeland	S	Printed designs
Jan 12	6	Thomas Goodfellow	T	Plate form
Jan 14	3	Davenports & Co.	Lpt	Teawares
Jan 14	3	Davenports & Co.	Lpt	Toiletwares
Jan 18	2	Davenports & Co.	Lpt	Teawares
Jan 18	2	Davenports & Co.	Lpt	Toiletwares
Jan 19	4	J. L. Gardner★	Ln	Ink bottle
Feb 4	9	James Parkhurst & Co.	H	Tureen form
Feb 10	2	George Wooliscroft	T	Dinnerwares
Feb 11	6	Worthington & Green	Sh	Moulded jug
Feb 12	3	Minton & Co.	S	Printed borders
Feb 17	4	W. S. Kennedy	B	Finger plates
Feb 26	5	W. T. Copeland	S	Moulded jug
Mar 4	12	Battam & Son★	L	Finger plates
Mar 10	2	J. & M. P. Bell & Co.	G	Printed design
Mar 17	5	J. W. Parkhurst & Co.	H	Teapot form
Mar 19	2	Minton & Co.	S	Printed design
April 2	9	C. Collinson & Co.	B	Water closet
April 4	6	J. Rose & Co.	Cpt	Moulded pot
April 23	2	W. Adams & Sons	T	Dinnerwares
May 7	5	John Alcock	C	Teaware forms
May 7	5	John Alcock	C	Dinnerwares

Jun 7	3	George Wood & Co.	Sh	Moulded jug
Jun 14	2	Livesley, Powell & Co.	H	Moulded jugs
Jun 22	3	James Parkhurst & Co.	H	Moulded jug
Jun 24	3	G. Wooliscroft	T	Eon print
Jun 24	11	Ridgway & Co.	Sh	Dinnerwares
July 18	4	John Edwards	L	Teapot form
July 20	2	J. H. Baddeley	Sh	Covered jars
Aug 8	1	Anthony Shaw	T	Printed design
Aug 10	2	Holland & Green	L	Tureen form
Sept 3	2	T. & R. Boote	B	Tureen form
Sept 6	3	Francis Morley & Co.	Sh	Dinnerwares
Sept 21	2	James Edwards	B	Dinnerwares
Oct 5	2	Venables, Mann & Co.	B	Teawares
Oct 5	2	Venables, Mann & Co.	B	Dinnerwares
Oct 6	5	J. Taylor & Son★	L	Lamp
Oct 10	3	Barrow & Co.	F	Covered dish
Oct 11	5	Ralph Scragg (modeller)	H	Covered dish
Oct 12	3	James Edwards	B	Covered dish
Oct 12	4	Livesley, Powell & Co.	H	Dinnerwares
Oct 12	4	Livesley, Powell & Co.	H	Teawares
Oct 19	4	Minton & Co.	S	Moulded teawares
Oct 22	1	T. J. & J. Mayer	B	Dinnerwares
Nov 24	2	T. Till & Son	B	Dinnerwares
Nov 26	2	W. T. Copeland	S	Panel
Nov 30	5	W. Adams & Sons	T	Printed design
Dec 6	6	John Alcock	C	Toiletwares
Dec 7	2	Ralph Scragg (modeller)	H	Moulded jug
Dec 24	3	Samuel Moore & Co.	Su	Aesop prints
Dec 24	4	John Alcock	C	Teawares

1854 (J at top)

Jan 30	4	S. Alcock & Co.	B	Moulded jug
Feb 23	3	W. T. Copeland	S	Moulded jug
Feb 28	2	Crosse & Blackwell★	Ln	Moulded jar
Mar 3	2	Thomas Jackson★	M	Bear jar print
Mar 11	4	S. Alcock & Co.	B	Printed design
Mar 20	1	T. Till & Son	B	Teapot form
Mar 22	2	James Edwards & Son	Lpt	Teawares
Mar 24	3	Minton & Co.	S	Floral printed design
Mar 27	3	George Baguley	H	Moulded jug
Mar 27	6	J. Deaville	H	Moulded jug
Mar 31	1	Holland & Green	L	Gothic jug
Mar 31	1	Holland & Green	L	Teawares
Mar 31	1	Holland & Green	L	Toiletwares
April 1	4	William Brownfield	C	Moulded jug
April 1	6	T. Till & Son	B	Teawares
April 4	3	Woolland & Hathesley★	Cam	Moulded jug
April 5	3	Ralph Scragg (modeller)	H	Moulded jug
April 6	3	S. Alcock & Co.	B	Toiletwares
April 10	3	J. Deaville	H	Moulded jug
April 10	4	S. Alcock & Co.	B	Moulded jug
April 11	5	Pearson, Farrall & Meakin	Sh	Dinnerwares

April 15	1	George Baguley	H	Moulded jug
April 21	3	Warburton & Britton	Lds	Moulded jug
May 4	4	J. Ridgway & Co.	Sh	Inhibitor
May 8	3	William Brownfield	C	Jardinere
Jun 3	2	T. Till & Son	B	Moulded jug
Jun 9	2	C. Meigh & Son	H	Moulded jug
Jun 21	5	T. & R. Boote	B	Toiletwares
July 18	2	T. & R. Boote	B	Teawares
July 18	4	S. Alcock & Co.	B	Printed design
Sept 4	2	J. Tylor & Sons★	Ln	Lamp
Sept 5	3	S. Alcock & Co.	B	Moulded edge
Sept 12	2	W. T. Copeland	S	Moulded jug
Oct 2	3	William Brownfield	C	Moulded edge
Oct 6	4	Davenports & Co.	Lpt	Teawares
Oct 9	4	T. J. & J. Mayer	B	Tureen form
Oct 31	2	George Ray	L	Moulded jug
Nov 10	5	J. Ridgway & Co.	Sh	Printed design
Dec 27	3	S. Alcock & Co.	B	Moulded jug
Dec 27	4	Parkhurst & Dimmock	H	Moulded jug
Dec 29	1	F. & R. Pratt & Co.	F	Printed pot lid

1855 (E at top)

Jan 4	2	Worthington & Green	Sh	Floral jug
Jan 6	4	S. Alcock & Co.	B	Moulded edge
Jan 15	2	Pinder, Bourne & Hope	B	Tureen form
Jan 15	4	Brougham & Mayer	T	Dinnerwares
Jan 15	4	Brougham & Mayer	T	Teawares
Jan 15	4	Brougham & Mayer	T	Toiletwares
Jan 19	3	Parkhurst & Dimmock	H	Moulded jug
Jan 30	1	John Edwards	L	Dinnerwares
Feb 3	4	J. & M. P. Bell & Co.	G	Anemone print
Feb 5	7	Coombs & Holland	Ws	Printed design
Feb 7	2	John Alcock	C	Dinnerwares
Feb 17	3	F. & R. Pratt & Co.	F	Moulded jugs
Feb 26	3	Lockett, Baguley & Cooper	Sh	Moulded edge
Feb 28	4	John Ridgway & Co.	Sh	Water closet
Mar 1	5	Minton & Co.	S	Toiletwares
Mar 1	5	Minton & Co.	S	Teawares
Mar 1	5	Minton & Co.	S	Moulded edge
Mar 5	3	Elsmore & Forster	T	Teapot form
Mar 13	4	Warburton & Britton	Lds	Moulded edge
Mar 17	1	William Baker	F	Tureen form
April 7	7	W. T. Copeland	S	Printed design
April 17	4	S. Hughes & Son	B	Tureen form
April 26	1	W. Brownfield	C	Moulded jugs
April 26	1	W. Brownfield	C	Plate form
April 28	7	Venables, Mann & Co.	B	Dinnerwares
May 10	5	Beech, Hancock & Co.	B	Jug form
May 14	3	Minton & Co.	S	Moulded jug
Jun 7	4	John Alcock	C	Dinnerwares
Jun 11	3	S. Alcock & Co.	B	"British Birds" print
July 4	5	Joseph Thompson	Dshire	Moulded jugs

July 24	1	C. Meigh & Son	H	Dinnerwares
July 24	1	C. Meigh & Son	H	Teawares
Aug 6	1	James Dudson	S	Moulded jug
Aug 8	5	James Edwards & Son	B	Dinnerwares
Aug 11	1	G. Grainger & Co.	W	Moulded edge
Aug 20	3	Thomas Ford	Sh	Teawares
Aug 27	2	Barrow & Co.	F	Toiletwares
Aug 27	2	Barrow & Co.	F	Moulded jug
Aug 27	2	Barrow & Co.	F	Teawares
Sept 3	1	S. Hughes & Son	B	Moulded jug
Sept 27	4	S. Bevington & Son	Sh	Moulded jugs
Oct 3	2	George Mayor & Co.	Ln	Covered pot
Oct 3	3	Minton & Co.	S	Teawares
Oct 17	8	M. Williamson	G	Vase forms
Oct 25	3	David Chetwynd (modeller)	C	Tureen form
Oct 29	6	G. W. Reade (Designer)	B	Dinnerwares
Nov 1	3	Josiah Wedgwood & Sons	E	Toilet jug
Nov 22	4	J. & M. P. Bell & Co.	G	Jug form
Nov 28	3	W. Brownfield	C	Moulded jug

1856 (L at top)

Jan 5	3	John Edwards	L	Toiletwares
Jan 15	4	James Pankhurst & Co.	H	Moulded jug
Jan 23	4	Minton & Co.	S	Moulded jug
Jan 31	4	Josiah Wedgwood & Sons	E	Toiletwares
Mar 11	1	Davenports & Co.	Lpt	Dessertwares
Mar 12	3	F. & R. Pratt & Co.	F	Printed designs
April 7	2	Anthony Shaw	T	Dinnerwares
April 7	2	Anthony Shaw	T	Teawares
April 7	3	J. & M. P. Bell & Co.	G	Printed design
April 18	2	William Beech	B	Moulded Jug
April 18	3	Ralph Scragg (modeller)	H	Covered dish
April 18	6	Edward Walley	C	Moulded jug
April 18	7	Ridgway & Abington	H	Moulded jug
April 30	3	W. Brownfield	C	Moulded jugs
May 8	2	Minton & Co.	S	Covered dish
May 22	1	Minton & Co.	S	Covered dish
Jun 13	3	C. Meigh & Son	H	Moulded jug
Jun 28	3	Worthington & Green	Sh	Moulded jug
Jun 30	7	Joseph Clementson	Sh	Printed design
July 28	3	Edward Challinor	T	Dora design
July 30	5	James Edwards & Son	B	Dinnerwares
Aug 12	2	F. & R. Pratt & Co.	F	Pot lid print
Aug 19	5	F. & R. Pratt & Co.	F	Hunting print
Aug 22	4	T. & R. Boote	B	Dinnerwares
Aug 22	4	T. & R. Boote	B	Toiletwares
Aug 22	4	T. & R. Boote	B	Teawares
Sept 1	3	W. T. Copeland	S	Printed designs
Oct 2	3	Henry Baggeley (modeller)	H	Royal Arms
Oct 14	4	John Roberts	Kent	Pipe
Oct 16	2	Minton & Co.	S	Jug forms
Oct 22	3	W. T. Copeland	S	Moulded jug

Nov 7	6	F. & R. Pratt & Co.	F	Pot lid print
Nov 14	9	Davenports & Co.	Lpt	Dinnerwares
Nov 27	3	Davenports & Co.	Lpt	Teawares
Nov 27	6	W. Brownfield	C	Tureen form
Nov 29	1	Edward Walley	C	Dinnerwares
Nov 29	1	Edward Walley	C	Teawares
Nov 29	1	Edward Walley	C	Toiletwares
Dec 11	4	W. T. Copeland	S	Printed design
Dec 18	2	Mayer Brothers & Elliot	Lpt	Oval tureen
Dec 23	4	Mayer Brothers & Elliot	Lpt	Circular tureen

1857 (K at top)

Jan 15	5	F. & R. Pratt & Co.	F	Pot lid print
Jan 26	7	James Edwards	B	Coffee pot
Feb 4	5	John Meir & Son	T	Dinnerwares
Feb 9	4	Minton & Co.	S	Moulded jug
Feb 17	3	Minton & Co.	S	Moulded bowl
Feb 23	9	Podmore, Walker & Co.	H	Moulded jug
Mar 20	4	John Alcock	C	Fluted teawares
April 16	1	John Alcock	C	Dinnerwares
April 29	1	W. T. Copeland	S	Printed designs
Jun 5	3	William Brownfield	C	Moulded shapes
Jun 19	1	W. T. Copeland	S	Printed design
Jun 19	2	Wilkinson & Rickhuss	H	Moulded jug
Jun 25	1	J. & M. P. Bell & Co.	G	Moulded jug
July 30	2	J. Ridgway, Bates & Co.	H	Filter
Aug 4	5	Taylor, Pears & Co.	F	Fluted dinner ware
Aug 11	3	Kerr & Binns	W	Dinnerwares
Sept 7	2	W. T. Copeland	S	Printed design
Oct 3	3	Doulton & Watts	Ln	Scent jars
Oct 14	1	Ridgway & Abington	H	Moulded jug
Oct 17	1	Mayer, Brothers & Elliot	B	Tureen form
Oct 17	2	T. & R. Boote	B	Teawares
Oct 22	1	Pratt & Co.	F	Printed figures
Nov 3	3	Maw & Co.	Br	Tiles
Nov 6	3	B. Richardson	Wy	Handle form
Nov 28	2	Kerr & Binns	W	Flower holder
Dec 4	4	Minton & Co.	S	Border form
Dec 9	2	William Brownfield	C	Moulded jug

1858 (B at top)

Jan 29	3	Cockson & Harding	H	Moulded jug
Jan 29	4	E. & W. Walley	C	Moulded jug
Feb 16	2	Crosse & Blackwell★	Ln	Moulded jar
Mar 25	2	Kerr & Binns	W	Candle holder
April 9	2	Kerr & Binns	W	Flower vase
April 17	4	Ridgway & Abington	H	Moulded border
April 22	5	T. & R. Boote	B	Dinnerwares
April 30	5	Minton & Co.	S	Vase form
May 6	4	John Edwards	L	Teawares
May 25	4	Anthony Shaw	T	Printed design
May 31	1	Holland & Green	L	Dinnerwares

May 31	1	Holland & Green	L	Teawares
May 31	1	Holland & Green	L	Toiletwares
May 31	4	William Adams (junior)	T	Dinnerwares
Jun 2	1	William Brownfield	C	Dinnerwares
Jun 23	6	S. Alcock & Co.	B	Fluted teawares
July 13	2	Mayer (&) Elliot	B	Tureen form
July 29	4	S. Alcock & Co.	B	Moulded jug
Aug 24	2	William Brownfield	C	Jug form
Sept 3	2	Sharpe Brothers & Co.	Sw	Moulded jug
Sept 6	5	James Edwards	L	Dinnerwares
Sept 10	3	John Edwards	L	Teapot form
Sept 10	6	Bridgwood & Clarke	B	Dinnerwares
Oct 5	2	Minton & Co.	S	Moulded jug
Oct 5	3	William Brownfield	C	Moulded jug
Oct 7	1	Ridgway & Abington	H	Moulded jug
Oct 18	3	Minton & Co.	S	Printed design
Oct 29	2	Benjamin Green	F	Moulded jug
Nov 3	8	James Stiff	Ln	Moulded form
Nov 5	5	William Savage*	Win	Jug form
Nov 11		E. & W. Walley	C	Moulded jug
Dec 8	11	T. & R. Boote	B	Teawares
Dec 8	11	T. & R. Boote	B	Toiletwares
Dec 17	6	W. T. Copeland	S	Printed design
Dec 23	2	Joseph Clementson	Sh	Toiletwares
Dec 23	9	W. T. Copeland	S	Toiletwares
Dec 27	4	Joseph Clementson	Sh	Dinnerwares

1859 (M at top)

Jan 25	4	W. T. Copeland	S	Printed border
Feb 2	3	T. & R. Boote	B	Oval tureen
Feb 3	2	Davenports & Co.	Lpt	Teawares
Feb 3	2	Davenports & Co.	Lpt	Toiletwares
Feb 8	6	Levison Hill	S	Moulded jug
Mar 19	1	Alsop, Downes, Spilsbury & Co.	Ln	Button
Mar 21	7	T. & R. Boote	B	"Atlantic" jug
Mar 29	7	T. & R. Boote	B	Teapot form
May 7	1	E. & W. Walley	C	Moulded jugs
May 10	2	S. Alcock & Co.	B	Saxon print
May 20	1	W. Brownfield	C	Moulded jug
May 26	1	Lockett, Baguley & Cooper	H	Moulded jug
July 2	2	W. T. Copeland	S	Plate design
Aug 6	7	F. & R. Pratt & Co.	F	Printed design
Aug 27	6	S. Alcock & Co.	B	Moulded jug
Sept 1	3	James Edwards & Son	Lpt	Dinnerwares
Oct 12	4	W. Adams, junior	T	Dinnerwares
Oct 14	4	W. T. Copeland	S	Printed border
Oct 25	1	Minton & Co.	S	Moulded jug
Oct 25	1	Minton & Co.	S	Ribbon edgings
Oct 28	1	Davenports & Co.	Lpt	Dinnerwares
Nov 2	3	Elsmore & Forster	T	Teawares
Nov 2	3	Elsmore & Forster	T	Toiletwares
Nov 2	3	Elsmore & Forster	T	Dinnerwares

Nov 5	4	W. Brownfield	C	Moulded jug
Nov 17	4	Minton & Co.	S	Printed designs
Nov 23	4	Minton & Co.	S	Printed design
Dec 10	5	J. Wedgwood & Sons	E	Jeddo design
Dec 14	2	E. & W. Walley	C	Moulded jug
Dec 15	3	Minton & Co.	S	Moulded design

1860 (Z at top)

Jan 10	4	W. T. Copeland	S	Printed border
Jan 23	7	Mayer & Elliot	Lpt	Tureen form
Feb 14	9	W. T. Copeland	S	Moulded vases
Mar 1	2	Bates, Brown-Westhead & Moore	Sh	Jug form
Mar 27	1	Bates, Brown-Westhead & Moore	Sh	Jug form
April 5	1	G. Grainger & Co.	W	Plate form
April 12	4	Minton & Co.	S	Moulded plate
May 2	2	John Meir & Son	T	Printed design
May 19	9	Lockett, Baguley & Cooper	H	Moulded jug
May 30	10	Edward Corn	B	Printed design
Jun 6	4	W. Brownfield	C	Moulded jug
Jun 6	4	W. Brownfield	C	Tureen form
Jun 6	4	W. Brownfield	C	Plate edging
Jun 19	4	John Phillpot★	Ln	Ham stand
Jun 22	2	Minton & Co.	S	Printed design
Jun 23	4	Sandford Estate Pottery Clay Co.	Wm	Moulded jug
Jun 23	4	Sandford Estate Pottery Clay Co.	Wm	Jardinere
Jun 28	2	Minton & Co.	S	Printed design
July 6	5	Sandford Estate Pottery Clay Co.	Wm	Moulded jugs
July 7	9	Sandford Estate Pottery Clay Co.	Wm	Moulded jugs
Aug 1	5	Sandford Estate Pottery Clay Co.	Wm	Moulded jugs
Aug 3	2	Sandford Estate Pottery Clay Co.	Wm	Moulded jug
Aug 21	2	John Wedge Wood	T	Printed design
Aug 23	9	Sandford Estate Pottery Clay Co.	Wm	Moulded jugs
Aug 28	5	Sandford Estate Pottery Clay Co.	Wm	Moulded jugs
Aug 28	5	Sandford Estate Pottery Clay Co.	Wm	Covered dish
Sept 24	3	Minton & Co.	S	Printed design
Sept 28	7	Sandford Estate Pottery Clay Co.	Wm	Jardinere
Sept 28	7	Sandford Estate Pottery Clay Co.	Wm	Moulded jug
Sept 29	7	Minton & Co.	S	Printed border
Oct 4	4	Sandford Estate Pottery Clay Co.	Wm	Moulded vase
Oct 13	5	Benjamin Green	F	Fluted teawares
Oct 18	4	Bates, Brown-Westhead & Moore	Sh	Toiletwares
Oct 18	4	Bates, Brown-Westhead & Moore	Sh	Dinnerwares
Oct 19	4	Joseph Clementson	Sh	Dinnerwares
Oct 19	4	Joseph Clementson	Sh	Teawares
Oct 19	4	Joseph Clementson	Sh	Toiletwares
Oct 19	5	Holland & Green	L	Dinnerwares
Oct 19	5	Holland & Green	L	Teawares
Oct 19	5	Holland & Green	L	Toiletwares
Oct 29	3	Minton & Co.	S	Moulded jug
Oct 29	9	W. Brownfield	C	Moulded jug
Nov 23	9	T. & R. Boote	B	Toiletwares
Nov 29	4	Sandford Estate Pottery Clay Co.	Wm	Moulded vases

Nov 29	4	Sandford Estate Pottery Clay Co.	Wm	Finger plate
Dec 3	3	Bates, Brown–Westhead & Moore	Sh	Printed designs
Dec 12	3	Bates & Co.	Sh	Moulded jug

1861 (R at top)

Jan 8	6	T. & R. Boote	B	Garibaldi jug
Jan 21	7	Wedgwood & Co.	T	Moulded jug
Feb 12	5	Sandford Estate Pottery Clay Co.	Wm	Flower holders
Feb 15	3	J. Furnival & Co.	C	Tureen form
Feb 27	5	James Edwards & Sons	Lpt	Dinnerwares
Mar 7	7	Turner & Tomkinson	T	Printed borders
Mar 19	3	W. T. Copeland	S	Printed design
Mar 19	4	W. H. Kerr & Co.	W	Ink & perfume pots
April 5	3	Pinder, Bourne & Hope	B	Moulded jug
April 6	1	Minton, Hollins & Co.	S	Tiles
April 12	3	Davenports & Co.	Lpt	Dinnerwares "Erie"
April 12	3	Davenports & Co.	Lpt	Teawares "Erie"
April 18	5	T. & R. Boote	B	Plate form
April 20	6	F. & R. Pratt & Co.	F	Printed designs
April 25	2	James Dudson	H	Moulded jug
May 1	5	Silicated Carbon Filter Co.★	S	Printed design
May 3	8	W. T. Copeland	S	Printed design
May 6	3	Hill Pottery Co.	B	Printed design
May 6	5	Old Hall Earthenware Co. Ltd.	H	Moulded jugs
May 9	3	Bates, Brown–Westhead & Moore	Sh	Printed design
May 9	3	Bates, Brown–Westhead & Moore	Sh	Jug form
May 13	7	Minton & Co.	S	Printed border
May 14	2	W. H. Kerr & Co.	W	Moulded bottle
May 25	2	W. H. Kerr & Co.	W	Dinnerwares
May 31	3	Cork, Edge & Malkin	B	Moulded jug
Jun 4	1	Bates, Brown–Westhead & Moore	Sh	Moulded jug
Jun 7	5	Hill Pottery Co.	B	Plate shape
Jun 11	2	W. T. Copeland	S	Printed design
Jun 11	2	W. T. Copeland	S	Jug form
Jun 13	6	Minton & Co.	S	Printed design
July 4	2	Lockett & Cooper	H	Moulded jug
July 5	2	Beech & Hancock	T	Moulded jug
July 6	2	William Brownfield	C	Moulded jug
July 18	4	J. Wedgwood & Sons	E	Printed designs
Aug 19	7	T. & R. Boote	B	Tureen form
Aug 22	7	Wedgwood & Co.	T	Moulded jug
Aug 23	2	G. W. Brade	C	Moulded jug
Sept 6	6	W. Brownfield	C	Printed design
Sept 12	6	J. & J. Peake	N	Printed design
Sept 17	2	W. T. Copeland	S	Printed design
Sept 18	7	William Beech	B	Jug form
Sept 26	7	John Cliff & Co.	Ln	Stoneware jar
Oct 10	5	W. H. Kerr	W	Teawares
Oct 11	3	Mountford & Scarratt	F	Jug forms
Oct 11	4	T. & R. Boote	B	Dinnerwares
Oct 15	3	Executors of Levison Hill	S	Moulded jug
Oct 18	3	W. T. Copeland	S	Printed design

Oct 24	5	Hulse, Nixon & Adderley	L	Coffee pot form
Oct 28	7	Bates, Brown-Westhead & Moore	Sh	Dinnerwares
Nov 18	3	Joseph Clementson	Sh	Dinnerwares
Nov 18	3	Joseph Clementson	Sh	Teawares
Nov 18	3	Joseph Clementson	Sh	Toiletwares
Nov 29	5	J. Wedgwood & Sons	E	"Doric" jug
Dec 4	7	W. Brownfield	C	Moulded jug
Dec 4	7	W. Brownfield	C	Jardinere
Dec 5	5	Till, Bullock & Smith	H	Moulded jug
Dec 20	7	Lockett & Cooper	H	Printed design
Dec 20	9	Wedgwood & Co.	T	Printed design

1862 (O at top)

Jan 11	5	W. Brownfield	C	Printed border
Jan 25	3	W. Brownfield	C	Moulded jug
Feb 1	4	Elliot Brothers	Lpt	Moulded jug
Feb 10	6	W. H. Kerr & Co.	W	Flower holder
Feb 10	8	Minton & Co.	S	Printed design
Feb 27	4	James Dudson	H	Moulded jugs
Mar 1	6	T. & R. Boote	B	Teapot
Mar 13	6	W. T. Copeland	S	Printed design
Mar 13	7	William Adams, junior	T	Dinnerwares
Mar 13	7	William Adams, junior	T	Teawares
Mar 14	8	Joseph Knight	F	Splash ornamentation
Mar 14	9	Wedgwood & Co.	T	Printed design
Mar 14	10	W. Brownfield	C	Printed design
Mar 14	10	W. Brownfield	C	Dinnerwares
Mar 21	6	Thompson Brothers	Dshire	Teapot form
Mar 22	9	T. & R. Boote	B	Toiletwares
Mar 27	5	J. & M. P. Bell & Co.	G	Printed design
Mar 27	5	J. & M. P. Bell & Co.	G	Tureen form
Mar 27	5	J. & M. P. Bell & Co.	G	Jug & candlestick
Mar 29	3	Minton & Co.	S	Toiletwares
April 1	5	J. Wedgwood & Sons	E	Tureen forms
April 4	2	Minton & Co.	S	Honey pot
April 4	5	J. & T. Furnival	C	Printed design
April 7	12	G. Grainger & Co.	W	Dinnerwares
April 9	3	Old Hall Earthenware Co. Ltd	H	Moulded jug
April 16	9	H. A. Abrahams	L	1862 Exhibition print
April 17	5	Thompson Brothers	Dshire	Fluted dish
April 24	2	Turner & Tomkinson	T	Printed design
May 1	7	Eardley & Hammersley	T	Printed design
May 3	3	G. L. Ashworth Bros	Sh	Dinnerwares
May 5	5	John Cliff	Ln	Water container
May 9	9	Brown-Westhead, Moore & Co.	Sh	Dinnerwares
May 9	9	Brown-Westhead, Moore & Co.	Sh	Toiletwares
May 14	3	George Jones & Co.	S	Printed designs
May 27	3	Edward Challinor	T	Printed design
May 29	5	J. Furnival & Co.	C	Moulded jug
Jun 24	5	Brown-Westhead, Moore & Co.	Sh	Printed design
July 2	4	Minton & Co.	S	Printed border
July 4	8	Joseph Clementson	Sh	Toiletwares

July 12	4	Joseph Clementson	Sh	Teawares
July 14	2	Beech & Hancock	T	Moulded jug
July 19	6	Joseph Clementson	Sh	Tureen form
July 31	3	Jones & Ellis	L	Printed design
July 31	4	Minton & Co.	S	Jug form
Aug 16	5	Richard Edwards	Lpt	Dinnerwares
Aug 16	7	J. H. Baddeley	H	Cheese dish
Aug 18	4	Hulse, Nixon & Adderley	L	Moulded jug
Aug 19	4	G. L. Ashworth & Bros.	Sh	Moulded jug
Aug 25	3	E. F. Bodley & Co.	B	Printed designs
Aug 25	8	F. Button & Sons	Notts	Printed border
Aug 30	3	Thomas Fell & Co.	NT	Printed design
Aug 30	4	T. & R. Boote	B	Moulded teapot
Sept 6	2	Malkin, Walker & Hulse	L	Printed design
Sept 11	3	Minton & Co.	S	Printed design
Sept 12	2	Thomas Cooper	L	Fluted jug
Sept 17	6	Hope & Carter	B	Tureen forms
Sept 22	7	Minton & Co.	S	Printed design
Sept 26	1	Hope & Carter	B	Dinnerwares
Sept 26	1	Hope & Carter	B	Toiletwares
Sept 26	1	Hope & Carter	B	Teawares
Oct 1	7	Thomas Fell & Co.	NT	Printed designs
Oct 9	3	Owners of Hill Pottery	B	Tureen form
Oct 15	2	Turner & Tomkinson	T	Printed design "Star"
Oct 23	8	William Baker & Co.	F	Toiletwares
Oct 23	8	William Baker & Co.	F	Teawares
Oct 23	8	William Baker & Co.	F	Dinnerwares
Nov 11	3	E. F. Bodley & Co.	B	Tureen form
Nov 19	5	George Woolliscroft	T	Tureen form
Nov 28	4	Minton & Co.	S	Vase form
Dec 3	5	Brown–Westhead, Moore & Co.	Sh	Tureen forms
Dec 5	2	W. Brownfield	C	Printed design
Dec 9	5	Thomas Cooper	H	Moulded jug
Dec 17	5	Old Hall Earthenware Co. Ltd	H	Tureen forms
Dec 18	3	George Jones	S	Printed design

1863 (G at top)

Jan 12	6	Davenport, Banks & Co.	E	Jug form
Jan 16	2	Minton & Co.	S	Moulded jug
Jan 16	8	Liddle Elliot & Sons	Lpt	Moulded jug
Jan 29	1	J. Wedgwood & Sons	E	Printed design
Jan 30	3	T. & R. Boote	B	Dinnerwares
Feb 2	3	Minton & Co.	S	Plate form
Feb 17	1	T. & R. Boote	B	Toiletwares
Feb 24	5	J. Stiff & Sons	Ln	Tile
Mar 6	2	G. L. Ashworth & Bros.	Sh	Teawares
Mar 13	2	Hope & Carter	B	Tureen forms
Mar 13	3	Wilkinson & Son	H	Moulded jug
Mar 20	8	Worthington & Green	H	Moulded jug
Mar 20	9	John Pratt & Co.	F	Moulded jug
Mar 20	9	John Pratt & Co.	F	Moulded cup or vase
Mar 21	2	Beech & Hancock	T	Moulded jug

Mar 21	4	Hulse, Nixon & Adderley	L	Moulded jug
Mar 21	5	J. Edwards & Son	B	Tureen form
Mar 23	2	Bodley & Harrold	B	Moulded jug
Mar 23	2	Bodley & Harrold	B	Printed design
Mar 27	4	J. Hinks & Son★	Bir	Lamp bases
April 11	1	James Macintyre	B	Moulded jug
April 15	5	F. A. Wint★	B	Vase form
April 23	4	Brown-Westhead, Moore & Co.	Sh	Toiletwares
April 25	1	Beech & Hancock	T	Moulded jug
April 30	3	Wilkinson & Son	H	Moulded jug
May 4	6	Harding & Cotterill	BT	Teapot form
May 11	3	Edward Pearson	C	Dinnerwares
May 11	3	Edward Pearson	C	Teawares
May 12	1	Bodley & Harrold	B	Printed design
May 15	10	Harding & Cotterill	BT	Moulded jug
May 22	4	W. T. Copeland	S	Printed design
May 22	4	W. T. Copeland	S	Jug form
May 26	9	Brown-Westhead, Moore & Co.	Sh	Dinnerwares
Jun 4	5	Old Hall Earthenware Co. Ltd	H	Printed design
Jun 8	15	Minton & Co.	S	Basket form
Jun 8	16	W. Brownfield	C	Jardinere
Jun 20	7	Edmund Ratcliff★	Bir	Lamp base
July 11	6	F. A. Wint★	B	Vase form
July 14	2	Turner & Tomkinson	T	Tureen form
July 15	3	Henry Venables	H	Printed design
July 20	3	W. Brownfield	C	Tureen form
July 24	3	W. T. Copeland	S	Printed designs
July 27	7	Architectural Pottery Co.	Poole	Mosaics
July 28	6	Minton & Co.	S	Printed design
Aug 1	2	Architectural Pottery Co.	Poole	Mosaics
Aug 11	3	Turner & Tomkinson	T	Printed designs
Aug 12	4	Hancock, Whittingham & Co.	B	Moulded jug
Aug 21	1	J. Clementson	H	Tureen form
Aug 28	5	Henry Venables	H	Printed design
Sept 7	6	T. & R. Boote	B	Toiletwares
Sept 28	4	Henry Venables	H	Vase form
Sept 28	6	J. Edwards & Son	B	Moulded plate
Sept 28	6	J. Edwards & Son	B	Teawares
Oct 2	5	Henry Venables	H	Vase form
Oct 6	5	Thompson Brothers	BT	Toiletwares
Oct 14	7	W. Brownfield	C	Moulded jug
Oct 15	2	F. Brewer & Son	L	Moulded plate
Oct 17	1	T. & R. Boote	B	Teapot form
Oct 22	5	Eardley & Hammersley	T	Printed design
Oct 24	5	J. Wedgwood & Sons	E	Dessertwares
Oct 26	7	Old Hall Earthenware Co. Ltd	H	Dinnerwares
Oct 26	7	Old Hall Earthenware Co. Ltd	H	Printed design
Oct 28	8	George Jones & Co.	S	Printed design
Oct 31	3	Edmund T. Wood	T	Dinnerwares
Oct 31	3	Edmund T. Wood	T	Toiletwares
Oct 31	3	Edmund T. Wood	T	Teawares
Nov 3	5	John Meir & Son	T	Printed design

Nov 4	7	T. & R. Boote	B	Dinnerwares
Nov 6	1	George Jones & Co.	S	Printed designs
Nov 16	10	William Kirkham	S	Moulded jug
Nov 26	12	W. Brownfield	C	Dinnerwares
Nov 27	3	Bodley & Harrold	B	Printed design
Dec 2	5	J. W. Pankhurst & Co.	H	Dinnerwares
Dec 2	6	T. & R. Boote	B	Plate form
Dec 18	4	F. & R. Pratt & Co.	F	Moulded jug
Dec 23	2	W. Brownfield	C	Jug form
Dec 30	1	Brown–Westhead, Moore & Co.	Sh	Tureen forms

1864 (N at top)

Jan 5	2	W. Brownfield	C	Dinnerwares
Jan 11	5	Malkin, Walker & Hulse	L	Printed design
Feb 2	5	J. Wedgwood & Sons	E	Flower vase
Feb 5	5	Hope & Carter	B	Plate edging
Feb 6	3	Thomas Goode & Co.★	Ln	Toiletwares
Feb 13	6	W. T. Copeland	S	Moulded jug
Feb 22	7	Cork, Edge & Malkin	B	Teapot form
Feb 25	6	Liddle Elliot & Son	L	Moulded jug
Feb 29	6	J. & D. Hampson	L	Fluted jug
Mar 1	1	Coalbrookdale Company	Cpt	Terracotta box
Mar 3	4	G. L. Ashworth & Bros.	H	Tureen form
Mar 5	3	F. A. Wint★	B	Candlesticks
Mar 12	5	Cork, Edge & Malkin	B	Jug form
Mar 18	1	Brown–Westhead, Moore & Co.	Sh	Tureen forms
Mar 22	3	Minton & Co.	S	Plate borders
Mar 23	4	Burgess & Leigh	B	Moulded jug
April 2	4	Coalbrookdale Company	Cpt	Wall bracket
April 9	4	J. Wedgwood & Sons	E	Tureen forms
April 15	4	George Jones	S	Printed design
April 18	5	Minton & Co.	S	Jardinere form
April 21	4	Brown–Westhead, Moore & Co.	Sh	Moulded jug
April 21	8	Liddle Elliot & Son	L	Tureen form
April 23	11	G. L. Ashworth & Bros.	H	Printed design
April 25	8	W. H. Ward★	Ln	Covered pot
April 26	3	Bodley & Harrold	B	Printed design
April 27	4	Hope & Carter	B	Printed design
April 29	2	W. Brownfield	C	"Argos" jug
May 9	3	R. T. Boughton & Co.	B	Shakespeare jug
May 10	5	George Jones & Co.	S	Printed designs
May 11	3	R. H. Grove	H	Printed design
May 12	5	Naylor & Co.	Ln	Centrepiece
May 18	5	George Ray	L	Teapot form
May 19	4	J. L. Lloyd	Bir	Moulded jug
May 21	1	J. & D. Hampson	L	Printed designs
Jun 9	7	Minton & Co.	S	Jug form
Jun 16	3	Hope & Carter	B	Jardinere forms
Jun 24	1	Johnston Fraser & Co.	G	Toiletwares
Jun 30	4	W. Brownfield	C	Printed design
Jun 30	10	Worcester Royal Porcelain Co. Ltd	W	Vase form
July 2	3	Wood & Sale	H	Moulded jug

July 9	5	Pinder, Bourne & Co.	B	Printed design
July 11	8	Pinder, Bourne & Co.	B	Tureen forms
July 18	6	Bodley & Harrold	B	Tray shape
July 18	7	Evans & Booth	B	Printed design
July 19	4	Hope & Carter	B	Tureen forms
July 22	5	J. Hinks★	Bir	Door furniture
July 28	4	Holland & Green	L	Dinnerwares
July 28	4	Holland & Green	L	Toiletwares
July 28	4	Holland & Green	L	Teawares
Aug 20	10	George Jones & Co.	S	Tureen form
Aug 26	5	Brown-Westhead, Moore & Co.	Sh	Toiletwares
Sept 6	5	W. T. Copeland	S	Printed designs
Sept 10	1	Minton & Co.	S	Toiletwares
Sept 12	2	Minton & Co.	S	Printed design
Sept 14	4	Bodley & Harrold	B	Tray form
Sept 16	6	G. L. Ashworth & Bros	H	Tureen forms
Sept 19	1	J. Wedgwood & Sons	E	Teawares
Sept 21	1	Minton & Co.	S	Printed borders
Sept 22	1	J. Hinks★	Bir	Lamp base
Sept 22	6	J. Wedgwood & Sons	E	Comport forms
Sept 22	6	J. Wedgwood & Sons	E	Flower vase
Sept 22	6	J. Wedgwood & Sons	E	Jug jardinere
Oct 4	2	George Jones & Co.	S	Printed border
Oct 12	4	W. Brownfield	C	Moulded jug
Oct 27	4	Evans & Booth	B	Oval tureen
Oct 28	2	Worcester Royal Porcelain Co.	W	Vase, hand form
Oct 28	4	Bodley & Harrold	B	Moulded jug
Oct 28	9	Minton & Co.	S	Cup form
Oct 29	2	C. Collinson & Co.	B	Moulded jug
Oct 31	3	Cork, Edge & Malkin	B	Moulded jug
Nov 1	7	W. T. Copeland	S	Circular container
Nov 4	3	Livesley Powell & Co.	H	Moulded jug
Nov 10	2	Elsmore & Foster	T	Dinnerwares
Nov 10	2	Elsmore & Foster	T	Teawares
Nov 10	3	Hope & Carter	B	Print "Dancers"
Nov 10	10	George Jones & Co.	S	Printed design
Nov 24	5	Brown-Westhead, Moore & Co.	Sh	Dinnerwares
Nov 29	1	Hope & Carter	B	Teapot form
Dec 9	1	William Kirkham	S	Moulded jug
Dec 10	8	Hope & Carter	B	Tureen forms
Dec 21	2	Coalbrookdale Company	Cpt	Vases, etc
Dec 31	6	George Jones & Co.	S	Printed design

1865 (W at top)

Jan 6	3	Hope & Carter	B	Printed design
Jan 6	4	Minton & Co.	S	Moulded jug
Jan 14	4	George Jones & Co.	S	Moulded dish
Feb 1	1	Minton & Co.	S	Printed designs
Feb 1	1	Minton & Co.	S	Light fitting
Feb 2	4	G. L. Ashworth & Bros.	H	Circular ornaments
Feb 13	7	F. & R. Pratt & Co.	F	Teapot form
Feb 14	4	Liddle Elliot & Son	Lpt	Tureen form

Feb 27	4	Livesley Powell & Co.	H	Fluted jug
Mar 31	3	Hope & Carter	B	"Odessa" print
April 1	4	W. Brownfield	C	Fluted jug
April 4	4	Minton & Co.	S	Printed design
April 22	5	T. Till & Sons	B	Printed design
April 22	7	J. Edwards & Sons	B	Moulded jug
April 26	5	J. Edwards & Sons	B	Tureen form
April 28	4	Hope & Carter	B	Tureen forms
April 28	7	Henry Alcock & Co.	C	Tureen forms
April 29	3	Worcester Royal Porcelain Co.	W	Vase, hand form
May 2	8	Livesley Powell & Co.	H	Jardinere
May 15	2	J. T. Hudden	L	"Toulon" print
May 17	2	Minton & Co.	S	Comport shape
Jun 6	6	J. T. Hudden	L	Printed designs
Jun 9	4	Worcester Royal Porcelain Co.	W	Basket centrepiece
Jun 13	5	Worcester Royal Porcelain Co.	W	Basket shape
Jun 14	6	Hill Pottery Co. Ltd.	B	Printed design
Jun 15	2	J. T. Hudden	L	"Choice" print
Jun 16	1	Evans & Booth	B	Printed border
Jun 17	5	Worcester Royal Porcelain Co.	W	Centrepiece–bust
Jun 29	2	Edward F. Bodley & Co.	B	Cobden print
Jun 29	2	Edward F. Bodley & Co.	B	Moulded jug
Jun 29	3	G. R. Ward★	Ln	Hand ornament
Jun 30	1	Hill Pottery Co. Ltd.	B	Teawares
July 3	7	Brown-Westhead, Moore & Co.	Sh	Openwork edgings
July 7	3	J. H. Battam★	Ln	Shell vase
July 12	3	J. Edwards & Son	B	Moulded jug
Aug 21	6	J. Furnival & Co.	C	Tureen form
Aug 23	5	J. Wedgwood & Sons	E	Moulded dish
Aug 24	5	Virgoe, Son & Co.	L	Paste pot
Aug 25	8	A. J. Claddo	Bir	Printed plate
Sept 11	4	R. T. Boughton & Co.	B	Tureen form
Sept 11	5	Thomas Cooper, executors of	H	Tureen form
Sept 14	2	Brown-Westhead, Moore & Co.	Sh	Centrepiece
Sept 18	6	Liddle Elliot & Son	Lpt	Tureen form
Sept 28	4	Minton & Co.	S	Printed border
Sept 30	4	S. Barker & Son	Sn	"York" print
Oct 13	8	Brown-Westhead, Moore & Co.	Sh	Dinnerwares
Oct 30	4	W. Brownfield	C	Tureen forms
Oct 30	4	W. Brownfield	C	Moulded jug
Nov 10	4	Pinder Bourne & Co with Anthony Shaw	B	Moulded edging
Nov 23	10	Old Hall Earthenware Co. Ltd	H	Vase form
Nov 29	8	J. Edwards & Son	B	Tureen forms
Dec 2	3	Worcester Royal Porcelain Co.	W	Ornament
Dec 23	3	James Dudson	H	Moulded jug

1866 (Q at top)

Jan 2	4	Pratt & Co.	F	Printed hunting design
Jan 3	6	J. T. Close & Co.	S	Dinnerwares
Jan 13	2	Edward F. Bodley & Co.	B	Coffee pot form
Jan 17	4	Burgess & Leigh	B	Printed design

Jan 24	1	Minton & Co.	S	Tureen forms
Jan 31	5	J. Edwards & Son	B	Jug form
Feb 2	7	W. T. Copeland	S	Covered box
Mar 1	9	Coalbrookdale Company	Cpt	Chimney pots
Mar 2	2	Ford, Challinor & Co.	T	Printed design
Mar 3	8	J. Robbins & Co.	Ln	Vase form
Mar 10	1	Old Hall Earthenware Co. Ltd	H	Plate form
April 14	6	Walker & Carter	L	Printed design
April 14	7	G. L. Ashworth & Bros.	H	Dinnerwares
April 14	7	G. L. Ashworth & Bros.	H	Teawares
April 14	7	G. L. Ashworth & Bros.	H	Toiletwares
April 16	8	Old Hall Earthenware Co. Ltd	H	Tureen form
April 18	4	J. Edwards & Son	B	Moulded jug
April 20	7	W. Brownfield	C	Tureen forms
April 20	7	W. Brownfield	C	Moulded jug
May 1	4	J. Furnival & Co.	C	Tureen forms
May 25	1	Hope & Carter	B	Moulded jug
May 25	1	Hope & Carter	B	Jardinere
Jun 4	4	J. Broadhurst	L	Printed design
Jun 12	1	J. Edwards	F	Dinnerwares
Jun 12	1	J. Edwards	F	Toiletwares
Jun 12	1	J. Edwards	F	Teawares
Jun 13	8	T. W. Cowan	Ws	Vases & brackets
Jun 21	4	Pinder Bourne & Co.	B	Tureen forms
Jun 30	4	Thomas Minshall	S	Printed design
July 19	5	J. T. Hudden	L	Printed design
July 25	3	George Jones	S	Tureen form
Aug 17	3	Morgan, Wood & Co.	B	Printed design
Aug 29	4	Edward F. Bodley & Co.	B	"Sydney" print
Sept 6	4	F. & R. Pratt & Co.	F	Moulded jug
Sept 13	9	T. & C. Ford	H	Dinnerwares
Sept 15	8	G. L. Ashworth & Bros	H	Printed design
Sept 20	8	Anthony Keeling	T	"Kew" print
Oct 8	3	Minton & Co.	S	Printed designs
Oct 8	3	Minton & Co.	S	Openwork edging
Oct 13	3	Thomas Furnival	C	Printed design
Nov 3	6	Minton & Co.	S	Moulded ewer
Nov 12	3	W. T. Copeland	S	Printed design
Nov 14	8	Brown-Westhead, Moore & Co.	Sh	Tureen & plate
Nov 15	4	G. Grainger & Co.	W	Moulded jug
Dec 13	4	Liddle Elliot & Son	B	Jug form
Dec 14	8	Samuel Barker & Son	Sn	Floral print
Dec 15	5	Brown-Westhead, Moore & Co.	Sh	Tureen form
Dec 19	5	J. Meir & Co.	T	Moulded jug
Dec 22	6	Pellatt & Co.★	Ln	Vase form
Dec 24	2	J. T. Hudden	L	"Oxford" print
Dec 29	2	Pellatt & Co.★	Ln	Teawares

1867 (T at top)

Jan 8	5	J. Edwards & Son	B	Moulded jug
Jan 17	3	Edward F. Bodley & Co.	B	Tureen form
Jan 23	2	Worcester Royal Porcelain Co.	W	Dove vase

Feb 9	1	Edward F. Bodley & Co.	B	Tureen form
Feb 23	5	Worthington & Harrop	H	Vase form
Mar 2	7	J. Wedgwood & Sons	E	Tureen form
Mar 4	4	Brown-Westhead, Moore & Co.	Sh	Dessert shapes
Mar 5	6	Powell & Bishop	H	Cheese dish
Mar 6	4	Old Hall Earthenware Co.	H	Oval tureen
Mar 9	3	John Edwards	F	Teawares
Mar 11	2	J. Wedgwood & Sons	E	Ornamental form
Mar 14	1	Davenport, Banks & Co.	E	Printed design
Mar 15	7	W. Brownfield	C	Jardinere
Mar 15	7	W. Brownfield	C	Vases & jug
Mar 15	7	W. Brownfield	C	Dessertwares
Mar 15	7	W. Brownfield	C	Tureen forms
Mar 18	5	Cockson, Chetwynd & Co.	C	Toiletwares
Mar 18	5	Cockson, Chetwynd & Co.	C	Teawares
Mar 19	5	James Edwards & Son	B	Plate design
Mar 20	2	J. Wedgwood & Sons	E	Printed design
Mar 21	10	James Edwards & Son	B	Tureen forms
Mar 25	3	J. Wedgwood & Sons	E	Jug form
Mar 26	4	Minton & Co.	S	Oyster plates
April 3	5	Minton & Co.	S	Strawberry dish
April 4	2	J. Wedgwood & Sons	E	Moulded edge
April 4	9	Elsmore & Foster	T	Dinnerwares
April 4	9	Elsmore & Foster	T	Teawares
April 17	1	Charles Hobson	B	Printed design
April 23	3	Adams, Scrivener & Co.	L	Dessertwares
April 24	2	W. T. Copeland & Sons	S	Teapot form
May 6	3	J. & M. P. Bell & Co.	G	Moulded jug
May 7	4	J. Meir & Son	T	Tureen form
May 8	6	Brown-Westhead, Moore & Co.	H	Dessertwares
May 18	7	William McAdam	G	Royal Arms jar
May 22	6	Clementson Brothers	H	Dinnerwares
May 22	6	Clementson Brothers	H	Jug form
Jun 6	3	J. Wedgwood & Sons	E	Moulded jug
Jun 11	6	Clementson Brothers	H	Teawares
Jun 11	7	Cockson, Chetwynd & Co.	C	Tureen forms
Jun 13	3	W. & J. A. Bailey	Alloa	Teawares
Jun 15	5	J. Cartland & Son★	Bir	Door handle
Jun 21	4	W. Brownfield	C	Moulded jug
Jun 21	8	E. & D. Chetwynd (modeller)	H	Tureen forms
Jun 24	4	E. & D. Chetwynd (modeller)	H	Tureen form
Jun 24	4	E. & D. Chetwynd (modeller)	H	Teapot form
Jun 28	1	J. G. Hughes★	Ln	Moulded edging
July 1	7	J. Ball, junior	L	Printed border
July 4	5	E. J. Ridgway	H	Fluted jug
July 8	3	G. L. Ashworth & Bros	H	Printed design
July 11	6	J. Johnson & Sons	Ln	Printed design
July 12	5	George Jones	S	Tureen form
July 15	2	J. Wedgwood & Sons	E	Printed design
July 17	2	E. & D. Chetwynd (modeller)	H	Oval tureen
July 17	2	E. & D. Chetwynd (modeller)	H	Teawares
July 25	3	Hope & Carter	B	Printed design

Aug 28	10	Worcester Royal Porcelain Co.	W	Vase form
Aug 29	3	James Miller	G	Water filter
Sept 16	7	Thomas Goode & Co.★	Ln	Toiletwares
Sept 17	3	Wedgwood & Co.	T	Printed design
Sept 21	1	G. L. Ashworth & Bros	Sh	Moulded jug
Sept 23	8	J. H. Battam★	Ln	Ornament
Sept 25	9	Powell & Bishop	H	Tureen form
Sept 25	9	Powell & Bishop	H	Teawares
Oct 2	1	Minton & Co	S	Printed design
Oct 3	5	Thompson Brothers	BoT	Teapot form
Oct 3	6	Minton & Co	S	Printed design
Oct 7	4	Minton & Co	S	Printed design
Oct 10	1	Thomas Booth	H	Moulded jug
Oct 24	5	Ford, Challinor & Co	T	Printed design
Oct 26	1	W. T. Copeland & Sons	T	Printed Xmas design
Oct 28	4	W. T. Copeland & Sons	T	Printed design
Oct 29	3	J. Wedgwood & Sons	E	Dessertwares
Oct 29	3	J. Wedgwood & Sons	E	Butter dish
Oct 30	3	J. T. Hudden	L	"Jewell" print
Oct 31	7	Powell & Bishop	H	Moulded jug
Nov 6	7	W. & J. A. Bailey	Alloa	Teapot form
Nov 7	4	J. Edwards & Son	B	Dinnerwares
Nov 18	9	Ford, Challinor & Co	T	Printed design
Nov 27	7	J. G. Hughes & Co★	L	Printed design
Dec 3	3	W. T. Copeland & Sons	S	Moulded jug
Dec 12	6	F. & R. Pratt & Co	F	Printed design
Dec 20	3	J. Wedgwood & Sons	E	Moulded jug
Dec 27	1	J. & J. B. Bebbington	H	Moulded jug

1868 (X at right)

Jan 3	1	Minton & Co	S	Egg cup stand
Jan 7	8	Thompson Brothers	BT	Moulded jug
Jan 7	11	Cockson, Chetwynd & Co	C	Dinnerwares
Jan 7	11	Cockson, Chetwynd & Co	C	Teawares
Jan 7	11	Cockson, Chetwynd & Co	C	Toiletwares
Jan 8	5	T. & R. Boote	B	Teawares
Jan 9	7	Taylor, Tunnicliffe & Co	H	Door fittings
Jan 10	2	Cork, Edge & Malkin	B	Printed design
Jan 11	2	W. Brownfield	C	Sardine dish
Jan 13	2	G. L. Ashworth & Bros	H	"Daisy" punt
Jan 16	13	Old Hall Earthenware Co Ltd	H	Printed border
Jan 18	7	Pellatt & Co★	Ln	Jug form
Jan 25	3	Hope & Carter	B	Scenic print
Jan 30	6	Jacob Furnival & Co	C	Moulded jug
Jan 31	8	J. Wedgwood & Sons	E	Centrepiece
Jan 31	14	T. & R. Boote	B	Tureen form
Feb 5	3	Carpi, Loly & Co★	Liv	Printed design
Feb 5	4	Adams, Scrivener & Co	L	Moulded jug
Feb 5	8	Elijah Hodgkinson	H	Moulded jug
Feb 10	8	Minton & Co	S	Openwork baskets
Feb 12	1	J. Wedgwood & Sons	E	Partridge pie dish
Feb 14	10	John Mortlock★	Ln	Moulded jug

Feb 18	1	J. Wedgwood & Sons	E	Jardinere
Feb 18	2	Brown-Westhead, Moore & Co	Sh	Moulded jug
Feb 18	2	Brown-Westhead, Moore & Co	Sh	Plate form
Feb 20	9	Minton & Co	S	Dish stand
Feb 25	6	J. Rose & Co	Cpt	Teawares
Feb 27	5	Alcock & Diggory	B	Dessertwares
Feb 28	7	W. & J. A. Bailey	Alloa	Teapot form
Mar 5	12	Thomas Goode & Co★	Ln	Dinnerwares
Mar 5	15	Minton & Co	S	Moulded jug
Mar 7	11	Battam & Son★	Ln	Finger plate
Mar 7	12	Frankham & Wilson★	Ln	China slides
Mar 16	4	Carpi, Loly & Co★	Liv	Printed design
Mar 25	7	W. T. Copeland & Sons	S	Acorn print
Mar 25	8	Worcester Royal Porcelain Co	W	Basket form
Mar 25	8	Worcester Royal Porcelain Co	W	Vase form
Mar 26	3	Walker & Carter	L	Moulded jug
April 1	6	Minton & Co	S	Teawares
April 6	5	Mary White	Fife	Wall brackets
April 6	6	Pinder, Bourne & Co	B	Printed designs
April 16	7	G. L. Ashworth & Bros	H	Printed design
April 21	6	Beech & Hancock	T	Printed border
April 23	8	R. Hammersley	T	"Gem" print
April 28	7	T. G. Green	BT	Teapot form
May 6	5	Pellatt & Co★	Ln	Jug form
May 13	1	Adams, Scrivener & Co	L	Moulded jug
May 14	2	Hope & Carter	B	Printed design
May 26	5	Brown-Westhead, Moore & Co	Sh	Printed design
May 26	6	Pinder, Bourne & Co	B	"Bird" prints
May 28	3	Holdcroft & Wood	T	Printed design
May 28	5	Minton & Co	S	Dinnerwares
May 28	5	Minton & Co	S	Divided dish
May 28	7	J. & T. Bevington	H	Cupid & shell
May 30	4	T. & R. Boote	B	Jug forms
Jun 8	4	Burgess & Leigh	B	"Oak" print
Jun 12	5	W. Brownfield	C	Teapot form
Jun 12	5	W. Brownfield	C	Jug form
Jun 16	4	W. P. & G. Phillips★	Ln	Fruit dish
Jun 18	6	Mary White★	Fife	Wall brackets
Jun 22	5	H. Minton & Co	S	Printed design
July 10	3	J. Wedgwood & Sons	E	Flower holder
July 16	3	Hackney & Co	L	Moulded jug
July 20	2	Hope & Carter	B	Printed borders
July 24	4	W. T. Copeland	S	Moulded jug
July 30	6	Adams, Scrivener & Co	L	Moulded jug
Aug 1	5	T. & R. Boote	B	Dinnerwares
Aug 1	5	T. & R. Boote	B	Teawares
Aug 13	1	J. Wedgwood & Sons	E	Printed design
Aug 15	8	J. Edwards & Son	B	Toiletwares
Aug 15	8	J. Edwards & Son	B	Dinnerwares
Aug 15	8	J. Edwards & Son	B	Teawares
Aug 17	2	Edward F. Bodley	B	Printed design
Aug 21	2	Ralph Malkin	F	Printed design

Aug 31	3	Ralph Malkin	F	Moulded jug
Aug 31	7	T. & R. Boote	B	Printed border
Sept 1	1	James Wardle	H	Vase forms
Sept 4	6	Gelson Brothers	H	Jug form
Sept 4	6	Gelson Brothers	H	Printed design
Sept 5	3	Brown–Westhead, Moore & Co	Sh	Plate form
Sept 5	6	D. McBinney	Bel	Moulded plate
Sept 5	6	D. McBinney	Bel	Vase forms
Sept 9	4	Hope & Carter	H	"Thames" print
Sept 9	5	Frederick Jones & Co	L	Moulded jug
Sept 9	6	Wedgwood & Co	T	Printed design
Sept 9	9	J. & T. Bevington	H	Eagle vase
Sept 12	3	Minton & Co	S	Printed border
Sept 12	3	Minton & Co	S	Plate form
Sept 14	4	Thomas Booth & Co	B	Printed design
Sept 17	4	T. C. Sambrook & Co	B	Printed design
Sept 21	4	George Ash	H	Vase forms
Sept 25	4	Minton & Co	S	Printed designs
Sept 25	13	Brown–Westhead, Moore & Co	Sh	Plate form
Sept 25	13	Brown–Westhead, Moore & Co	Sh	Cup form
Oct 8	7	Minton & Co	S	Printed design
Oct 9	2	Joseph Holdcroft	S	Vase form
Oct 9	3	Hope & Carter	B	Moulded jug
Oct 9	5	Davenports & Co	Lpt	Dinnerwares
Oct 9	5	Davenports & Co	Lpt	Toiletwares
Oct 9	5	Davenports & Co	Lpt	Teawares
Oct 14	8	George Jones	S	Moulded jug
Oct 17	4	Minton & Co	S	Jardinere
Oct 21	8	W. P. & G. Phillips★ (produced by W. Brownfield)	Ln	Jug form
Oct 22	1	D. McBinney	Bel	Teawares
Oct 22	5	James Edwards & Son	B	Jug forms
Nov 3	5	Minton & Co	S	Printed design
Nov 3	5	Minton & Co	S	Shaped dish
Nov 3	6	Brown–Westhead, Moore & Co	Sh	Plate form
Nov 6	13	Powell & Bishop	H	Butter pot
Nov 9	5	J. Wedgwood & Sons	E	Divided dish
Nov 16	3	Knapper & Blackhurst	T	Printed design
Nov 17	1	Moore Brothers	C	Dinnerwares
Nov 17	1	Moore Brothers	C	Teawares
Nov 21	5	Minton & Co	S	Moulded jug
Nov 24	5	Brown–Westhead, Moore & Co	Sh	Plate form
Nov 25	4	Cork, Edge & Malkin	B	"Ruth" jug form
Nov 25	6	D. Hulett & Co	Ln	Stove
Dec 1	4	Brown–Westhead, Moore & Co	Sh	Tureen forms
Dec 3	5	Worcester Royal Porcelain Co	W	Comport-vase
Dec 11	5	Edward F. Bodley & Co	B	Printed design
Dec 12	4	W. Brownfield	C	Dish form
Dec 14	7	Cockson, Chetwynd & Co	C	Teaware forms
Dec 23	5	Minton & Co	S	Shell dish
Dec 23	6	Worcester Royal Porcelain Co	W	Vase

Dec 31	6	G. L. Ashworth & Bros	H	Moulded jug
Dec 31	7	Ralph Hammersley	T	Printed design

1869 (H at right)

Jan 1	8	George Jones	S	Oval tureen
Jan 4	4	Minton & Co	S	Dove vase
Jan 7	6	T. Goode & Co	Ln	Bird ornament
Jan 21	6	Minton & Co	S	Toiletwares
Jan 21	6	Minton & Co	S	Plate form
Jan 22	5	Gelson Bros	H	Plate form
Jan 22	13	Brown-Westhead, Moore & Co	Sh	Tureen forms
Jan 25	3	Worthington & Son	H	Printed design
Jan 28	5	Minton & Co	S	Printed design
Jan 28	10	George Ash	H	Vase forms
Feb 1	7	Brown-Westhead, Moore & Co	Sh	Teaware forms
Feb 2	4	George Yearsley	L	Parian figure
Feb 9	5	Minton & Co	S	Ornament - boots
Feb 11	10	George Jones	S	"Grecian" print
Feb 15	1	Thomas Booth & Co	B	Printed design
Feb 19	2	J. Wedgwood & Sons	E	Printed border
Feb 22	6	J. Wedgwood & Sons	E	Tobacco jar
Feb 22	11	D. McBirney	Bel	Teawares
Feb 22	13	Pinder, Bourne & Co	B	Printed design
Feb 27	5	J. Wedgwood & Sons	E	Cigar ash tray
Mar 1	8	Worthington & Son	H	Teapot form
Mar 1	8	Worthington & Son	H	Jug form
Mar 1	8	Worthington & Son	H	Printed design
Mar 3	8	T. Till & Son	H	Printed design
Mar 4	6	J. Lawton	Bir	Knob form
Mar 6	8	F. Primavesi & Sons★	Cf	Printed design
Mar 8	6	F. & R. Pratt & Co	F	Cruet shape
Mar 9	1	George Jones	S	Dessertwares
Mar 9	1	George Jones	S	"Crete" print
Mar 9	3	George Jones	I	Ornamental tray
Mar 10	10	F. Primavesi & Sons★	Cf	Printed design
Mar 18	12	R. H. Grove	L	Printed design
Mar 18	12	R. H. Grove	L	Knife sharpener
Mar 24	1	James F. Wileman	F	Moulded jug
April 1	1	Wood & Pigott	T	Printed design
April 2	6	W. Brownfield	C	Jardinere
April 2	7	Minton & Co	S	Flower holder - dove
April 6	3	Baker & Chetwynd	B	Teawares
April 6	3	Baker & Chetwynd	B	Jug forms
April 7	2	Minton & Co	S	Butterfly handle
April 7	4	Worcester Royal Porcelain Co	W	Birds nest vase
April 12	4	Taylor, Tunnicliffe & Co	H	Door furniture
April 12	5	Liddle Elliot & Son	B	Dinnerwares
April 12	5	Liddle Elliot & Son	B	Toiletwares
April 12	5	Liddle Elliot & Son	B	Teawares
April 20	5	Liddle Elliot & Son	B	Tureen forms
April 28	13	J. & T. Bevington	H	Cupid centrepiece
May 4	3	Trachtenberg & Pantes★	Odessa	Printed design

May 11	1	Adams, Scrivener & Co	L	Teawares
May 13	16	J. Edwards & Son	B	Tureen forms
May 21	1	Worthington & Son	H	Printed design
May 26	4	Thomas Booth	H	Moulded jug
May 27	8	Davenports & Co	Lpt	Dinnerwares – vine
May 27	8	Davenports & Co	Lpt	Toiletwares – vine
May 27	8	Davenports & Co	Lpt	Teawares – vine
Jun 3	6	D. McBirney	Bel	Dish form
Jun 8	7	Phillip & Pearce★	Ln	Flower trough
Jun 19	5	W. Brownfield	C	Moulded teapot
Jun 19	5	W. Brownfield	C	"Severn" jug
Jun 25	4	J. Edwards & Son	B	Jug form
Jun 26	9	Minton & Co	S	Swan vase
July 3	9	J. Wedgwood & Sons	E	Strawberry dish
July 3	9	J. Wedgwood & Sons	E	Supper set
July 6	3	J. Meir & Son	T	"Talbot" print
July 16	8	Charles Stanley	Sn	Printed design
July 19	8	J. Wardle	H	Vase form
July 20	2	J. Wedgwood & Sons	E	Printed border
July 21	6	George Ash	H	Bird vases
July 23	6	Minton & Co	S	Nut dish
July 24	4	W. T. Copeland & Sons	S	Cup & stand
July 26	4	Levison Hill, executors of	S	Cupid vase
July 27	4	J. T. Hudden	L	"Regent" print
Aug 2	6	W. T. Copeland & Sons	S	Shell ornament
Aug 3	5	John Edwards	F	Teawares
Aug 4	4	Tomkinson Bros & Co	H	Dinnerwares
Aug 11	13	Phillip & Pearce★	Ln	Flower trough
		(produced by Royal Worcester)		
Aug 19	6	W. T. Copeland & Sons	S	Teawares
Aug 26	6	W. T. Copeland & Sons	S	Covered box
Aug 31	6	John Pratt & Co	F	Printed designs
Aug 31	12	W. T. Copeland & Sons	S	Teawares
Sept 4	3	Minton & Co	S	Tureen – lobster
Sept 8	5	W. T. Copeland & Sons	S	Teawares
Sept 8	6	Pinder, Bourne & Co	B	Printed design
Sept 9	3	John Pratt & Co	F	Printed design
Sept 10	4	Minton & Co	S	Printed design
Sept 15	1	J. Cartland & Son	Bir	Door furniture
Sept 21	7	Gelson Bros	H	Dinnerwares
Sept 22	10	W. & J. A. Bailey	Alloa	Teapot form
Sept 30	8	Brown-Westhead, Moore & Co	Sh	Jug forms
Sept 30	8	Brown-Westhead, Moore & Co	Sh	Jardinere
Sept 30	9	F. Lloyd & Co★	Ln	Cigar holder
Oct 1	3	Minton & Co	S	Bird dish
Oct 1	3	Minton & Co	S	Printed design
Oct 4	6	Minton & Co	S	Pineapple pot
Oct 14	3	D. McBirney & Co	Bel	Spill vase
Oct 15	6	George Jones	S	Cake stand
Oct 23	4	George Jones	S	Cigar ash tray
Oct 26	2	James Ellis & Son	H	Moulded jug
Oct 27	4	Smith & Chamberlain★	Bir	Screen base

Oct 27	5	D. McBirney & Co	Bel	Egg holder
Oct 29	3	Minton & Co	S	Tray – birds
Oct 29	3	Minton & Co	S	Tray – rabbit
Oct 29	4	Powell & Bishop	H	Dinnerwares
Oct 29	4	Powell & Bishop	H	Teawares
Nov 2	12	Edward Clarke	T	Teawares
Nov 2	12	Edward Clarke	T	Toiletwares
Nov 3	12	Brown–Westhead, Moore & Co	Sh	Plate form
Nov 8	1	D. McBirney & Co	Bel	Vase forms
Nov 8	2	Brown–Westhead, Moore & Co	Sh	Spill vase
Nov 9	11	Tams & Lowe	L	"Tonia" print
Nov 10	3	W. Brownfield	C	Dinnerwares
Nov 13	5	D. McBirney & Co	Bel	Sailor-boy boxes
Nov 15	8	Liddle Elliot & Son	B	Printed designs
Nov 18	5	Alcock & Diggory	B	Teawares
Nov 18	6	J. S. Crapper★	H	Spittoon
Nov 19	12	Worcester Royal Porcelain Co	W	Elephant vase
Nov 20	8	T. Goode & Co★	Ln	Teapot form
Nov 20	9	J. Mortlock★	Ln	Swan jug
Nov 23	1	D. McBirney & Co	Bel	Cheese stand
Nov 24	4	Minton & Co	S	Cat ornament
Nov 26	3	Minton & Co	S	Printed border
Dec 1	3	George Jones	S	Printed design
Dec 3	9	W. Brownfield	C	Covered dish
Dec 14	4	J. S. Crapper★	H	Spittoon
Dec 17	7	Minton & Co	S	Printed border
Dec 18	2	Powell & Bishop	H	Toiletwares
Dec 18	2	Powell & Bishop	H	Teawares
Dec 20	8	George Ash	H	Bird vase
Dec 22	7	George Jones	S	Nut tray
Dec 24	1	Gelson Bros	H	Tureen form
Dec 28	2	John Pratt & Co	F	Printed design
Dec 31	2	Minton & Co	S	Printed design

1870 (C at right)

Jan 1	5	Brown–Westhead, Moore & Co	Sh	Jardinere
Jan 3	4	George Jones	S	Tureen form
Jan 7	9	Pellatt & Co★	Ln	Swan vase
Jan 15	12	Liddle Elliot & Son	B	Printed borders
Jan 27	8	C. Hobson	S	Teapot & jug
Jan 29	3	Minton & Co	S	Butterfly plate
Feb 1	6	Brown–Westhead, Moore & Co	Sh	Dessertwares
Feb 3	13	Brown–Westhead, Moore & Co	Sh	Jug forms
Feb 3	13	Brown–Westhead, Moore & Co	Sh	Toilet wares
Feb 3	13	Brown–Westhead, Moore & Co	Sh	Dressing table set
Feb 4	7	Powell & Bishop	H	Moulded teapot
Feb 7	5	Wiltshaw, Wood & Co	B	Covered pot
Feb 7	6	W. & J. A. Bailey	Alloa	Moulded teapot
Feb 9	2	J. Wedgwood & Sons	E	Printed design
Feb 10	8	Minton & Co	S	Flower trough
Feb 11	12	Phillip & Pearce★	Ln	Flower troughs
		(produced by Royal Worcester)		

Feb 15	6	Brown-Westhead, Moore & Co	Sh	Dessertwares
Feb 25	2	Minton & Co	S	Asparagus dish
Feb 28	6	Minton & Co	S	Printed design
Mar 2	4	Minton & Co	S	Bird ornament
Mar 7	6	C. Hobson	B	Printed design
Mar 8	1	George Jones	S	Bird trays
Mar 10	1	George Jones	S	Toilet jug
Mar 10	9	Powell & Bishop	H	Dinnerwares
Mar 11	8	Levison Hill, executors of	S	Figure vase
Mar 14	4	Brown-Westhead, Moore & Co	Sh	Dessert edging
Mar 15	6	T. Till & Sons	B	Tureen forms
Mar 16	2	Minton & Co	S	Flower trough
Mar 16	2	Minton & Co	S	Bird dish
Mar 17	4	D. McBirney & Co	Bel	Vases
Mar 17	7	Worcester Royal Porcelain Co	W	Vase
Mar 17	9	J. Mortlock★	Ln	Butterfly vase
Mar 18	1	W. Cadman★	Ln	Lobster dish
Mar 18	6	Minton & Co	S	Printed design
Mar 23	9	J. Blackshaw & Co	S	Vase & Jug
Mar 25	4	Hope & Carter	B	Dinnerwares
Mar 25	5	Minton & Co	S	Circular stand
Mar 25	5	Minton & Co	S	Scuttle ornament
Mar 26	1	Minton & Co	S	Leaf dish
Mar 26	1	Minton & Co	S	Figure centrepiece
Mar 26	2	Worthington & Son	H	Teapot form
Mar 28	9	Old Hall Earthenware Co Ltd	H	Tureen form
April 7	9	Cork, Edge & Malkin	B	Printed design
April 7	10	Baker & Co	F	Printed designs
April 7	11	Harvey Adams & Co	L	Moulded jug
April 9	1	Minton & Co	S	Printed design
April 11	3	Worcester Royal Porcelain Co Ltd	W	Dove basket
April 13	4	T. Goode & Co★	Ln	Breakfastwares
April 14	7	Minton & Co	S	Ribbon edge
May 5	1	James Oldham & Co	H	Moulded jug
May 6	5	D. McBirney & Co	Bel	Ribbon motif
May 6	5	D. McBirney & Co	Bel	Fern ornament
May 10	4	George Ash	H	Bird vases
May 11	9	J. S. Crapper★	H	Condenser
May 13	8	Brown-Westhead, Moore & Co	Sh	Toiletwares
May 17	7	Brown-Westhead, Moore & Co	Sh	Shell salt
May 18	6	Bates Elliot & Co	B	Printed borders
May 21	6	Old Hall Earthenwares Co Ltd	H	Tureen forms
May 21	12	J. Edwards & Son	B	Toiletwares
May 25	7	J. Edwards & Son	B	Jug form
May 26	5	Minton	S	Toiletwares
May 27	11	C. Christodulo	Liv	Printed design
May 30	15	George Jones	S	Tureen form
Jun 3	8	F. & R. Pratt & Co	F	Jug form
Jun 7	15	Hope & Carter	B	Printed border
Jun 7	16	Thomas Booth	H	Teapot form
Jun 9	3	Brown-Westhead, Moore & Co	Sh	Flower trough
Jun 10	1	W. Brownfield	C	Toiletwares

Jun 10	1	W. Brownfield	C	Teapot & jug
Jun 11	3	J. Edwards & Son	B	Fluted jug
Jun 17	7	Minton Hollins & Co	S	Printed tiles
Jun 22	1	Harvey Adams & Co	L	Teawares
Jun 22	1	Harvey Adams & Co	L	Dessertwares
Jun 22	3	Minton Hollins & Co	S	Printed tiles
Jun 22	4	Worcester Royal Porcelain Co	W	Flower holder
Jun 27	1	George Jones	S	Pineapple teapot
July 5	5	Baker & Co	F	Printed design
July 8	7	James Wardle	H	Vase designs
July 12	6	Joseph Parkes★	Ln	Moulded jug
July 13	8	J. Edwards & Son	B	Moulded jug
July 14	9	Minton Hollins & Co	S	Printed tiles
July 14	10	Worcester Royal Porcelain Co	W	Printed design
July 15	1	W. T. Copeland & Sons	S	Moulded jug
July 16	2	J. Wardle	H	Vase
July 19	6	F. & R. Pratt & Co	F	Printed border
July 20	5	T. Booth	H	Moulded jug
July 21	1	T. Booth	H	Moulded teapot
July 22	1	Cork, Edge & Malkin	B	Moulded jug
July 27	1	Beech, Unwin & Co	L	Band print
Aug 1	2	R. G. Scrivener & Co	H	Cup forms
Aug 4	4	J. Wardle	H	Elephant vase
Aug 4	5	James Broadhurst	S	Crest motifs
Aug 9	2	W. Brownfield	C	Dessertwares
Aug 22	4	T. & R. Boote	B	Dinnerwares
Aug 22	4	T. & R. Boote	B	Toiletwares
Aug 23	6	George Jones	S	Figure dish
Aug 25	5	T. & R. Boote	B	Teawares
Sept 7	7	Bailey & Cooke	H	Basket ornament
Sept 10	9	Minton & Co	S	Plate form
Sept 16	5	Minton & Co	S	Printed design
Sept 19	2	W. Brownfield	C	Jug form
Sept 27	4	Elsmore Foster & Co	T	Dinnerwares
Sept 27	6	Phillips & Pearce★	Ln	Jardinere
Sept 28	11	Gelson Bros	H	Moulded jug
Oct 4	7	Joseph Holdcroft	L	Bird dish
Oct 4	8	Minton & Co	S	Toiletwares
Oct 6	4	Minton & Co	S	Printed design
Oct 6	5	James Broadhurst	L	Printed border
Oct 7	3	Minton & Co	S	Plate form
Oct 8	9	Powell & Bishop	H	Printed design
Oct 19	2	George Jones	S	Divided dish
Oct 19	2	George Jones	S	Biscuit barrel
Oct 22	2	W. Brownfield	C	Teawares
Oct 25	6	Brown-Westhead, Moore & Co	Sh	Teawares
Nov 4	9	Brown-Westhead, Moore & Co	Sh	Dinnerwares
Nov 9	7	Blumberg & Co★	Ln	Dressing table set
Nov 9	8	J. Meir & Son	T	Printed design
Nov 9	9	Pellatt & Co★	Ln	Divided dish
Nov 10	5	Minton & Co	S	Covered box – log
Nov 10	5	Minton & Co	S	Condiment
Nov 10	5	Minton & Co	S	Teawares

Nov 10	10	W. Brownfield	C	Dinnerwares
Nov 10	10	W. Brownfield	C	Moulded jug
Nov 12	3	D. McBirney & Co	Bel	Teawares
Nov 12	8	Minton Hollins & Co	S	Printed tiles
Nov 21	5	Joseph Partners★	Ln	Jug designs
Nov 22	3	George Jones	S	Dinnerwares
Nov 24	3	Minton & Co	S	Ornamental basket
Nov 24	8	Bates Elliot & Co	B	Printed design
Nov 25	1	Minton & Co	S	Bamboo vase
Nov 25	2	Turner Goddard & Co	T	Jug form
Nov 26	9	T. & R. Boote	B	Dinnerwares
Nov 26	9	T. & R. Boote	B	Toiletwares
Nov 26	9	T. & R. Boote	B	Teawares
Dec 1	7	W. Brownfield	C	Cheese stand
Dec 2	11	Brown-Westhead, Moore & Co	Sh	Tureen form
Dec 5	4	Minton Hollins & Co	S	Printed tiles
Dec 8	4	Blumberg & Co★	Ln	Teawares
Dec 16	5	Bates Elliot & Co	B	Printed border
Dec 17	11	Bates Elliot & Co	B	Bird print
Dec 19	9	Harvey Adams & Co	L	Moulded plate
Dec 27	4	J. Edwards & Son	B	Moulded jug

1871 (A at right)

Jan 2	2	Gelson Bros	H	Tureen form
Jan 6	3	Minton & Co	S	Jardinere
Jan 7	8	Bates, Elliot & Co	B	Printed design
Jan 9	4	D. McBirney & Co	Bel	Shell teawares
Jan 10	7	George Jones	S	Dog covered box
Jan 11	4	J. Mortlock★	Ln	Water can ornament
Jan 12	7	D. McBirney & Co	Bel	Jug form
Jan 12	12	Soane & Smith★	Ln	Dressing set
Jan 24	4	Soane & Smith★	Ln	Teawares
Jan 26	8	Minton, Hollins & Co	S	Tile designs
Jan 27	9	Worcester Royal Porcelain Co	W	Pierced edging
Jan 30	2	Gelson Bros	H	Tureen form
Jan 30	7	R. Minton Taylor & Co	S	Tile design
Feb 2	3	J. Edwards & Son	B	Tureen form
Feb 6	5	D. McBirney	Bel	Tureen & dish
Feb 6	5	D. McBirney	Bel	Honey pot
Feb 6	5	D. McBirney	Bel	Border design
Feb 8	9	J. Macintyre & Co	B	Door furniture
Feb 11	9	Brown-Westhead, Moore & Co	Sh	Dessertwares
Feb 13	6	Edge, Malkin & Co	B	Teapot form
Feb 13	7	Worthington & Son	H	Candleholder
Feb 13	9	Powell & Bishop	H	Dinnerwares
Feb 13	10	Edward F. Bodley & Co	B	Candleholder
Feb 15	7	Powell & Bishop	H	Teawares
Feb 17	7	Thomas Peake	T	Tile designs
Feb 20	2	Elsmore & Forster	T	Dinnerwares
Feb 20	2	Elsmore & Forster	T	Toiletwares
Feb 28	8	Watcombe Terra Cotta Clay Co Ltd	Wat	Jar
Mar 9	4	J. & T. Bevington	H	Flower vase

Mar 14	4	John Pratt & Co	F	Printed border
Mar 15	10	Bates, Elliot & Co	B	Printed border
Mar 16	5	George Skey	Tm	Gas stoves
Mar 27	1	W. Brownfield	C	Teapot
Mar 29	1	T. Furnival & Son	C	Jug & decoration
April 4	4	D. McBirney & Co	Bel	Printed shell border
April 22	4	J. Pratt & Co	F	Printed border
April 24	4	J. Wedgwood & Sons	E	Bambo teapot
April 26	12	Minton, Hollins & Co	S	Tile design
April 27	7	Wood & Clarke	B	Printed designs
April 27	8	Phillip & Pearce★	Ln	Comport
April 27	8	Phillip & Pearce★	Ln	Candelabra
April 28	1	Wood & Clarke	B	Printed design
April 29	6	Wood & Clarke	B	Printed design
April 29	7	J. Edwards & Son	B	Covered dish
May 1	9	Brown–Westhead, Moore & Co	Sh	Flower troughs
May 2	3	Ambrose Bevington	H	Vase
May 2	4	W. Brownfield & Son	C	Dessertwares
May 2	4	W. Brownfield & Son	C	Toiletwares
May 2	4	W. Brownfield & Son	C	Jug and pot
May 3	4	J. Jackson & Co	Y	Printed design
May 6	1	Phillips & Pearce★	Ln	Jug forms
May 9	9	Liddle Elliot & Co	B	Printed border
May 11	13	Powell & Bishop	H	Toiletwares
May 13	6	Elsmore, Forster & Co	T	Teawares
May 22	8	J. Lawton	Bir	Bedstead unit
May 22	9	D. McBirney & Co	Bel	Flower trough
May 24	10	J. Meir & Son	T	Dinnerwares
Jun 2	4	Brown–Westhead, Moore & Co	Sh	Teawares
Jun 7	7	Grove & Stark	L	Flower vase
Jun 16	9	John Twigg	Y	Printed designs
Jun 17	3	Minton & Co	S	Toiletwares
Jun 17	3	Minton & Co	S	Printed border
Jun 19	9	Pinder, Bourne & Co	B	Fish print
Jun 19	9	Pinder, Bourne & Co	B	Washstand
Jun 22	1	T. Till & Sons	B	Printed border
Jun 23	9	Bates, Elliot & Co	B	Printed design
July 4	8	W. T. Copeland & Sons	S	Teawares
July 14	6	Taylor, Tunnicliffe & Co	H	Door furniture
July 15	2	Thomas Booth	H	Moulded jug
July 19	2	Ambrose Bevington	H	Printed border
July 22	8	Haviland & Co	Fr	Tureen form
July 22	8	Haviland & Co	Fr	Teapot forms
July 25	12	Bates, Elliot & Co	B	Printed border
July 29	6	Hope & Carter	B	Dinnerwares
Aug 2	3	Robinson & Leadbeater	S	Owl ornament
Aug 9	7	Bates, Elliot & Co	B	Printed design
Aug 18	10	Pratt & Co	F	Meat pot
Aug 28	5	James Wardle	H	Leaf dish
Aug 29	2	George Jones	S	Fish dish
Aug 30	4	Thomas Barlow	L	Jug form
Aug 31	9	J. H. & J. Davis	H	Printed design

Sept 15	7	J. Bevington & Co	H	Jug form
Sept 15	10	Thomas Barlow	L	Moustache cup
Sept 19	2	Minton & Co	S	"Delft" print
Sept 25	8	Brown-Westhead, Moore & Co	Sh	Jug form
Sept 28	5	Thomas Booth & Co	T	Printed design
Oct 4	7	Minton & Co	S	Tile designs
Oct 4	9	Pinder, Bourne & Co	B	Printed design
Oct 6	6	Moore & Son	L	Teapot
Oct 6	6	Moore & Son	L	Mirror frame
Oct 6	6	Moore & Son	L	Floral bowl
Oct 9	8	E. J. Ridgway & Son	H	Dinnerwares
Oct 10	3	J. T. Hudden	L	"Tichborne" print
Oct 10	6	Brown-Westhead, Moore & Co	Sh	Toiletwares
Oct 11	4	D. McBirney & Co	Bel	Vase
Oct 14	6	Thomas Booth & Co	T	Printed ribbon design
Oct 14	7	J. Wedgwood & Sons	E	Dinnerwares
Oct 18	4	Moore & Son	L	Teapot form
Oct 19	6	W. T. Copeland & Sons	S	Moulded jug
Oct 24	3	Robert Cooke	H	Boat ornament
Oct 31	5	Minton & Co	S	"Danish" print
Oct 31	6	Edge, Hill & Palmer	L	Match holder
Nov 3	4	R. G. Scrivener	H	Dish form
Nov 3	4	R. G. Scrivener	H	Teawares
Nov 3	5	J. F. Wileman	F	Printed design
Nov 15	4	J. Thomson & Son	G	"Birds" print
Nov 23	6	Thomas Ford	H	Dessertwares
Dec 1	6	George Jones	S	Bird tray
Dec 15	5	Robinson & Leadbeater	S	Monkey vase
Dec 16	7	D. McBirney & Co	Bel	Centrepiece
Dec 22	6	F. & R. Pratt	F	Fluted jar
Dec 23	3	George Jones	S	Camel box
Dec 23	3	George Jones	S	Comfort
Dec 23	5	Robert Cooke	H	Moulded teapot
Dec 29	10	Brown-Westhead, Moore & Co	Sh	Basket – dish

1872 (I at right)

Jan 1	5	Moore & Son	L	Teapot
Jan 1	6	Edge, Malkin & Co	B	Moulded jug
Jan 5	3	D. McBirney & Co	Bel	Centrepiece
Jan 6	1	Minton & Co	S	Fancy dish
Jan 18	6	Worcester Royal Porcelain Co Ltd	W	Teapot
Jan 20	6	George Jones	S	Comport
Jan 30	7	W. T. Copeland	S	Teawares
Feb 2	2	Moore & Son	L	Fan – dish
Feb 2	11	Turner & Tomkinson	T	Printed border
Feb 3	4	George Jones	S	Comport
Feb 3	4	George Jones	S	Flower container
Feb 7	3	Ambrose Bevington	H	Patterned plate
Feb 15	3	Powell & Bishop	H	Moulded jug
Feb 16	6	D. McBirney & Co	Bel	Teapot
Feb 16	7	George Jones	S	Strawberry dish
Feb 16	7	George Jones	S	Comports

Feb 19	6	W. H. Goss	S	Brooch
Feb 20	4	Worcester Royal Porcelain Co Ltd	W	Squirrel vase
Feb 22	3	Minton & Co	S	Lily bowl
Feb 26	6	E. Wood★	Ln	Tobacco jar
Mar 4	3	George Jones	S	Elephant vase
Mar 4	4	Minton & Co	S	Tile design
Mar 4	4	Minton & Co	S	Floral print
Mar 4	6	Minton, Hollins & Co	S	Printed tile
Mar 7	7	Harvey Adams & Co	L	Teawares
Mar 7	10	Bates, Elliot & Co	B	Floral jug
Mar 8	5	Minton, Hollins & Co	S	Printed tiles
Mar 9	1	D. McBirney & Co	Bel	Dragon teapot
Mar 13	8	Minton, Hollins & Co	S	Printed tile
Mar 16	6	Minton & Co	S	Printed tile
Mar 18	6	Minton & Co	S	Openwork edge
Mar 20	10	Worcester Royal Porcelain Co Ltd	W	Candle snuffer
Mar 21	14	R. Minton Taylor & Co	F	Printed design
Mar 22	5	Joseph Holdcroft	L	Fancy dish
Mar 22	8	Brown-Westhead, Moore & Co	Sh	Dinnerwares
Mar 26	3	Robinson & Leadbeater	S	Parian ornament
Mar 26	3	Robinson & Leadbeater	S	Parian cow
Mar 26	6	Phillips & Pearce★	Ln	Basket
April 5	4	Wedgwood & Co	T	Printed border
April 5	5	Minton & Co	S	Teawares
April 6	1	Joseph Holdcroft	L	Bird dishes
April 9	6	Brown-Westhead, Moore & Co	Sh	Ship's jug
April 10	11	T. Furnival & Son	C	Jug
April 17	13	E. J. Ridgway & Son	H	Toiletwares
April 19	5	Minton, Hollins & Co	S	Printed tile
April 24	5	J. Pratt & Co Ltd	F	Printed border
April 27	9	Moore & Son	L	Boy in canoe
May 2	9	Harvey Adams & Co	L	Teawares
May 2	9	Harvey Adams & Co	L	Floral vase
May 2	11	T. Furnival & Son	C	Prints for jugs
May 3	9	Minton & Co	S	Monkey vase
May 3	9	Minton & Co	S	Pineapple tureen
May 3	11	Bates, Elliot & Co	B	Toiletwares
May 6	3	Moore & Son	L	Jardinere
May 6	3	Moore & Son	L	Fan vase
May 6	3	Moore & Son	L	Bird wall-pocket
May 6	8	Bates, Elliot & Co	B	Printed border
May 6	9	Minton Hollins & Co	S	Printed tiles
May 10	1	Moore & Son	L	Wall vase
May 11	4	T. Booth & Sons	H	Punch prints
May 14	6	Thomson & Kelley★	Ln	Pot lid designs
May 27	1	George Jones	S	Jug - foxes
May 27	3	Minton Hollins & Co	S	Printed tile
May 29	2	George Jones	S	Match box
May 29	5	G. Grainger & Co	W	Teapot designs
May 29	5	G. Grainger & Co	W	Plate edging
May 30	1	Minton & Co	S	Vase
May 30	1	Minton & Co	S	Divisional dish

Jun 3	6	Watcombe Terra Cotta Clay Co	Wat	Jug
Jun 5	3	Hope & Carter	B	Printed border
Jun 6	6	W. Brownfield & Son	C	Dinnerwares
Jun 7	4	Minton, Hollins & Co	S	Tile design
Jun 11	5	J. Wedgwood & Sons	E	Tureen form
Jun 11	12	W. T. Copeland & Sons	S	Jug form
Jun 18	3	G. L. Ashworth & Bros	Sh	Fluted kettle
Jun 18	3	G. L. Ashworth & Bros	Sh	Teapot
Jun 18	4	Minton, Hollins & Co	S	Tile design
Jun 21	7	Minton, Hollins & Co	S	Tile designs
Jun 22	5	Minton & Co	S	Tile design
Jun 22	8	W. Brownfield & Son	C	Fancy dishes
Jun 27	1	Brown–Westhead, Moore & Co	Sh	Dinnerwares
July 2	2	Robinson & Leadbeater	S	Dog match holders
July 2	3	J. Wedgwood & Sons	E	Mask match pot
July 13	5	Gelson Bros	H	Gravy dish
July 15	4	Robinson & Leadbeater	S	Parian group
July 16	5	Minton, Hollins & Co	S	Tile design
July 19	5	R. Minton Taylor	F	Tile designs
July 20	3	George Jones	S	Flower–holder
July 20	3	George Jones	S	Lily dish
July 24	2	W. & T. Adams	T	Printed armorials
July 29	7	J. Dimmock & Co	H	Dinnerwares
July 31	3	Minton & Co	S	Designs for tiles
Aug 2	1	E. J. Ridgway & Son	H	Printed designs
Aug 14	4	T. Booth & Co	T	Printed design
Aug 16	1	W. Brownfield & Son	C	Comports
Aug 16	1	W. Brownfield & Son	C	Divided dish
Aug 19	4	W. E. Cartlidge	H	Low bowl
Aug 19	5	W. & J. A. Bailey	Alloa	Teapot
Sept 2	3	D. McBirney & Co	Bel	Vase
Sept 2	8	Bates, Elliot & Co	B	Jug
Sept 7	14	George Skey	Tam	Stoves
Sept 12	6	Minton Hollins & Co	S	Tile design
Sept 25	9	Minton Hollins & Co	S	Tile designs
Sept 26	2	Frederick Jones	L	Fluted teawares
Sept 26	5	W. E. Cartlidge	H	Jug
Oct 7	7	Brown–Westhead, Moore & Co	Sh	Jardinere
Oct 11	5	J. Wedgwood & Sons	E	Jardineres
Oct 11	5	J. Wedgwood & Sons	E	Toiletwares
Oct 11	5	J. Wedgwood & Sons	E	Match holder
Oct 11	5	J. Wedgwood & Sons	E	Vase
Oct 12	10	Bates, Elliot & Co	B	Teapot
Oct 12	10	Bates, Elliot & Co	B	Jug
Oct 14	4	Minton Hollins & Co	S	Tile design
Oct 17	8	J. Wedgwood & Sons	E	Match holders
Oct 18	5	G. Jones	S	Jug
Oct 18	5	G. Jones	S	Basket
Oct 18	5	G. Jones	S	Honey pot
Oct 18	7	Masbro Stove Co	Y	Tiles
Oct 30	2	J. F. Wileman	F	Printed design
Oct 30	5	Brownhills Pottery Co	T	Toiletwares

Oct 30	9	Maw & Co	Br	Fireplace
Nov 2	6	Worcester Royal Porcelain Co	W	Teawares
Nov 2	6	Worcester Royal Porcelain Co	W	Flower trough
Nov 4	3	G. Grainger & Co	W	Swan ornament
Nov 11	2	W. E. Cartlidge	H	Teapot
Nov 12	4	Minton & Co	S	Printed design
Nov 14	13	W. Brownfield & Son	C	Centrepiece
Nov 14	13	W. Brownfield & Son	C	Teapot
Nov 14	13	W. Brownfield & Son	C	Candlelabra
Nov 14	14	Moore Brothers	L	Cupid vase
Nov 18	3	Holland & Green	L	Printed design
Nov 30	8	Belfield & Co	Sc	Teapot
Dec 2	5	Brown-Westhead, Moore & Co	Sh	Teawares
Dec 4	3	John Pratt & Co Ltd	F	Printed border
Dec 10	2	Minton & Co	S	Printed designs
Dec 11	8	Old Hall Earthenware Co Ltd	H	Tureen forms
Dec 11	8	Old Hall Earthenware Co Ltd	H	Jug
Dec 14	5	W. Brownfield & Son	C	Jug
Dec 14	5	W. Brownfield & Son	C	Tureen forms
Dec 24	1	Cockson & Chetwynd	C	Jug
Dec 27	4	John Adams – executors of	L	Teawares
Dec 27	5	R.G. Scrivener & Co	H	Jug
Dec 27	8	Meir & Son	T	Printed design
Dec 28	1	Charles Ellis	L	Bottle form
		(manufactured by Doultons, Lambeth)		

1873 (F at right)

Jan 10	1	G. Jones	S	Plate shape
Jan 13	4	W. T. Copeland & Sons	S	Toiletwares
Jan 14	8	J. Defries & Sons★	Ln	Printed design
Jan 15	2	Worthington & Son	H	Jug form
Jan 29	1	Minton, Hollins & Co	S	Tile designs
Jan 29	2	Moore Brothers	L	Leaf teawares
Jan 29	2	Moore Brothers	L	Fan dishes
Feb 1	1	Minton, Hollins & Co	S	Tile designs
Feb 10	2	W. & J. A. Bailey	Alloa	Teapot
Feb 12	4	Bates, Elliot & Co	B	Plate shape
Feb 15	1	Minton & Co	S	Tile design
Feb 19	14	J. & T. Bevington	H	Jug
Feb 19	14	J. & T. Bevington	H	Swan ornament
Feb 25	6	G. Jones	S	Jug
Feb 27	4	T. Till & Sons	B	Printed border
Feb 27	8	Minton, Hollins & Co	S	Tile design
Mar 6	1	Minton & Co	S	Tile designs
Mar 6	9	Brownhills Pottery Co	T	Covered jar
Mar 15	10	J. Lawton & Sons	Bir	Bedstead units
Mar 26	6	G. Jones	S	Tureen
Mar 26	6	G. Jones	S	Leaf dish
April 3	6	Minton & Co	S	Openwork edge
April 15	4	Taylor, Tunnicliffe & Co	H	Bedstead knob
April 19	1	T. Davidson, junior & Co	G	Teapot forms
April 19	2	Minton & Co	S	Teapot forms

April 23	6	Gelson Brothers	H	Toiletwares
April 28	5	Powell & Bishop	H	Printed designs
April 29	3	G. Jones	S	Strawberry set
April 29	3	G. Jones	S	Teawares
April 29	3	G. Jones	S	Breakfastwares
May 2	8	W. Whiteley★ (manufactured by A. Bevington)	Ln	Teapot
May 3	2	T. Till & Sons	B	Tureen forms
May 3	7	W. Brownfield & Son	C	Footbath
May 3	7	W. Brownfield & Son	C	Pail
May 3	7	W. Brownfield & Son	C	Centrepiece
May 3	7	W. Brownfield & Son	C	Cupid dish
May 3	8	Minton & Co	S	Tile designs
May 6	2	Minton & Co	S	Moulded plate
May 12	8	Brown-Westhead, Moore & Co	Sh	Jug
May 14	2	F. Atkins & Co	Ln	Filter
May 14	7	Moore Brothers	L	Dessertwares
May 16	6	Minton, Hollins & Co	S	Tile design
May 22	5	Worthington & Co	H	Oval dish
May 26	7	Moore Brothers	L	Jardinere
May 26	7	Moore Brothers	L	Basket dish
May 26	8	Soane & Smith★	Ln	Tea kettle
May 29	4	Worthington & Son	H	Printed design
May 29	8	T. Ford	H	Teawares
May 30	15	Brown-Westhead, Moore & Co	Sh	Jug
Jun 11	4	Bates, Elliot & Co	B	Pot lid prints
Jun 17	3	Taylor, Tunnicliffe & Co	H	Castor
Jun 19	3	Pinder, Bourne & Co	B	Jug
Jun 28	4	T. Goode & Co★	Ln	Plate border
Jun 30	3	Minton, Hollins & Co	S	Tile designs
July 3	9	Minton, Hollins & Co	S	Tile designs
July 4	7	Brown-Westhead, Moore & Co	Sh	Welled plate
July 28	2	Charles Hobson	B	Printed design
July 28	8	J. Meir & Sons	T	Printed design
July 29	3	D. McBirney & Co	Bel	Lighthouse ornament
July 31	1	Mintons	S	Menu holders
Aug 5	2	Baker & Chetwynd	B	Basket dish
Aug 5	3	George Skey	Tam	Gas stove
Aug 14	10	Brown-Westhead, Moore & Co	Sh	Teawares
Aug 25	1	G. Jones	S	Castle box
Aug 25	1	G. Jones	S	Tortoise box
Aug 27	1	Worcester Royal Porcelain Co Ltd	W	Bird ornament
Aug 30	2	Brown-Westhead, Moore & Co	Sh	Fluted jug
Sept 2	8	Edge, Malkin & Co	B	"Tiger" print
Sept 4	3	Mintons	S	Recessed plate
Sept 10	7	Powell & Bishop	H	Dinnerwares
Sept 15	3	Brown-Westhead, Moore & Co	Sh	Toiletwares
Sept 16	4	Brown-Westhead, Moore & Co	Sh	Toiletwares
Sept 17	8	Worcester Royal Porcelain Co Ltd	W	Bird ornament
Sept 19	4	Brown-Westhead, Moore & Co	Sh	Teawares
Sept 25	8	Harvey Adams & Co	L	Trinket set
Sept 25	10	Jane Beech	B	Washington jug

Sept 29	2	W. Brownfield & Son	C	Teapot
Oct 4	3	Moore Brothers	L	Cupid centrepiece
Oct 4	3	Moore Brothers	L	Wall pocket
Oct 4	3	Moore Brothers	L	Swan ornament
Oct 4	4	Heath & Blackhurst	B	"Rustic" print
Oct 6	6	Brown–Westhead, Moore & Co	Sh	Teawares
Oct 11	6	Mintons	S	Printed design
Oct 13	3	G. Jones	S	Printed designs
Oct 22	6	Mintons	S	Printed design
Nov 3	3	Hope & Carter	B	Printed design
Nov 3	4	G. Jones	S	Bird dish
Nov 3	4	G. Jones	S	Dish – birds
Nov 3	4	G. Jones	S	Bird honey pot
Nov 6	6	Wedgwood & Co	T	Printed design
Nov 10	7	Brown–Westhead, Moore & Co	Sh	Toiletwares
Nov 12	3	Worthington & Son	H	Jug
Dec 2	6	Taylor, Tunnicliffe & Co	H	Inkstand
Dec 2	6	Taylor, Tunnicliffe & Co	H	Elephant lamp
Dec 2	6	Taylor, Tunnicliffe & Co	H	Flower centrepiece
Dec 2	6	Taylor, Tunnicliffe & Co	H	Flower holder
Dec 4	6	Old Hall Earthenware Co Ltd	H	Printed design
Dec 5	1	Harvey Adams & Co	L	Teawares
Dec 5	8	W. Brownfield & Son	C	Cupid flower holder
Dec 10	12	G. Jones	S	Bird dish
Dec 22	7	J. Blashfield	Lincs	Chimney pot
Dec 27	7	G. Jones & Sons	S	Game pie dish

1874 (U at right)

Jan 1	3	Bates, Elliot & Co	B	4-seasons prints
Jan 10	15	Davenports & Co	Lpt	Menu tablets
Jan 20	3	Powell & Bishop	H	Printed design
Jan 21	7	W. T. Copeland & Sons	S	Teapot
Jan 23	2	Charles Southwell★	Ln	Fluted teawares
Jan 23	5	J. Meir & Son	T	Tureen forms
Jan 30	4	Haviland & Co	Fr	Tureen forms
Jan 30	4	Haviland & Co	Fr	Dish forms
Feb 9	4	Worcester Royal Porcelain Co Ltd	W	"Terrier" jug
Feb 9	5	Bodley & Co	B	Jug
Feb 11	2	T. Booth & Sons	H	Teapot
Feb 14	9	Worthington & Son	H	Jug
Feb 19	1	G. Jones & Sons	S	Jug
Feb 25	6	Robinson & Leadbeater	S	Dove basket
Feb 25	7	G. Jones & Sons	S	Bird dish
Feb 26	7	Minton, Hollins & Co	S	Tile designs
Mar 2	1	D. McBirney & Co	Bel	Egg cup basket
Mar 3	4	G. Jones & Sons	S	Printed design
Mar 4	3	Mintons	S	Printed design
Mar 4	8	Worcester Royal Porcelain Co Ltd	W	Dessert comports
Mar 13	6	J. Dimmock & Co	H	Dinnerwares
Mar 14	2	Mintons	S	Printed menu tablet
Mar 17	5	Powell & Bishop	H	"Autumn" print
Mar 21	5	Powell & Bishop	H	Bird printed designs

Mar 24	4	Mintons	S	Menu tablet
Mar 27	2	Worthington & Son	H	Jug
Mar 28	3	G. Jones & Sons	S	Sardine box
Mar 28	3	G. Jones & Sons	S	Flower & card holder
Mar 30	1	Worthington & Son	H	Teapot
April 7	4	Worcester Royal Porcelain Co Ltd	W	Egg cup stand
April 14	4	Ambrose Bevington	H	Teawares
April 15	7	Mintons	S	Vase
April 20	7	Minton, Hollins & Co	S	Tile designs
April 21	8	G. Jones & Sons	S	Printed design
April 22	1	W. Brownfield & Son	C	Sauceboat
April 23	8	Brown-Westhead, Moore & Co	Sh	Fluted teapot
April 25	2	G. Jones & Sons	S	Jug
April 29	7	Ridgway, Sparks & Ridgway	H	Printed border
April 29	9	T. Furnival & Son	C	Printed design
April 30	2	T. Booth & Sons	H	Jug
May 5	3	Bates, Elliot & Co	B	Printed design
May 7	7	Crosse & Blackwell★	Ln	Covered pot
May 9	3	G. Jones & Sons	S	Centrepiece
May 9	3	G. Jones & Sons	S	Garden seat
May 11	2	Moore Brothers	L	Camel teapot
May 11	2	Moore Brothers	L	Flower bowl
May 11	2	Moore Brothers	L	Squirrel jug
May 11	3	J. Thomson & Sons	G	"Oaknut" print
May 11	4	Holland & Green	L	Jug
May 20	11	Bates, Elliot & Co	B	Printed design
May 21	5	Mintons	S	Figure menu
May 22	8	Mintons	S	Figure menu
May 23	4	G. Jones & Sons	S	Flower centrepiece
May 23	4	G. Jones & Sons	S	Wall vase
Jun 1	7	Worcester Royal Porcelain Co Ltd	W	Hanging ornament
Jun 6	2	W. Brownfield & Son	C	Menu holder
Jun 6	2	W. Brownfield & Son	C	Dog flower holder
Jun 6	2	W. Brownfield & Son	C	Teapot
Jun 6	2	W. Brownfield & Son	C	Lamp holder
Jun 6	5	Charles Ford	H	Teacup
Jun 10	8	Daniel Pearce★	Ln	Menu holder
Jun 16	6	Cockson & Chetwynd	C	Tureen form
Jun 17	7	Edge, Malkin & Co	B	Jug
Jun 18	1	Mintons	S	Pierced edging
Jun 23	3	Williamson & Son	L	Printed design
Jun 23	7	Worcester Royal Porcelain Co Ltd	W	Nest wall pocket
Jun 25	5	Thomas Ford	H	Wall pockets
Jun 25	5	Thomas Ford	H	Menu stands
Jun 26	4	Pinder, Bourne & Co	B	Jug
July 10	2	Mintons	S	Leaf dish
July 13	6	Brown-Westhead, Moore & Co	Sh	Tea kettle
July 13	6	Brown-Westhead, Moore & Co	Sh	Printed border
July 25	7	J. Curling Hope★	Hgs	Fisherman match holder
July 27	1	Hulse & Adderley	L	Printed border
July 30	5	Minton, Hollins & Co	S	Tile design
Aug 1	8	Mintons	S	Tile designs

Aug 1	9	Cockson & Chetwynd	C	Teawares
Aug 6	7	Brown-Westhead, Moore & Co	Sh	Toilet jug
Aug 8	2	W. Brownfield & Son	C	Jardinere
Aug 8	2	W. Brownfield & Son	C	Vase – boot
Aug 10	7	John Moir & Son★	Ln	Jar form
Aug 15	4	Bates, Elliot & Co	B	Teawares
Aug 22	6	J. T. Hudden	L	Printed design
Aug 28	4	G. Jones & Sons	S	Jardinere
Aug 28	4	G. Jones & Sons	S	Tray form
Aug 31	6	T. J. & J. Emberton	T	Vine print
Sept 1	3	T. Till & Sons	B	Jug
Sept 3	12	Cockson & Chetwynd	C	Jugs
Sept 4	3	Mintons	S	Teawares
Sept 5	4	Worcester Royal Porcelain Co Ltd	W	Figure menu card
Sept 5	4	Worcester Royal Porcelain Co Ltd	W	Dove flower holder
Sept 5	7	T. Furnival & Son	C	Printed border
Sept 7	3	T. Booth & Sons	H	Jugs
Sept 10	3	W. Brownfield & Son	C	Toiletwares
Sept 12	1	Mintons	S	Printed border
Sept 15	2	G. Jones & Sons	S	Oyster plate
Sept 17	4	R. Britton & Sons	Lds	Printed design
Sept 19	8	James McKee★	Ln	Washstand
Sept 30	4	W. Brownfield & Son	C	Pair figures
Oct 2	5	G. Grainger & Co	W	Wall pocket
Oct 2	5	G. Grainger & Co	W	Baskets
Oct 3	4	Moore Brothers	L	Cat ornaments
Oct 3	4	Moore Brothers	L	Centrepiece – bowl
Oct 3	4	Moore Brothers	L	Frame
Oct 6	3	Mintons	S	Printed design
Oct 6	4	Grove & Stark	L	Jug form
Oct 10	4	Mintons	S	Cat jug
Oct 12	2	Powell & Bishop	H	Toiletwares
Oct 17	8	Bates, Elliot & Co	B	Printed design
Oct 21	8	G. Jones & Sons	S	Menu holder
Oct 21	8	G. Jones & Sons	S	Napkin holder
Oct 24	3	Robinson & Leadbeater	S	Shell matchbox
Oct 24	3	Robinson & Leadbeater	S	Butler matchbox
Oct 27	1	George Ash	H	Flower vase
Oct 28	9	Pinder, Bourne & Co	B	Printed border
Oct 30	5	Benjamin Green	F	Printed design
Nov 2	3	J. Edwards & Son	B	Tureen form
Nov 3	4	W. & E. Corn	B	Dinnerwares
Nov 3	4	W. & E. Corn	B	Teawares
Nov 3	4	W. & E. Corn	B	Jug forms
Nov 6	3	W. Brownfield & Son	C	Dessertwares
Nov 7	4	Thomas Ford	H	Wall pockets
Nov 7	4	Thomas Ford	H	Shell dishes
Nov 7	4	Thomas Ford	H	Shell condiment
Nov 10	3	G. Jones & Sons	S	Flower vase
Nov 12	3	Mintons	S	Printed design
Nov 12	12	Bates, Elliot & Co	B	Printed design
Nov 20	12	F. & R. Pratt & Co	F	Jug

Nov 25	7	Minton, Hollins & Co	S	Tile designs
Dec 1	5	W. T. Copeland & Sons	S	Candlestick
Dec 4	6	Thomas Barlow	L	Teawares
Dec 5	4	Holmes & Plant	B	Knob form
Dec 7	8	Brown-Westhead, Moore & Co	Sh	Baskets
Dec 7	8	Brown-Westhead, Moore & Co	Sh	Spittoon
Dec 7	8	Brown-Westhead, Moore & Co	Sh	Brush stand
Dec 8	2	G. Jones & Sons	S	Jug
Dec 10	4	Pinder, Bourne & Co	B	Jug
Dec 10	11	Worcester Royal Porcelain Co Ltd	W	Menu holders
Dec 12	3	G. Jones & Sons	S	Cheese stand
Dec 12	5	Port Dundas Pottery Co	G	Teapot
Dec 18	4	T. Barlow	L	Teawares
Dec 18	6	G. Jones & Sons	S	Trinket set
Dec 18	7	Ambrose Bevington	H	Plate form
Dec 18	9	G. Grainger & Co	W	Menu holder
Dec 18	11	Minton, Hollins & Co	S	Tile designs

1875 (S at right)

Jan 2	4	Brown-Westhead, Moore & Co	Sh	Dinnerwares
Jan 2	4	Brown-Westhead, Moore & Co	Sh	Teawares
Jan 6	3	Minton, Hollins & Co	S	Tile designs
Jan 11	11	W. Toogood★	Ln	Animal ornaments
Jan 12	3	Worcester Royal Porcelain Co Ltd	W	Menu card
Jan 16	9	Brownhills Pottery Co	T	Jug
Jan 18	8	Brown-Westhead, Moore & Co	Sh	Dog ornament
Jan 20	3	Robinson & Leadbeater	S	Flower holder
Jan 20	4	W. Brownfield & Son	C	Teawares
Jan 20	4	W. Brownfield & Son	C	Leaf dishes
Jan 20	4	W. Brownfield & Son	C	Menu holder
Jan 20	4	W. Brownfield & Son	C	Cruet
Jan 21	2	G. Jones & Sons	S	Dinnerwares
Jan 23	9	Brown-Westhead, Moore & Co	Sh	Dinnerwares
Jan 23	9	Brown-Westhead, Moore & Co	Sh	Toiletwares
Jan 28	4	C. Denham★	Ln	Spoonwarmer
Jan 28	5	Mintons	S	Teawares
Jan 29	1	Worthington & Son	H	Teapot
Jan 29	1	Worthington & Son	H	Jug
Feb 3	7	Charles Ford	H	Menu holder
Feb 5	5	T. & R. Boote	B	Tureen form
Feb 6	2	Moore Brothers	L	Cat ornament
Feb 9	1	Pinder, Bourne & Co	B	Printed designs
Feb 9	2	G. Jones & Sons	S	Strawberry set
Feb 12	6	J. Maddock & Sons	B	Dinnerwares
Feb 15	2	Moore Brothers	L	Kitten & basket
Feb 17	7	Mintons	S	Bird comports
Feb 23	5	J. Maddock & Sons	B	Dinnerwares
Feb 23	6	G. Jones & Sons	S	Spill vase
Feb 23	8	George Ash	H	Small vases
Feb 24	3	Stephen Clive	T	Printed design
Mar 5	2	W. Brownfield & Son	C	Cat ornament
Mar 12	5	G. Jones & Sons	S	Jugs

Mar 12	5	G. Jones & Sons	S	Sardine dish
Mar 24	13	Minton, Hollins & Co	S	Tile design
Mar 24	14	Brown-Westhead, Moore & Co	Sh	Teawares
Mar 30	1	T. Booth & Sons	H	Jug
Mar 31	5	W. Brownfield & Sons	C	Fan dish
Mar 31	5	W. Brownfield & Sons	C	Cat flower stand
Mar 31	8	James McKee★	Ln	Jug
April 3	7	J. Dimmock & Co	H	Covered dish
April 3	9	Edward F. Bodley & Son	B	Teawares
April 7	3	Mintons	S	Jug – oak leaf
April 9	6	W. Brownfield & Son	C	Candlelabra
April 9	6	W. Brownfield & Son	C	Menu tablet
April 9	6	W. Brownfield & Son	C	Name tablet
April 10	7	Powell & Bishop	H	Teawares
April 10	7	Powell & Bishop	H	Printed design
April 15	5	Ralph Malkin	F	Printed design
April 17	1	Pinder, Bourne & Co	B	Vase
April 20	1	J. Dimmock & Co	H	Slipper ornament
April 20	2	Mintons	S	Ornamental stand
April 21	5	Stephen Clive	T	Printed design
April 22	3	W. P. & G. Phillips★	Ln	Flower troughs
April 22	4	Minton, Hollins & Co	S	Tile designs
May 7	7	G. Jones & Sons	S	Trinket stand
May 7	8	Burgess & Leigh	B	Jug
May 11	5	J. Jeckyle★	Ln	Tile design
May 11	6	T. Goode & Co★	Ln	Bear ornament
May 20	1	Bates, Elliot & Co	B	Printed design
May 20	3	J. Dimmock & Co	H	Oval dish
May 22	1	Holland & Green	L	Printed design
May 26	6	Brown-Westhead, Moore & Co	Sh	Jugs
May 26	6	Brown-Westhead, Moore & Co	Sh	Tureen form
May 28	10	Campbellfield Pottery Co	G	Teapot
May 31	8	G. Jones & Sons	S	Flower pot
May 31	18	Ridgway, Sparks & Ridgway	H	"Chelsea" print
Jun 2	9	Minton, Hollins & Co	S	Tile designs
Jun 5	7	W. P. & G. Phillips★ (manufactured by Brownfields)	Ln	Figures with baskets
Jun 7	3	W. & T. Adams	T	Printed border
Jun 8	4	Worcester Royal Porcelain Co Ltd	W	Flower holder
Jun 10	6	W. Brownfield & Son	C	Printed designs
Jun 12	6	Maddock & Gates	B	Tureens
Jun 12	10	T. Furnival & Sons	C	Printed designs
Jun 15	5	J. Wedgwood & Sons	E	Beer set
Jun 19	6	T. Till & Sons	B	Printed border
Jun 26	2	G. Jones & Sons	S	Tea & dessertwares
July 5	1	W. Brownfield & Son	C	Fruit basket
July 7	8	Moore Brothers	L	Cupid centrepiece
July 7	8	Moore Brothers	L	Swan centrepiece
July 8	5	Moore Brothers	L	Lily vase
July 20	4	Edwin J. D. Bodley	B	Basket
July 23	10	Brown-Westhead, Moore & Co	Sh	Garden seat
July 27	5	Grove & Stark	L	Printed design

July 28	7	Minton, Hollins & Co	S	Tile design
Aug 19	7	Grove & Stark	L	Printed design
Aug 28	6	W. P. & G. Phillips★	Ln	Figures
Sept 2	3	Thomas Elsmore & Son	T	Tureen form
Sept 13	2	G. Jones & Sons	S	Punch centrepiece
Sept 13	2	G. Jones & Sons	S	Jug
Sept 14	9	Minton, Hollins & Co	S	Tile design
Sept 18	2	G. Jones & Sons	S	Flower holders
Sept 21	1	R. Cockran & Co	G	Printed border
Sept 22	9	J. Graham & Co	G	Brackets
Sept 24	2	H. Aynsley & Co	L	Printed design
Sept 25	3	Grove & Stark	L	Printed design
Sept 25	4	W. Toogood★	Ln	Cupid vase
Sept 25	4	W. Toogood★	Ln	Ornamental basket
Sept 28	6	Brown–Westhead, Moore & Co	Sh	Tureen forms
Sept 30	4	John Edwards	F	Dinnerwares
Sept 30	4	John Edwards	F	Jug
Oct 2	6	J. Wedgwood & Sons	E	Tureen forms
Oct 6	4	Robert Cooke	H	Teawares
Oct 11	4	Powell & Bishop	H	Toilet jug
Oct 11	10	Brownhills Pottery Co	T	Jug
Oct 11	10	Brownhills Pottery Co	T	Vase form
Oct 16	8	Burgess & Leigh & Co	B	Printed border
Oct 28	3	Minton, Hollins & Co	S	Printed tile
Oct 30	9	W. P. & G. Phillips★	Ln	Child figures
Nov 5	3	G. Jones & Sons	S	Ornamental trays
Nov 8	4	Minton, Hollins & Co	S	Tile designs
Nov 8	8	W. T. Copeland & Sons	S	Jug
Nov 12	1	G. Jones & Sons	S	Centrepiece
Nov 12	2	Burgess, Leigh & Co	B	Cheese dish
Nov 13	8	Worcester Royal Porcelain Co Ltd	W	Figure menu holder
Dec 1	2	W. Brownfield & Sons	C	Vase
Dec 1	9	Gelson Brothers	H	Dinnerwares
Dec 3	4	G. Jones & Sons	S	Fruit tray
Dec 6	8	J. Meir & Son	T	Toiletwares
Dec 10	3	Mintons	S	Teapot
Dec 10	8	A. Care & Co★	Ln	Fancy baskets
Dec 11	5	Grove & Stark	L	Printed border
Dec 11	8	Soane & Smith★	Ln	Vase
Dec 13	8	Minton, Hollins & Co	S	Tile designs
Dec 15	2	Mintons	S	Teawares
Dec 15	3	Mintons	S	Printed designs
Dec 24	4	Charles Ford	H	Wall pockets
Dec 24	6	Bates, Walker & Co	B	Printed design
Dec 29	5	Edge, Malkin & Co	B	Teapot
Dec 29	6	Brown–Westhead, Moore & Co	Sh	Jug
Dec 29	6	Brown–Westhead, Moore & Co	Sh	Spoon warmer
Dec 30	2	Mintons	S	Figure
Dec 30	6	William Toogood★	Ln	Figure menu – holder
Dec 30	8	Minton, Hollins & Co	S	Tile design

1876 (V at right)

Jan 4	4	Mintons	S	Japanese style vase
Jan 6	2	Moore Brothers	L	Cupid centrepiece
Jan 11	7	Edwin J. D. Bodley	B	Cup form
Jan 21	13	Bale & Co	E	Printed designs
Jan 22	6	George Jones & Sons	S	Strainer dish
Jan 22	6	George Jones & Sons	S	Ornamental dishes
Jan 22	8	Charles Ford	H	Menu tablet
Jan 24	1	Mintons	S	Teapot
Jan 24	6	Bates, Walker & Co	B	Printed design
Jan 24	6	Bates, Walker & Co	B	Jug
Jan 26	2	Edge, Malkin & Co	B	Covered bowl
Jan 26	3	Powell & Bishop	H	Jug
Jan 28	8	J. Edwards & Son	B	Jug
Jan 29	3	W. Brownfield & Son	C	Flower holder
Jan 29	3	W. Brownfield & Son	C	"Yeddo" jug
Jan 29	3	W. Brownfield & Son	C	Flower trough
Feb 1	2	W. Brownfield & Son	C	Figures with baskets
Feb 2	7	J. Wedgwood & Sons	E	Canoe dishes
Feb 2	12	Ridgway, Sparks & Ridgway	H	Print - shells
Feb 3	5	Powell & Bishop	H	Jug
Feb 4	6	Mintons	S	Eagle vase
Feb 4	12	Worcester Royal Porcelain Co Ltd	W	Jardinere
Feb 4	12	Worcester Royal Porcelain Co Ltd	W	Swan flower vase
Feb 8	9	Bates, Walker & Co	B	Printed design
Feb 15	5	G. Curling Hope★	Hgs	Fisherman match holder
Feb 19	5	G. Jones & Sons	S	Strawberry dish
Feb 21	4	Worcester Royal Porcelain Co Ltd	W	Nest wall pocket
Feb 22	3	Minton, Hollins & Co	S	Tile designs
Feb 29	9	J. Dimmock & Co	H	Toiletwares
Feb 29	11	W. Toogood★	Ln	Wall pocket
Mar 2	8	T. Gelson & Co	H	Jug forms
Mar 2	8	T. Gelson & Co	H	Tureen form
Mar 2	11	Brownhills Pottery Co	T	Tureen form
Mar 10	8	Minton, Hollins & Co	S	Tile designs
Mar 14	5	Brown-Westhead, Moore & Co	Sh	Jug
Mar 17	5	Mintons	S	Figure group
Mar 18	3	Robinson & Chapman	L	Printed design
Mar 23	8	Edwin J. D. Bodley	B	Jug
Mar 24	7	Bates, Walker & Co	B	Tureen form
Mar 28	8	W.E. Withinshaw	B	Toilet jug
Mar 30	4	G. Jones & Sons	S	Jardinere
Mar 30	4	G. Jones & Sons	S	Wall pocket
Mar 30	4	G. Jones & Sons	S	Teapot
April 8	6	Bates, Walker & Co	B	Printed border
April 11	4	T. Gelson & Co	H	Jug
April 12	4	Powell & Bishop	H	Printed design
April 12	11	J. Dimmock & Co	H	Teapot
April 21	7	Minton, Hollins & Co	S	Tile design
April 21	10	T. Furnival & Son	C	Printed designs
April 22	5	Worcester Royal Porcelain Co Ltd	W	Flower holder
April 27	3	Mintons	S	Jug

May 8	7	Brown-Westhead, Moore & Co	Sh	Strawberry dish
May 8	7	Brown-Westhead, Moore & Co	Sh	Baskets
May 10	3	G. Jones & Sons	S	Bird tray
May 11	9	F. & R. Pratt & Co	F	Cold cream print
May 16	7	Mintons	S	Menu stands
May 16	7	Mintons	S	Pair figures
May 22	3	Moore Brothers	L	Bird dish
May 22	4	J. Wedgwood & Sons	E	Teapot
May 22	4	J. Wedgwood & Sons	E	Jug forms
May 23	7	Haviland & Co	Fr	Tureen forms
May 24	3	Mintons	S	Monkey ornament
May 25	6	Moore Brothers	L	Owl ornament
May 29	8	G. Jones & Sons	S	Teawares
Jun 3	2	Mintons	S	Fan-shape box
Jun 3	7	J. S. Crapper	H	Swan, spittoon
Jun 3	5	Edwin J. D. Bodley	B	Teawares
Jun 3	5	Edwin J. D. Bodley	B	Dinnerwares
Jun 3	5	Edwin J. D. Bodley	B	Cruet
Jun 7	1	T. Gelson & Co	H	Tureen
Jun 8	4	Mintons	S	Candlestick
Jun 9	6	W. T. Copeland & Sons	S	Toilet forms
Jun 15	1	H. Meir & Son	T	"Indian Star" print
Jun 15	9	Minton, Hollins & Co	S	Tile designs
Jun 19	2	J. Wedgwood & Sons	E	Jug
Jun 19	7	T. Whetstone★	Ln	Welsh tea party print
Jun 19	9	J. Holdcroft	L	Wall pocket
Jun 20	3	T. Whetstone★	Ln	Plate ornamentation
Jun 21	4	Mintons	S	Figure menu holder
Jun 22	4	T. Gelson & Co	H	Tureen form
Jun 23	5	Mintons	S	Jardinere
Jun 26	6	Minton, Hollins & Co	S	Tile designs
Jun 28	8	J. Aynsley	L	Pierced edging
July 1	3	Mintons	S	Monkey ornament
July 1	3	Mintons	S	Pillar ornament
July 1	4	John Tams	L	"Shamrock" print
July 3	2	Ford & Challinor	T	Teapot
July 5	1	T. Till & Sons	B	Jug
July 5	7	W. T. Copeland & Sons	S	Hanging parrot
July 10	3	T. Gelson & Co	H	Ashtray
July 12	2	Edwin J. D. Bodley	B	Comport
July 18	3	Soane & Smith★	Ln	Water ewer
July 26	3	G. Jones & Sons	S	Hat flower holder
July 28	10	T. Gelson & Co	H	Tureen form
July 28	11	Powell & Bishop	H	Tureen form
July 31	8	G. Grainger & Co	W	Eagle vase
Aug 8	1	Robinson & Chapman	L	Printed design
Aug 25	8	F. & R. Pratt & Co	F	Swan print
Sept 5	5	Bates, Walker & Co	B	Printed designs
Sept 6	9	Pinder, Bourne & Co	B	Jug
Sept 6	10	W. Brownfield & Sons	C	Jug
Sept 9	8	Worthington & Son	H	Printed design
Sept 9	9	Brown-Westhead, Moore & Co	Sh	Jug

Sept 11	1	Edwin J. D. Bodley	B	Teawares
Sept 12	6	G. Jones & Sons	S	Fish & lobster tureens
Sept 18	10	G. L. Ashworth & Bros	H	Printed design
Sept 20	3	Hollinshead & Kirkham	B	Toiletwares
Sept 22	3	Powell & Bishop	H	Toiletwares
Sept 25	4	W. Toogood★	Ln	Monkey & cat basket
Sept 26	5	Hope & Carter	B	Printed design
Sept 26	10	Brown-Westhead, Moore & Co	Sh	Bread tray
Sept 28	2	Moore Brothers	L	Rustic flower holder
Sept 28	2	Moore Brothers	L	Cupid flower holder
Sept 28	10	Hope & Carter	B	Jug
Oct 3	2	W. B. Simpson & Sons	Ln	Tile design
Oct 7	2	W. Harrop	H	Embossed jug
Oct 7	3	W. Brownfield & Sons	C	Table ornaments
Oct 7	4	J. Wedgwood & Sons	E	Dinnerwares
Oct 7	6	W. Adams	T	Jug
Oct 7	6	W. Adams	T	Teapot
Oct 9	1	G. Jones & Sons	S	Egg basket
Oct 9	1	G. Jones & Sons	S	Sardine box
Oct 12	8	Ambrose Bevington	H	Oval tureen
Oct 17	4	Brown-Westhead, Moore & Co	Sh	Toilet jug
Oct 17	9	Wardle & Co	H	Jug
Oct 19	3	Burgess, Leigh & Co	B	Jug
Oct 20	2	Mintons	S	Printed designs
Oct 21	1	Edge, Malkin & Co	B	Jug
Oct 23	2	Mintons	S	Printed designs
Oct 31	2	W. Brownfield & Sons	C	Teapot forms
Oct 31	2	W. Brownfield & Sons	C	Spittoon
Oct 31	2	W. Brownfield & Sons	C	Leaf dish
Nov 1	2	Moore Brothers	L	Candlelabra
Nov 4	16	W. Stokes & Co	Du	Battle form
Nov 7	3	Robert Jones	H	Toilet mirror
Nov 8	3	G. Jones & Sons	S	Jug
Nov 8	9	W. Brownfield & Sons	C	Elephant vase
Nov 9	10	Belfield & Co	Sc	Leaf dessertware
Nov 11	9	Moore Brothers	L	Chicken teapot
Nov 13	3	Mintons	S	Printed border
Nov 14	2	J. Wedgwood & Sons	E	Candlestick
Nov 14	8	Clementson Brothers	H	Teawares
Nov 17	3	Banks & Thorley	H	Jug
Nov 18	3	Minton, Hollins & Co	S	Tile design
Nov 18	7	Minton, Hollins & Co	S	Tile design
Nov 18	9	Worcester Royal Porcelain Co Ltd	W	Flower holder
Nov 23	5	W. Adams	T	Printed design "Pearl"
Nov 24	15	T. Furnival & Sons	C	Printed borders
Nov 28	2	W. Hudson & Son	L	Flower prints
Nov 29	11	T. Furnival & Sons	C	Jug
Dec 5	2	Wedgwood & Co	T	Printed design
Dec 8	2	Wittman & Roth★	Ln	Gladstone figure
Dec 8	2	Wittman & Roth★	Ln	Disraeli figure
Dec 11	2	J. Tams	L	Printed design
Dec 12	11	Campbell Brick & Tile Co	S	Tile design

Dec 14	1	Harvey Adams & Co	L	Masonic menu
Dec 14	11	J. Dimmock & Co	H	Jug
Dec 18	9	James Beech	L	Oak print
Dec 20	7	J. & T. Bevington	H	Napkin ring
Dec 21	2	Grove & Stark	L	Jug
Dec 23	5	Charles Ford	H	Handle form
Dec 27	15	Campbell Brick & Tile Co	S	Tile design
Dec 28	6	Harvey Adams & Co	L	Cup form

1877 (P at right)

Jan 4	10	Campbellfield Pottery Co	G	Teapot form
Jan 17	5	Worcester Royal Porcelain Co Ltd	W	Wall pocket
Jan 20	2	Grove & Stark	L	Printed design – birds
Jan 24	10	W. Brownfield & Sons	C	Printed design – Puck
Jan 25	6	Wood & Co	B	Jug
Jan 25	7	G. Jones & Sons	S	Wall pocket
Jan 25	7	G. Jones & Sons	S	Teawares
Jan 25	7	G. Jones & Sons	S	Basket
Jan 26	3	Mintons	S	Tile design
Jan 26	4	Powell & Bishop	H	Teapot
Feb 1	6	J. Edwards & Son	B	Teapot
Feb 2	7	Worcester Royal Porcelain Co Ltd	W	Water carrier figure
Feb 2	7	Worcester Royal Porcelain Co Ltd	W	Jug
Feb 2	7	Worcester Royal Porcelain Co Ltd	W	Flower holder
Feb 3	4	Minton, Hollins & Co	S	Tile designs
Feb 5	2	D. McBirney & Co	Bel	Cupid print
Feb 5	2	D. McBirney & Co	Bel	Toiletwares
Feb 7	3	Holland & Green	L	Toiletwares
Feb 7	7	W. Brownfield & Sons	C	Printed designs
Feb 7	7	W. Brownfield & Sons	C	Cheese dish
Feb 7	7	W. Brownfield & Sons	C	Dessertwares
Feb 9	7	Robinson & Co	L	Floral print
Feb 9	11	Brown-Westhead, Moore & Co	Sh	Animal prints
Feb 12	3	James Beech	L	Orchid design
Feb 14	16	Worcester Royal Porcelain Co Ltd	W	Figures with baskets
Feb 15	10	Minton, Hollins & Co	S	Tile design
Feb 16	9	J. Rose & Co	Cpt	Tureen forms
Feb 19	2	W. Brownfield & Sons	C	Toiletwares
Feb 20	8	G. Grainger & Co	W	Wall pocket
Feb 21	6	Mintons	S	Plate edging
Feb 21	9	W. T. Copeland & Sons	S	Parrot
Feb 24	3	Thomas Hughes	B	Printed design
Feb 27	2	Mintons	S	Cup form
Mar 1	4	Hallam, Johnson & Co	L	Biblical prints
Mar 8	14	W. T. Copeland & Sons	S	Lamp
Mar 10	7	G. Jones & Sons	S	Strawberry basket
Mar 14	9	Campbell Brick & Tile Co	S	Tile design
Mar 20	3	Clementson Brothers	H	Dinnerwares
Mar 20	3	Clementson Brothers	H	Teawares
Mar 20	3	Clementson Brothers	H	Toiletwares
Mar 20	8	J. Dimmock & Co	H	Tureen form
Mar 20	9	W. B. Simpson & Sons	Ln	Tile design

Mar 22	14	Edwin J. D. Bodley	B	Dessertwares
Mar 24	1	Powell & Bishop	H	Printed designs
Mar 31	7	E.F. Bodley & Co	B	Vine print
April 3	1	Powell & Bishop	H	Jug
April 4	5	John Mortlock★	Ln	Pie dish
April 5	2	Ford, Challinor & Co	T	Jug
April 12	11	John Dimmock & Co	H	Printed design – Moses
April 12	12	T. S. Bale	H	Candlestick
April 21	11	Silber & Fleming★	Ln	Printed design
April 23	4	J. Tams	L	Jug
April 26	2	J. & T. Bevington	H	Basket form
April 26	7	Worcester Royal Porcelain Co Ltd	W	Teawares
April 27	10	J. Rose & Co	Cpl	Teawares
May 2	2	G. Jones & Sons	S	Flower trough
May 2	2	G. Jones & Sons	S	Flower basket
May 2	2	G. Jones & Sons	S	Wall pocket
May 2	2	G. Jones & Sons	S	Caviare set
May 4	13	Old Hall Earthenware Co Ltd	H	Jug
May 5	4	J. Wedgwood & Sons	E	Printed border
May 12	7	T. Furnival & Sons	C	Jug
May 16	5	W. Brownfield & Sons	C	Flower basket
May 18	6	J. Wedgwood & Sons	E	Jug
May 22	5	W. Brownfield & Sons	C	Bear ornament
May 22	5	W. Brownfield & Sons	C	Sack biscuit box
May 22	5	W. Brownfield & Sons	C	Monkey ornament
May 24	8	Brown-Westhead, Moore & Co	Sh	Centrepiece
May 30	13	T. Furnival & Sons	C	Tureen
Jun 1	2	J. & R. Hammersley	H	Jug form
Jun 5	6	Edwin J. D. Bodley	B	Dinnerwares
Jun 7	1	Edwin J. D. Bodley	B	Cat ornament
Jun 7	2	J. Holdcroft	L	Jug
Jun 8	7	Minton, Hollins & Co	S	Tile designs
Jun 9	3	Baker & Co	F	Dinnerwares
Jun 9	3	Baker & Co	F	Teawares
Jun 13	2	Baker & Co	F	Animal ornament
Jun 15	7	Ridgway, Sparks & Ridgway	H	"Indus" print
Jun 19	4	Ford & Challinor	T	Printed design
Jun 19	6	Murray & Co	G	Teapot
Jun 22	3	Walker & Carter	S	Printed design
Jun 22	13	Steele & Wood	S	Tile designs
Jun 22	14	Edward F. Bodley & Co	B	Printed shell design
Jun 26	11	T. Furnival & Sons	C	Printed designs
Jun 28	9	T. Furnival & Sons	C	Printed design
Jun 29	10	Sherwin & Cotton	H	Tile designs
July 2	3	W. T. Copeland & Sons	S	Jug
July 6	2	Mintons	S	Pierced border
July 7	4	Ridge, Meigh & Co	L	Printed design
July 9	2	Minton, Hollins & Co	S	Tile design
July 14	2	J. Tams	L	Printed designs
July 17	9	J. Edwards & Son	B	Plate design
July 17	9	J. Edwards & Son	B	Finger plates
July 17	9	J. Edwards & Son	B	Jug

July 20	7	Haviland & Co	Fr	Tureen forms
July 20	7	Haviland & Co	Fr	Jug
July 20	15	Taylor, Tunnicliffe & Co	H	Water bottle
July 20	15	Taylor, Tunnicliffe & Co	H	Jug & spittoon
July 23	2	J. Edwards	F	Dinnerwares
July 23	2	J. Edwards	F	Teawares
July 25	5	Ford, Challinor & Co	T	Jug
July 26	6	Minton, Hollins & Co	S	Tile designs
July 31	1	D. McBirney & Co	Bel	Printed design
July 31	2	Minton, Hollins & Co	S	Tile design
Aug 1	4	Holmes, Stonier & Hollinshead	H	Printed design
Aug 1	12	J. Vernon	Sc	Toilet jug
Aug 3	14	Campbell Brick & Tile Co	S	Tile design
Aug 13	5	Haviland & Co	Fr	Jug
Aug 15	7	Campbell Brick & Tile Co	S	Tile design
Aug 15	10	G. Picket*	Ln	Water filter
Aug 17	11	Ridgway, Sparks & Ridgway	H	Dinnerwares
Aug 18	6	Minton, Hollins & Co	S	Tile designs
Aug 18	7	Furnival & Son	C	Printed border
Aug 23	6	W. Hudson & Son	L	Printed design
Aug 25	2	W. Wood & Co	B	Finger plate
Aug 25	2	W. Wood & Co	B	Printed design
Aug 25	3	Minton, Hollins & Co	S	Tile designs
Aug 28	9	Brown-Westhead, Moore & Co	Sh	Printed design
Sept 11	3	G. W. Turner & Sons	T	Printed design
Sept 19	5	Minton, Hollins & Co	S	Tile design
Sept 20	3	J. Wedgwood & Sons	E	Toiletwares
Sept 22	7	Mintons	S	Printed design
Sept 22	7	Mintons	S	Teawares
Sept 22	13	Minton, Hollins & Co	S	Tile – squirrel
Sept 25	5	Mintons	S	Basket
Sept 28	9	J. Holdcroft	L	Jug
Oct 2	7	Bates, Walker & Co	B	Printed design
Oct 3	2	Robinson & Leadbeater	S	Flower holder
Oct 4	4	J. & T. Bevington	H	Dog ornament
Oct 4	4	J. & T. Bevington	H	Cat ornament
Oct 10	3	John Edwards	F	Lion ornament
Oct 10	5	W. Brownfield & Sons	C	Toiletwares
Oct 15	2	G. Jones & Sons	S	Jardinere – lily
Oct 15	2	G. Jones & Sons	S	Jardinere – swan
Oct 16	6	Powell & Bishop	H	Teawares
Oct 19	8	Minton, Hollins & Co	S	Tile design
Oct 19	13	Brown-Westhead, Moore & Co	Sh	Fruit box
Oct 24	10	Grove & Stark	L	Printed design
Oct 24	14	F. & R. Pratt & Co	F	Jug
Oct 30	7	Wedgwood & Co	T	Tureen form
Oct 31	6	G. Jones & Sons	S	Jardinere
Nov 5	4	Powell & Bishop	H	Cleopatra's Needle
Nov 6	11	W. Brownfield & Sons	C	Jug
Nov 6	11	W. Brownfield & Sons	C	Flower holder
Nov 6	11	W. Brownfield & Sons	C	Cat, basket
Nov 6	11	W. Brownfield & Sons	C	Dog, basket

Nov 7	1	Edwin J. D. Bodley	B	Flower holder
Nov 7	1	Edwin J. D. Bodley	B	Ewer & basin
Nov 7	1	Edwin J. D. Bodley	B	Wall pocket
Nov 7	2	Mintons	S	Tile design
Nov 7	10	Pinder, Bourne & Co	B	Jug
Nov 9	8	Taylor, Tunnicliffe & Co	H	Knob form
Nov 15	12	Brown–Westhead, Moore & Co	Sh	Vase
Nov 20	9	J. Edwards & Son	B	Tureen form
Nov 21	8	Davenports & Co	Lpt	Lily toiletware
Nov 22	1	Old Hall Earthenware Co Ltd	H	Tureen forms
Nov 22	13	B. & S. Hancock	S	Printed design
Nov 24	7	J. Dimmock & Co	H	Printed design
Nov 29	3	J. Holdcroft	L	Teaset on tray
Dec 1	5	J. Holdcroft	L	Bird cruet
Dec 1	6	Oakes, Clare & Chadwick	B	Jug
Dec 5	2	Edwin J. D. Bodley	B	Cat and basket
Dec 6	4	Mintons	S	Dinnerwares
Dec 7	14	Joseph Unwin	L	Printed design
Dec 14	1	J. Dimmock & Co	H	Tureen form
Dec 15	10	Worcester Royal Porcelain Co Ltd	W	Dessert forms
Dec 15	10	Worcester Royal Porcelain Co Ltd	W	Pierced edging
Dec 21	6	Mintons	S	Boar's head tureen
Dec 21	10	T. Furnival & Son	C	Dinnerwares
Dec 22	5	W. Brownfield & Sons	C	Bear honey-pot
Dec 22	5	W. Brownfield & Sons	C	Jug
Dec 29	6	Brown–Westhead, Moore & Co	Sh	Toilet jug

1878 (D at right)

Jan 3	4	Minton, Hollins & Co	S	Tile designs
Jan 9	4	Brownhills Pottery Co	T	Printed design
Jan 9	4	Brownhills Pottery Co	T	Vase
Jan 9	4	Brownhills Pottery Co	T	Jug
Jan 10	12	J. Mortlock & Co★	Ln	Fluted dish
Jan 14	1	J. Maddock & Sons	B	Tureen form
Jan 14	2	Cotton & Rigby	B	Teapot
Jan 14	3	W. Adams	T	Dinnerwares
Jan 14	6	Minton, Hollins & Co	S	Tile design
Jan 15	5	J. Wedgwood & Sons	E	Tureen form
Jan 18	5	Taylor, Tunnicliffe & Co	H	Rope guides
Jan 22	6	J. Dimmock & Co	H	Printed pattern
Jan 24	6	W. T. Copeland & Sons	S	Cupid wall pocket
Jan 25	9	W. Brownfield & Sons	C	Spoon warmer
Jan 25	9	W. Brownfield & Sons	C	Vase
Jan 28	11	Brown–Westhead, Moore & Co	Sh	Dessertwares
Jan 30	3	G. Jones & Sons	S	Jug
Jan 30	3	G. Jones & Sons	S	Vase
Jan 30	15	Brownhills Pottery Co	T	Jug
Jan 30	15	Brownhills Pottery Co	T	Vase
Jan 31	1	B. & S. Hancock	S	Swallows print
Feb 1	4	G. Jones & Sons	S	Jardinere
Feb 1	11	Minton, Hollins & Co	S	Tile designs
Feb 1	16	Derby Crown Porcelain Co Ltd	D	Vases

Feb 1	16	Derby Crown Porcelain Co Ltd	D	Figure centrepiece
Feb 5	5	Campbell Brick & Tile Co	S	Tile design
Feb 9	6	J. Dimmock & Co	H	Printed design
Feb 11	5	Brown–Westhead, Moore & Co	Sh	Toiletwares
Feb 12	5	Derby Crown Porcelain Co Ltd	D	Vases
Feb 12	5	Derby Crown Porcelain Co Ltd	D	Wall pocket
Feb 20	6	Minton, Hollins & Co	S	Tile design
Feb 20	7	Worcester Royal Porcelain Co Ltd	W	Printed design
Feb 21	10	W. E. Cartlidge	B	Teapot
Feb 22	8	Campbell Brick & Tile Co	S	Tile design
Feb 28	3	Dunn, Bennett & Co	H	Jug
Mar 5	2	Grove & Stark	L	Oval tureen
Mar 6	5	Minton, Hollins & Co	S	Tile design
Mar 7	4	J. Edwards	F	Oval tureen
Mar 9	1	Brownhills Pottery & Co	T	Tureen
Mar 9	1	Brownhills Pottery & Co	T	Printed design
Mar 9	8	Moore Brothers	L	Floral bowl
Mar 9	11	Powell & Bishop	H	Toiletwares
Mar 11	1	Taylor, Tunnicliffe & Co	H	Knob forms
Mar 13	1	Mintons	S	Printed design
Mar 13	7	J. & T. Bevington	H	Cupid centrepiece
Mar 13	10	W. T. Copeland & Sons	S	Jug
Mar 15	10	J. Rose & Co	Cpt	Teawares
Mar 23	8	Derby Crown Porcelain Co Ltd	D	Centrepieces
Mar 25	9	F. J. Emery	B	Jug
Mar 27	6	G. W. Turner & Sons	T	Printed design
Mar 27	15	Minton, Hollins & Co	S	Tile design
April 2	6	Belfield & Co	Sc	Teapot
April 10	4	Mintons	S	"Denmark" print
April 13	9	D. McBirney	Bel	Printed design
April 15	11	Nestle & Huntsman★	Ln	Ornamental figures
April 17	4	Mintons	S	Teapot
April 17	14	Ridgway, Sparks & Ridgway	S	Printed designs
April 20	2	T. Furnival & Sons	C	Dinnerwares
April 20	2	T. Furnival & Sons	C	Teawares
April 20	6	Worcester Royal Porcelain Co Ltd	W	Horn flower holder
April 24	2	W. Brownfield & Sons	C	Strawberry tray
April 27	12	D. McBirney & Co	Bel	Teawares
April 30	7	J. Wedgwood & Sons	E	Sardine box
April 30	7	J. Wedgwood & Sons	E	Oyster tray
May 3	2	J. Wedgwood & Sons	E	Jug
May 3	9	Robinson & Leadbeater	S	Match stand
May 8	8	Nestle & Huntsman★	Ln	Figures
May 8	8	Nestle & Huntsman★	Ln	Fan ornament
May 8	9	Bates & Bennett	C	Printed designs
May 14	6	Elsmore & Son	T	Printed design
May 17	12	J. Dimmock & Co	H	Shell form box
May 20	9	Derby Crown Porcelain Co Ltd	D	Flower vases
May 21	11	Banks & Thorley	H	Jug
May 23	3	J. Wedgwood & Sons	E	Sardine box
May 23	4	Moore Brothers	L	Figure flower holder
May 24	2	J. Wedgwood & Sons	E	Oyster tray

May 27	20	Edwin J. D. Bodley	B	Fancy box
May 29	9	Minton, Hollins & Co	S	Inlaid tile
Jun 1	5	J. Mortlock & Co★	Ln	Menu stand
Jun 4	9	T. Furnival & Sons	C	Jug
Jun 5	14	W. T. Copeland & Sons	S	Dish forms
Jun 7	1	G. Jones & Sons	S	Printed designs
Jun 8	8	W. Wood & Co	B	Circular dish
Jun 12	10	Harvey Adams & Co	L	Moulded plate
Jun 13	2	John Tams	L	Teapot
Jun 13	3	D. McBirney & Co	Bel	Moulded plate
Jun 19	7	Edward F. Bodley & Co	B	Toiletwares
Jun 21	8	Allen & Green	F	Card holder
Jun 27	7	J. Wedgwood & Sons	E	Butter churn
Jun 29	1	Wood, Son & Co	C	Oval tureen
July 1	1	Burgess & Leigh	B	Jug
July 3	2	Mintons	S	Tile design
July 8	6	J. Wedgwood & Sons	E	Jug
July 9	8	Mintons	S	Tureen forms
July 9	8	Mintons	S	Bowl
July 9	9	J. Wedgwood & Sons	E	Dejeune set
July 9	10	J. Dimmock & Co	H	Toiletwares
July 10	14	Bates & Bennett	C	Printed design
July 11	1	Soane & Smith★	Ln	Toiletwares
July 11	11	W. & J. A. Bailey	Sc	Teapot
July 12	4	J. Wedgwood & Sons	E	Butter dish
July 12	13	Samuel Lear	H	Jug
July 12	15	Brown-Westhead, Moore & Co	Sh	Printed designs
July 15	1	Pratt & Simpson	F	Ornamental designs
July 17	9	W. Adams	T	Printed portrait
July 18	2	Ambrose Bevington	H	Oval tureen
July 20	1	James Bevington	H	Fish shape basket
July 20	6	J. Meir & Son	T	Jug
July 20	11	Edwin J. D. Bodley	B	Teawares
July 20	11	Edwin J. D. Bodley	B	Dinnerwares
July 26	3	J. Wedgwood & Sons	E	Match holder
July 30	2	J. Wedgwood & Sons	E	Brandy set – Punch
July 30	6	Powell, Bishop & Stonier	H	Royal Arms motif
July 30	12	Edward Clarke	Lpt	Oval tureen
July 31	8	Mintons	S	Teawares
July 31	13	J. Edwards & Son	B	Oval tureen
Aug 6	3	Moore Brothers	L	Flower holder
Aug 7	3	T. Hughes	B	Printed design
Aug 9	10	Derby Crown Porcelain Co Ltd	D	Centrepiece
Aug 9	12	Craven Dunnill & Co Ltd	Shrop	Tile designs
Aug 16	9	Campbell Brick & Tile Co	S	Tile design
Aug 23	1	Moore Brothers	L	Flower holder, peas
Aug 23	7	J. Dimmock & Co	H	Printed design
Sept 5	3	Moore Brothers	L	Flower holder
Sept 9	5	W. Brownfield & Sons	C	Candlelabra
Sept 9	5	W. Brownfield & Sons	C	Cart flower holder
Sept 9	5	W. Brownfield & Sons	C	Shell cachepot
Sept 10	2	J. Wedgwood & Sons	E	Printed designs

Sept 10	5	T. Hughes	B	Printed design
Sept 12	6	James Bevington	H	Kitten ornament
Sept 13	5	G. L. Ashworth & Bros	H	Toiletwares
Sept 13	16	Worcester Royal Porcelain Co Ltd	W	Printed borders
Sept 20	19	R. Wotherspoon & Co	G	Preserving jar
Sept 24	3	Thomas Bevington	H	Printed border
Sept 27	1	G. Stubbs	W	Crested tiles
Sept 28	5	Minton, Hollins & Co	S	Peacock basket
Sept 30	1	Mintons	S	Tortoise teapot
Oct 1	10	Fyfe & Robinson★	Ln	Tile design
Oct 2	2	Mintons	S	Fish teapot
Oct 3	8	J. T. Hudden	L	Printed design
Oct 4	8	F. & R. Pratt & Co	F	"Cyprus" print
Oct 5	13	Worcester Royal Porcelain Co Ltd	W	Dr Wall design
Oct 8	6	Moore Brothers	L	Bird handle
Oct 8	7	Bates, Gildea & Walker	B	Jug
Oct 9	9	J. Wedgwood & Sons	E	Strawberry service
Oct 11	8	Minton, Hollins & Co	S	Tile design
Oct 14	8	W. T. Copeland & Sons	S	Bird handles
Oct 23	1	Brownhills Pottery Co	T	Jug
Oct 23	11	Pinder, Bourne & Co	B	Teawares
Oct 23	11	Pinder, Bourne & Co	B	Printed design
Oct 24	1	T. Furnival & Son	C	Printed design
Oct 24	2	J. Dimmock & Co	H	Toiletwares
Oct 24	13	Worcester Royal Porcelain Co Ltd	W	Teawares
Oct 26	4	W. Brownfield & Co	C	Cup shape
Oct 30	3	Minton, Hollins & Co	S	Tile design
Nov 1	3	J. Bevington	H	Basket
Nov 4	1	Edge, Malkin & Co	B	Jug
Nov 5	11	Henry Burgess	B	Tureen form
Nov 5	17	Edwin J. D. Bodley	B	Jug
Nov 6	3	Samuel Lear	H	Teapot
Nov 13	13	J. Rose & Co	Cpt	Teawares
Nov 15	1	Craven, Dunnill & Co Ltd	Shrop	Tile design
Nov 15	11	F. & R. Pratt & Co	F	Marmalade pot
Nov 16	5	J. Dimmock & Co	H	Printed design
Nov 23	2	E. & C. Challinor	F	"Lorne" print
Nov 26	14	T. & R. Boote	B	Printed design
Nov 27	9	J. McIntyre & Co	B	Letter weight
Nov 29	14	W. & E. Corn	B	Coffee pot
Dec 2	7	Brown-Westhead, Moore & Co	Sh	Jug
Dec 3	9	J. McIntyre & Co	B	Salt cellar
Dec 4	2	W. Brownfield & Sons	C	Bowl, boat form
Dec 6	3	Mintons	S	Printed design
Dec 7	2	Anthony Shaw	B	Printed design
Dec 19	8	Thomas Hughes	B	Printed design
Dec 27	13	T. & R. Boote	B	Tile design
Dec 28	4	J. Gaskell, Son & Co	B	Door knob

1879 (Y at right)

Jan 7	7	W. T. Copeland & Sons	S	Teapot
Jan 8	11	Minton, Hollins & Co	S	Tile design

Jan 9	8	W. Brownfield & Sons	C	Toiletwares
Jan 9	8	W. Brownfield & Sons	C	Fish vase
Jan 14	5	New Wharf Pottery & Co	B	Printed design
Jan 14	6	Campbell Brick & Tile Co	S	Tile design
Jan 16	3	B. & S. Hancock	S	Printed border
Jan 16	13	F. & R. Pratt & Co	F	Jug
Jan 20	15	Derby Crown Porcelain Co Ltd	D	Baskets – donkey
Jan 22	4	Dunn, Bennett & Co	H	Jug
Jan 28	11	W. T. Copeland & Sons	S	Printed design
Jan 29	2	T. Furnival & Son	C	Jug
Jan 29	3	T. Bevington	H	Basket – shell
Jan 29	15	Edwin J. D. Bodley	B	Plate form
Feb 1	13	Clementson Brothers	H	Jug
Feb 3	1	J. Wedgwood & Sons	E	Jardinere
Feb 5	7	Mintons	S	Figure ornaments
Feb 8	1	Mintons	S	Pierced flower holder
Feb 10	5	William Oppenheim★	Ln	Lamp base
Feb 14	4	T. Furnival & Sons	C	Oval tureen
Feb 15	2	Campbell Brick & Tile Co	S	Tile design
Feb 17	6	D. McBirney	Bel	Flower vase
Feb 24	2	W. P. Jervis	S	Tile design
Feb 24	3	W. & T. Adams	T	Printed designs
Feb 25	4	Mintons	S	Jug
Feb 28	1	Elijah Chetwynd (modeller)	Sh	Oval tureen
Feb 28	7	Clementson Brothers	H	Covered dish
Mar 1	1	T. Furnival & Sons	C	Jug
Mar 4	4	Grove & Stark	L	Jug
Mar 6	10	Powell, Bishop & Stonier	H	Printed design
Mar 12	4	Edge, Malkin & Co	B	Teapot
Mar 12	12	W. T. Copeland & Sons	S	Printed design
Mar 13	1	W. Davenport & Co	Lpt	Dinnerwares
Mar 13	1	W. Davenport & Co	Lpt	Toiletwares
Mar 13	14	Clementson Brothers	H	Jug
Mar 14	9	Edward Clarke	Lpt	Oval tureen
Mar 17	2	Powell, Bishop & Stonier	H	"Aster" print
Mar 18	1	J. Wedgwood & Sons	E	Jug
Mar 19	2	John Hawthorne	C	Oval tureen
Mar 25	10	E. Quinter & Co	Paris	Figure centrepieces
Mar 26	17	Worcester Royal Porcelain Co Ltd	W	Candlestick
Mar 26	17	Worcester Royal Porcelain Co Ltd	W	Teawares
Mar 27	9	Candy & Co	De	Ornamental brick
Mar 28	6	Clementson Brothers	H	Jug
Mar 29	4	Beck, Blair & Co	L	Printed design
April 3	9	Brown-Westhead, Moore & Co	Sh	Jug
April 4	12	Pinder, Bourne & Co	B	Printed design
April 9	5	H. Alcock & Co	C	Oval tureen
April 10	12	Brown-Westhead, Moore & Co	Sh	Jug
April 12	1	Worcester Royal Porcelain Co Ltd	W	Flower holder
April 15	6	Brown-Westhead, Moore & Co	Sh	Toiletwares
April 22	2	Linder & Co	Bir	Printed design
April 23	8	Brown-Westhead, Moore & Co	Sh	Toiletwares
April 24	3	J. Wedgwood & Sons	E	Printed designs

May 2	5	Ambrose Bevington	H	Printed design
May 5	1	T. Furnival & Sons	C	Printed design
May 5	1	T. Furnival & Sons	C	Tureen form
May 5	6	Bates, Gildea & Walker	B	Jug form
May 6	7	S. Bridgwood & Son	L	Jug forms
May 6	7	S. Bridgwood & Son	L	Cup stand
May 7	11	Worcester Royal Porcelain Co Ltd	W	Floral print
May 9	15	Worcester Royal Porcelain Co Ltd	W	Jug
May 13	4	Pinder, Bourne & Co	B	Jug
May 13	4	Pinder, Bourne & Co	B	Toiletwares
May 13	8	Clementson Brothers	H	Printed design
May 14	9	Brown-Westhead, Moore & Co	Sh	Printed design
May 14	13	Edwin J. D. Bodley	B	Vase
May 14	13	Edwin J. D. Bodley	B	Cup form
May 19	1	W. Brownfield & Sons	C	Bottle vase
May 19	1	W. Brownfield & Sons	C	Centrepiece
May 21	5	Harvey Adams & Co	L	Cup form
May 23	2	Sampson Bridgwood & Son	L	Jug
May 23	2	Sampson Bridgwood & Son	L	Covered box
May 23	14	Harvey Adams & Co	L	Teawares
May 29	2	J. Tams	L	"Stork" print
May 29	12	Pinder, Bourne & Co	B	Jug
May 30	3	D. McBirney & Co	Bel	Wash basin
May 30	10	J. Dimmock & Co	H	Printed pattern
May 30	12	Grove & Stark	L	Printed bird pattern
May 31	4	Minton, Hollins & Co	S	Tile design
Jun 10	4	T. Furnival & Sons	C	Printed design
Jun 11	8	T. Till & Sons	B	Jug
Jun 13	13	Brown-Westhead, Moore & Co	Sh	Jug
Jun 18	4	Grove & Stark	L	Jug
Jun 24	11	J. Wedgwood & Sons	E	Oval tureen
Jun 25	1	Clementson Brothers	H	Cup form
Jun 26	13	Haviland & Co	Fr	Fluted stand
Jun 26	13	Haviland & Co	Fr	Dish forms
Jun 27	11	Shorter & Boulton	S	Jug
Jun 30	12	Birks, Brothers & Seddon	C	Toiletwares
Jun 30	12	Birks, Brothers & Seddon	C	Teapot
July 2	2	J. Wedgwood & Sons	E	Printed design
July 7	2	James F. Wileman	F	Printed design
July 8	1	Mintons	S	Jardinere
July 8	16	Brown-Westhead, Moore & Co	Sh	Printed design
July 9	12	Brown-Westhead, Moore & Co	Sh	Jug
July 10	2	T. Bevington	H	Shell basket
July 10	3	Moore Brothers	L	Floral vase
July 16	4	Ambrose Bevington & Co	H	Printed design
July 16	14	Brown-Westhead, Moore & Co	Sh	Printed jug design
July 18	18	Stuart & Smith	Sd	Floral design
July 25	4	Mintons	S	Sauce tureen
July 26	6	Minton, Hollins & Co	S	Tile design
July 28	6	G. G. MacWilliams★	Ln	Washbasin
July 31	2	Mintons	S	Ornate vase
Aug 2	2	H. M. Williamson & Sons	L	Printed design

Aug 5	12	J. Mortlock & Co★	Ln	Centrepieces
Aug 6	6	Wardle & Co	H	Jardinere
Aug 13	2	Grove & Stark	L	Bullfinch print
Aug 22	4	D. McBirney	Bel	Printed border
Aug 27	13	Bates, Gildea & Walker	B	Printed design
Sept 4	6	Brown-Westhead, Moore & Co	Sh	Printed design
Sept 10	13	Brown-Westhead, Moore & Co	Sh	Printed design
Sept 17	4	W. Brownfield & Sons	C	Tureen forms
Sept 26	4	Brown-Westhead, Moore & Co	Sh	Printed design
Sept 26	4	J. T. Hudden	L	Printed design
Sept 29	3	Edge, Malkin & Co	B	Jug
Sept 29	12	W. T. Copeland & Sons	S	Dish
Oct 9	6	Bates, Gildea & Walker	B	Jug
Oct10	2	Brown-Westhead, Moore & Co	Sh	Plate form
Oct 11	5	Edwin J. D. Bodley	B	Teawares, bamboo
Oct 15	1	Mintons	S	Jug
Oct 16	5	Joseph Roth★	Ln	Printed design
Oct 16	16	Minton, Hollins & Co	S	Tile design
Oct 17	2	G. L. Ashworth & Bros	H	Tureen form
Oct 18	3	J. Wedgwood & Sons	E	Strawberry dish
Oct 23	12	Pillivuyt & Co	Fr	Oval dish
Oct 24	4	Campbell Brick & Tile Co	S	Tile designs
Oct 27	9	Edward F. Bodley & Co	B	Jug
Oct 29	5	Mintons	S	Printed design
Oct 29	7	Clementson Brothers	H	Moulded edge
Oct 29	15	F. D. Bradley	L	Figures box
Oct 30	4	Mintons	S	Printed design
Oct 31	8	G. A. Stubbs	Ln	Tiles
Nov 3	12	Minton, Hollins & Co	S	Tile design
Nov 3	14	Tundley, Rhodes & Procter	B	Printed design
Nov 6	2	J. Wedgwood & Sons	E	Covered dish
Nov 6	3	Moore Brothers	L	Cupid flower bowls
Nov 6	4	Wilcox & Co	Lds	Pressed tiles
Nov 12	11	Worcester Royal Porcelain Co Ltd	W	Coffee pot
Nov 15	12	Charles Ford	H	Printed floral design
Nov 15	16	W. T. Copeland & Sons	S	Tureen forms
Nov 15	16	W. T. Copeland & Sons	S	Fluted dinnerwares
Nov 17	2	Powell, Bishop & Stonier	H	Oval tureen
Nov 19	5	Powell, Bishop & Stonier	H	Oval tureen
Nov 20	4	Elsmore & Son	T	Printed designs
Nov 21	6	Mintons	S	Jug
Nov 21	14	Soane & Smith★	Ln	Dahlia bowl
Nov 22	7	Worcester Royal Porcelain Co Ltd	W	Shell wall pocket
Nov 28	5	W. Brownfield & Sons	C	Menu tablet
Nov 28	6	Ambrose Bevington	H	Printed floral design
Nov 29	3	Mintons	S	Oyster plate
Nov 29	4	Brown-Westhead, Moore & Co	Sh	Printed border
Dec 1	2	J. Holdcroft	L	Teapot
Dec 2	4	Brown-Westhead, Moore & Co	Sh	Tureen
Dec 2	4	Brown-Westhead, Moore & Co	Sh	Plate form
Dec 2	5	Elsmore & Son	T	Printed design
Dec 2	17	J. Aynsley & Sons	L	Comport

Dec 6	2	T. & R. Boote	B	Printed designs
Dec 10	9	Clementson Brothers	H	Oval tureen
Dec 11	4	Moore Brothers	L	Floral bowls
Dec 11	4	Moore Brothers	L	Centrepiece
Dec 17	11	Ridgways	S	Tureen form
Dec 19	1	Clementson Brothers	H	Cup form
Dec 20	5	J. Wedgwood & Sons	E	Covered box
Dec 22	2	Mintons	S	Leaf dish
Dec 24	2	Sherwin & Cotton	H	Tile design

1880 (J at right)

Jan 3	1	Sherwin & Cotton	H	Tile design
Jan 7	3	T. Bevington	H	Floral bowls
Jan 7	4	T. & R. Boote	B	Printed design
Jan 7	5	Soane & Smith★	Ln	Toiletwares
Jan 7	8	Minton, Hollins & Co	S	Tile design
Jan 8	9	Old Hall Earthenware Co Ltd	H	Dinnerwares
Jan 9	3	Sherwin & Cotton	H	Tile design
Jan 9	12	T. George Allen	Ln	"London" print
Jan 13	1	Brown-Westhead, Moore & Co	Sh	Printed design
Jan 14	11	Worcester Royal Porcelain Co Ltd	W	Printed designs
Jan 16	8	S. Fielding & Co	S	Jug – shell
Jan 16	14	Brockwell & Son★	Ln	Salad bowl
Jan 21	7	Pinder, Bourne & Co	B	Printed design
Jan 21	7	Pinder, Bourne & Co	B	Dish & jug
Jan 22	2	Mintons	S	Plate form
Jan 22	8	Minton, Hollins & Co	S	Tile designs
Jan 26	11	W. Brownfield & Sons	C	Teapot
Jan 27	13	Wardle & Co	H	Jug
Jan 28	3	Brown-Westhead, Moore & Co	Sh	Jug
Jan 28	4	J. Aynsley & Sons	L	Tray form
Jan 28	12	Powell, Bishop & Stonier	H	"Hong Kong" print
Jan 29	9	Edwin J. D. Bodley	B	Covered boxes
Jan 30	2	Taylor, Tunnicliffe & Co	H	Tablet
Feb 3	11	Powell, Bishop & Stonier	H	Spoon warmer
Feb 9	14	Albert Meisel★	NY	Oyster plate
Feb 9	18	Whittingham, Ford & Riley	B	Printed figure design
Feb 10	4	Mintons	S	Printed design
Feb 10	4	Mintons	S	Tureen form
Feb 10	4	Mintons	S	Tile design
Feb 11	10	T. Bevington	H	Basket – child
Feb 12	4	W.A. Adderley	L	Printed design
Feb 12	7	W. Brownfield & Sons	C	Teawares
Feb 14	14	Bates, Gildea & Walker	B	Jug
Feb 18	12	Derby Crown Porcelain Co Ltd	D	Printed design
Feb 24	2	Mintons	S	Cigar stand
Feb 24	11	W. Harrop & Co	H	Printed design
Feb 25	18	Clementson Brothers	H	Tureen
Feb 25	23	Sherwin & Cotton	H	Tile design
Feb 26	6	Minton, Hollins & Co	S	Tile designs
Feb 27	7	Moore Brothers	L	Vase
Feb 27	7	Moore Brothers	L	Figure vases

Mar 2	6	J. Holdcroft	L	Shell bowl
Mar 4	8	Soane & Smith★	Ln	Fancy bowls
Mar 8	4	T. Furnival & Sons	C	Floral print
Mar 8	10	W. Harrop & Co	H	Jug
Mar 10	15	E. Quinter & Co★	Paris	Bowl – cupids
Mar 12	4	W .A. Adderley	L	Jug
Mar 16	3	J. F. Wileman & Co	F	Printed design
Mar 16	11	Sherwin & Cotton	H	Tile design
Mar 16	12	J. Macintyre & Co	B	Egg cup
Mar 16	12	J. Macintyre & Co	B	Ash tray
Mar 17	6	J. Wedgwood & Sons	E	Garden pot
Mar 18	3	Moore Brothers	L	Floral bowls
Mar 18	3	Moore Brothers	L	Centrepieces, figures
Mar 22	4	Powell, Bishop & Stonier	H	Tureen
Mar 23	4	Taylor, Tunnicliffe & Co	H	Menu slate
Mar 25	6	Mintons	S	Butterfly box
Mar 30	4	Sherwin & Cotton	H	Tile design
Mar 31	3	T. Peake	T	Edging tile
April 12	6	Bates, Gildea & Walker	B	Printed designs
April 15	11	Ridgways	Sh	Printed design
April 19	11	Worcester Royal Porcelain Co Ltd	W	Teawares
April 19	11	Worcester Royal Porcelain Co Ltd	W	Jug
April 22	4	Sherwin & Cotton	H	Tile designs
April 22	5	W. H. Grindley & Co	T	Jug & decoration
April 26	1	T. Furnival & Sons	C	Printed design
April 27	11	Moore Brothers	L	Lily basket
April 27	11	Moore Brothers	L	Double vase
April 27	11	Moore Brothers	L	Figure centrepiece
April 27	13	Worcester Royal Porcelain Co Ltd	W	Figure candle-snuffers
April 29	4	Mintons	S	Menu card
April 29	4	Mintons	S	Divisional dish
April 30	6	T. Furnival & Sons	C	Jug
May 3	3	W. Brownfield & Sons	C	Dessertwares
May 3	3	W. Brownfield & Sons	C	Menu card
May 5	11	E. Quinter★	Paris	Figure ornaments
May 5	13	S. Fielding & Co	S	Jug
May 10	6	Powell, Bishop & Stonier	H	Printed design – roses
May 11	15	Soane & Smith★	Ln	Fish strainer
May 12	3	G. Skey & Co Ltd	Tam	Bear flower-holder
May 13	8	Mintons	S	Dish forms
May 13	15	Minton, Hollins & Co	S	Tile design
May 14	26	Bates, Gildea & Walker	B	Bowl
May 25	4	W. Brownfield & Sons	C	Jug
May 26	6	Mintons	S	Strawberry dishes
Jun 1	4	Mintons	S	Printed design
Jun 2	3	Sherwin & Cotton	H	Tile design
Jun 7	6	J. Dimmock & Co	H	Printed design
Jun 8	1	G. Jones & Sons	S	Jug, fish design
Jun 10	3	Sherwin & Cotton	H	Tile design
Jun 10	4	Edwin J. D. Bodley	B	Jug
Jun 10	12	J. Dimmock & Co	H	Oval tureen
Jun 11	3	J. Wedgwood & Sons	E	Jug

Jun 14	12	Joseph Roth★	Ln	Floral encrustation
Jun 15	4	Buckley, Wood & Co	B	Jug
Jun 16	3	Wedgwood & Co	T	"Beatrice" print
Jun 17	4	Samuel Lear	H	Jug
Jun 17	15	Ridgways	H	Printed floral design
Jun 17	26	J. Macintyre & Co	B	Menu slab
Jun 17	20	Crystal Porcelain Co Ltd	H	Jug
Jun 17	21	J. Dimmock & Co	H	Oval tureen
Jun 19	11	J. Wedgwood & Sons	E	Butter dish
Jun 19	15	Joseph Roth★	Ln	Floral bowl
Jun 22	1	W. H. Grindley & Co	T	Printed designs
Jun 26	13	Worcester Royal Porcelain Co Ltd	W	Figure centrepieces
July 7	4	Sherwin & Cotton	H	Tile design
July 7	5	Mintons	S	Centrepiece
July 7	15	F. J. Emery	B	Jug
July 12	4	Mintons	S	Jug, ribbon motif
July 13	12	Thomas Barlow	L	Covered box
July 15	3	Dunn, Bennett & Co	H	Jug
July 15	4	Grove & Stark	L	Printed design
July 16	9	Sherwin & Cotton	H	Tile design
July 16	10	Moore Brothers	L	Cupid flower bowl
July 16	19	S. Fielding & Co	S	Teapot
July 23	9	S. & H. Levi★	Ln	Egg stand
July 28	2	Brownhills Pottery Co	T	Printed design
July 31	8	Old Hall Earthenware Co Ltd	H	Printed design
Aug 4	3	Pinder, Bourne & Co	B	Printed design
Aug 11	14	Clementson Brothers	H	Printed design
Aug 14	12	W. Davenport & Co	Lpt	Toiletwares
Aug 14	12	W. Davenport & Co	Lpt	Basket dish
Aug 17	6	Sherwin & Cotton	H	Tile design
Aug 18	3	J. Wedgwood & Sons	E	Jug, Longfellow
Aug 18	14	Dean & Morris	H	Wine funnel
Aug 18	14	Dean & Morris	H	Pie preserver
Aug 21	2	Sherwin & Cotton	H	Tile design
Aug 21	10	W. A. Adderley	L	Printed design
Aug 23	5	Jackson & Gosling	F	Printed design
Aug 23	6	Brown-Westhead, Moore & Co	Sh	Printed design
Aug 24	10	Edwin J. D. Bodley	B	Teawares, bamboo
Sept 3	3	Brown-Westhead, Moore & Co	Sh	Toilet jug
Sept 4	7	J. Beech & Son	L	Teawares
Sept 11	3	W. Brownfield & Sons	C	Vase forms
Sept 14	6	Mintons	S	Printed design
Sept 15	6	G. L. Ashworth & Bros	H	Teapot
Sept 15	12	Minton, Hollins & Co	S	Tile design
Sept 23	3	Ambrose Wood★	H	Tile design
Sept 25	6	Minton, Hollins & Co	S	Tile designs
Sept 25	13	J. A. Briart & Co★	Ln	Stoneware bottle
Sept 27	5	John Marshall & Co	Sc	Printed designs
Sept 29	3	Brownhills Pottery Co	T	Toiletwares
Sept 30	4	Worcester Royal Porcelain Co Ltd	W	Jug
Oct 1	3	Wade & Colclough	B	Teapot – Gladstone
Oct 6	4	J. Wedgwood & Sons	E	Jug

Oct 12	4	Mintons	S	Jardinere
Oct 13	5	J. Wedgwood & Sons	E	Jug
Oct 20	10	Burgess & Leigh	B	Jug – Roman
Oct 21	3	Worcester Royal Porcelain Co Ltd	W	Flower vases
Oct 22	4	Edward F. Bodley & Son	B	Teapot
Oct 22	12	J. Aynsley & Sons	L	Jug
Oct 26	13	Minton, Hollins & Co	S	Tile designs
Oct 27	5	Taylor, Tunnicliffe & Co	H	Menu slab
Oct 27	20	John Tams	L	Jug
Oct 27	21	G. Woolliscroft & Son	E	Fireplace surround
Oct 28	2	Sherwin & Cotton	H	Tile design
Oct 30	6	Jones & Hopkinson	H	Jug
Nov 2	2	W. H. Grindley & Co	T	Jug
Nov 4	4	W. & T. Adams	T	Printed, crab, design
Nov 4	15	Minton, Hollins & Co	S	Tile designs
Nov 9	4	J. Wedgwood & Sons	E	Ink pot
Nov 10	2	Wilcock & Co	Lds	Drain designs
Nov 10	13	Bednall & Heath	H	Jug
Nov 18	3	Samuel Radford	L	Printed leaf border
Nov 18	14	Mintons	S	Bottle & decoration
Nov 19	15	Crown Derby Porcelain Co Ltd	D	Printed design
Nov 24	4	Grove & Stark	L	"Yeddo" print
Nov 24	5	Bates, Gildea & Walker	B	"Kioto" print
Dec 6	2	Powell, Bishop & Stonier	H	Printed design
Dec 7	10	Pinder, Bourne & Co	H	Dinnerwares
Dec 7	10	Pinder, Bourne & Co	H	Toiletwares
Dec 7	10	Pinder, Bourne & Co	H	Printed design, fruit
Dec 8	5	Wittman & Roth★	Ln	Fancy flower holders
Dec 15	15	W. Brownfield & Sons	C	Vase forms
Dec 15	15	W. Brownfield & Sons	C	Jardinere
Dec 15	15	W. Brownfield & Sons	C	Menu holder
Dec 18	2	Bates, Gildea & Walker	B	Printed design
Dec 24	8	Brown-Westhead, Moore & Co	Sh	Printed design, leaf
Dec 29	7	Doulton & Co	Ln	Mug designs
Dec 29	7	Doulton & Co	Ln	Sporting jug
Dec 29	7	Doulton & Co	Ln	Covered jar
Dec 31	1	Old Hall Earthenware Co Ltd	H	Floral print
Dec 31	4	Sherwin & Cotton	H	Tile designs

1881 (E at right)

Jan 5	7	Joseph Roth★	Ln	Floral motifs
Jan 6	2	B. & S. Hancock	S	Printed design
Jan 6	8	F. D. Bradley	L	Flower bowl
Jan 7	13	Sherwin & Cotton	H	Tile design
Jan 12	5	Sherwin & Cotton	H	Tile design
Jan 14	1	C. F. Boseck & Co★	Ln	Printed designs
Jan 14	10	Worcester Royal Porcelain Co Ltd	W	Floral print
Jan 14	18	Edwin J. D. Bodley	B	Teawares
Jan 15	4	Holmes, Stonier & Hollinshead	H	Printed designs
Jan 20	3	Mintons	S	Two dimensional dish
Jan 21	11	W. & T. Adams	T	Eagle device
Jan 26	4	Minton, Hollins & Co	S	Tile design

Jan 27	15	Worcester Royal Porcelain Co Ltd	W	Teapot
Jan 28	3	G. Woolliscroft & Son	H	Tile design
Feb 8	5	Grove & Stark	L	Printed design
Feb 8	6	W. Brownfield & Sons	C	Toiletwares
Feb 8	6	W. Brownfield & Sons	C	Teapot forms
Feb 11	10	F. J. Emery	B	Jug
Feb 15	6	W. A. Adderley	L	Printed design
Feb 16	3	F. D. Bradley	L	Rose bowl
Feb 17	2	Murray & Co	G	Teapot
Feb 18	3	Samuel Radford	L	Printed design
Feb 21	4	Taylor, Waine & Bates	L	National emblems
Feb 24	8	W. Harrop & Co	H	Vase
Feb 25	14	J. MacIntyre & Co	B	Menu holder
Feb 28	9	Edwin J. D. Bodley	B	Teawares
Mar 3	5	J. Dimmock & Co	H	Jug, swan
Mar 7	11	J. Aynsley & Sons	L	Printed borders
Mar 8	3	Grove & Stark	L	Jug
Mar 10	12	Martin Gray★	Ln	Oval tureen
Mar 14	1	Edwin J. D. Bodley	B	Teawares
Mar 17	9	Shorter & Boulton	S	Jug
Mar 19	4	Mintons	S	Tile design
Mar 19	4	Mintons	S	Printed design
Mar 23	4	Mintons	S	Boy ornament
Mar 24	2	T. S. Pinder	B	Printed design
Mar 24	3	W. A. Adderley	L	Jug
Mar 29	6	T. A. Simpson	H	Tile design
Mar 31	2	J. T. Hudden	L	Printed design
April 7	2	Sherwin & Cotton	H	Tile design
April 7	9	Old Hall Earthenware Co Ltd	H	Printed design
April 8	2	W. Harrop & Co	H	"Pekin" print
April 8	3	Wedgwood & Co	T	"Louise" print
April 8	14	Worcester Royal Porcelain Co Ltd	W	Boy with basket
April 9	5	R. H. Plant & Co	L	Jug
April 11	1	A. Bevington & Co	H	Oval tureen
April 12	4	Mintons	S	Dish forms
April 12	4	Mintons	S	Plate shape
April 14	10	Mintons	S	Printed design
April 16	17	J. Marshall & Co	G	Floral print
April 19	3	Sherwin & Cotton	H	Tile design
April 19	5	T. & R. Boote	B	Tile design
April 21	4	Sherwin & Cotton	H	Tile design
April 21	5	Edwin J. D. Bodley	B	Teawares, floral
April 21	5	Edwin J. D. Bodley	B	Marmalade pot
April 23	7	J.F. Wileman	F	"Swallow" print
April 28	12	W. T. Copeland & Sons	S	Printed design
April 30	3	Trubshaw, Hand & Co	L	Printed design
April 30	4	J. Wedgwood & Sons	E	Carlyle print
May 3	4	William Wood & Co	B	Menu holder or tablet
May 3	5	Sherwin & Cotton	H	Tile design
May 4	2	Sherwin & Cotton	H	Tile design
May 4	3	W. Brownfield & Sons	C	Plate form
May 4	3	W. Brownfield & Sons	C	Teawares

May 4	3	W. Brownfield & Sons	C	Jug
May 5	2	W. & T. Adams	T	Printed design
May 6	4	R. H. Plant & Co	L	Jug
May 11	3	J. Tams	L	"Violet" fruit
May 13	2	Mintons	S	Plate form
May 16	2	J. Wedgwood & Sons	E	Beaconsfield jug
May 17	8	S. & H. Levi★	Ln	Vase forms
May 17	9	J. Mortlock & Co★	Ln	Tureen form
May 17	9	J. Mortlock & Co★	Ln	Plate form
May 20	11	W. A. Adderley	L	Teapot
May 21	3	Powell, Bishop & Stonier	H	Teawares
May 24	5	G. L. Ashworth & Bros	H	Toiletwares
May 24	6	Mintons	S	Tile designs
May 24	7	F. J. Emery	B	Measure-jug
May 25	3	Powell, Bishop & Stonier	H	Teawares
May 25	9	Worcester Royal Porcelain Co Ltd	W	National figures
May 25	10	J. Wedgwood & Sons	E	Umbrella stands
May 26	7	G. Woolliscroft & Son	H	Tile design
May 30	1	T. Furnival & Sons	C	Printed design
May 30	2	Decorative Art Tile Co	H	Tile design
Jun 1	3	Mintons	S	Tile design
Jun 1	13	J. Mortlock & Co★ (manufactured by Doulton & Co)	Ln	Stoneware jug
Jun 3	4	S. P. Ledward	L	Printed design
Jun 4	3	T. Furnival & Sons	C	Printed border
Jun 4	4	Decorative Art Tile Co	H	Tile design
Jun 7	3	Edward F. Bodley & Sons	B	Spittoon
Jun 7	4	Decorative Art Tile Co	H	Tile designs
Jun 7	17	Worcester Royal Porcelain Co Ltd	W	National figures
Jun 8	6	Crystal Porcelain Co Ltd	H	Tile design
Jun 13	1	Samuel Lear	H	Teapot
Jun 13	4	S. P. Ledward	L	Printed design
Jun 16	8	S. Fielding & Co	S	Fan jug
Jun 16	8	S. Fielding & Co	S	Fan plate
Jun 18	1	Jackson & Gosling	F	Floral print
Jun 21	13	Birks, Brothers & Seddon	C	Teawares
Jun 21	13	Birks, Brothers & Seddon	C	Toiletwares
Jun 21	13	Birks, Brothers & Seddon	C	Tureen form
Jun 21	20	Gildea & Walker	B	Printed pattern
July 2	1	D. McBirney & Co	Bel	Moulded plate
July 2	5	T. Furnival & Sons	C	Printed design
July 6	7	J. Wedgwood & Sons	E	Tureen form
July 9	10	Wardle & Co	H	Toiletwares
July 14	6	Brown-Westhead, Moore & Co	Sh	Toiletwares
July 16	3	Trubshaw, Hand & Co	L	Teawares – grape
July 25	2	John H. Davis	H	Printed border
July 28	3	D. McBirney & Co	Bel	Shell border
July 28	4	A. Wood★	H	Tile design
July 28	14	Ridgways	H	Fern print
July 29	2	Sherwin & Cotton	H	Tile design
July 29	3	Whittman & Roth★	Ln	Owl lamp
July 30	3	Sampson Bridgwood & Son	L	Comport

July 30	4	Sherwin & Cotton	H	Tile design
July 30	5	Mintons	S	Garden seat
July 30	15	W. T. Copeland & Sons	S	Tureen form
Aug 2	1	Edwin J. D. Bodley	B	Printed design
Aug 5	12	Pinder, Bourne & Co	B	Chandelier
Aug 10	13	Old Hall Earthenware Co Ltd	H	Jug
Aug 20	11	Worcester Royal Porcelain Co Ltd	W	John Bull
Aug 23	3	Grove & Stark	L	"Nankin" print
Aug 24	11	T. & R. Boote	B	Fireplace surround
Aug 26	16	W. B. Simpson & Sons	Ln	Tile designs
Aug 27	3	Samuel Lear	H	Jug
Aug 27	9	Gildea & Walker	B	Printed design
Aug 27	9	Gildea & Walker	B	Jug
Aug 29	7	W. & T. Adams	T	Printed mark
Aug 30	7	R. M. Brundige★	NY	Lamp base
Sept 2	4	Dale, Page & Goodwin	L	Printed design
Sept 3	11	T. A. Simpson	H	Tile design
Sept 6	1	Derby Crown Porcelain Co Ltd	D	Printed design
Sept 7	10	Adams & Sleigh	B	Floral print
Sept 9	11	Worcester Royal Porcelain Co Ltd	W	Printed design
Sept 10	12	Joseph Roth★	Ln	Floral encrustation
Sept 16	10	G. Jones & Sons	S	Tureen
Sept 22	9	S. Bold & M. Michelson★	H	President Garfield
Sept 23	21	Minton, Hollins & Co	S	Tile designs
Sept 27	9	Pinder, Bourne & Co	B	Printed design
Sept 28	4	Edwin J. D. Bodley	B	Tureen
Sept 28	13	Gildea & Walker	B	Tureen
Sept 29	3	G. Jones & Sons	S	Printed ivy design
Sept 30	3	Davenports Ltd	Lpt	Toiletwares
Sept 30	15	Mintons	S	Garden seat
Sept 30	15	Mintons	S	Oyster plate & dishes
Oct 4	6	W. Brownfield & Sons	C	Jug
Oct 6	5	T. & R. Boote	B	Teapot
Oct 6	7	Campbell Brick & Tile Co	S	Tile design
Oct 7	27	Mintons	S	Jug
Oct 13	3	Adderley & Lawson	L	Printed design
Oct 13	5	T. & R. Boote	B	Oval tureen
Oct 20	1	F. J. Emery	B	Parnell print
Oct 20	2	Robinson & Chapman	L	Printed border
Oct 22	1	Mintons	S	Tureen
Oct 25	14	W. B. Simpson	Ln	Tile designs
Oct 26	8	Mintons	S	Printed design
Oct 26	16	Brown-Westhead, Moore & Co	Sh	Cuff-links
Oct 27	1	Robinson & Chapman	L	Printed border
Oct 29	3	T. & R. Boote	B	Tile design
Oct 29	4	W. Brownfield & Sons	C	Printed design U.S.A.
Oct 29	11	Wardle & Co	H	Jug
Oct 29	14	Minton, Hollins & Co	S	Tile design
Nov 2	1	Brown-Westhead, Moore & Co	Sh	Jug forms
Nov 3	12	Worcester Royal Porcelain Co Ltd	W	Floral print
Nov 4	24	Worcester Royal Porcelain Co Ltd	W	Teawares
Nov 8	1	T. & R. Boote	B	Tile design

Nov 9	6	Grove & Stark	L	Toiletwares
Nov 9	7	Edwin J. D. Bodley	B	Jugs
Nov 9	7	Edwin J. D. Bodley	B	Floral cup
Nov 10	2	Brough & Blackhurst	L	Printed design
Nov 14	10	W. B. Simpson & Sons	Ln	Tile designs
Nov 19	3	Sampson Bridgwood & Son	L	Plate form
Nov 19	12	Worcester Royal Porcelain Co Ltd	W	Tureen
Nov 21	1	John Bevington	H	Ewer – swan
Nov 22	9	John Tams	L	Oval tureen
Nov 22	17	Ambrose Wood★	H	Tile design
Nov 23	13	Shorter & Boulton	S	Jug
Nov 25	1	Adams & Sleigh	B	Jug
Nov 25	15	Joseph Roth★	Ln	Sunflower motif
Nov 26	1	W. G. MacWilliam★	Ln	Condiment
Nov 26	1	W. G. MacWilliam★	Ln	Floral border
Nov 29	6	James Hill★	Ln	Door furniture
Nov 29	10	Worcester Royal Porcelain Co Ltd	W	Acorn condiment
Dec 2	16	Joseph Roth★	Ln	Rose motif
Dec 5	11	J. Rose & Co	Cpt	Teawares
Dec 8	9	Adderley & Lawson	L	Floral print
Dec 9	2	Edwin J. D. Bodley	B	Menu tablet
Dec 9	12	J. Defries & Sons★	Ln	Floral prints
Dec 10	7	Brown-Westhead, Moore & Co	Sh	Plate form
Dec 12	12	John Fell	L	Butter dish
Dec 16	3	Mintons	S	Printed border
Dec 20	9	Bednall & Heath	H	Jug
Dec 21	3	Frederick Grosvenor	G	Teapot
Dec 21	9	Worcester Royal Porcelain Co Ltd	W	Teapot
Dec 24	5	James Broadhurst	F	Printed design

1882 (L at right)

Jan 3	6	Holmes, Plant & Maydew	B	Printed design
Jan 4	2	W. T. Copeland & Sons	S	Toiletwares
Jan 4	7	Joseph Roth★	Ln	Floral reliefs
Jan 4	9	F. & R. Pratt & Co	F	Teapot
Jan 7	2	W. H. Grindley & Co	T	Printed design
Jan 7	11	Ridgways	H	"Chintz" print
Jan 10	5	Samuel Lear	H	Jug
Jan 11	1	Minton, Hollins & Co	S	Tile designs
Jan 13	4	Decorative Art Tile Co	H	Tile designs
Jan 18	10	Robinson & Son	L	Printed design
Jan 24	1	W. H. Micklethwaite & Co	Y	Printed design
Jan 26	5	J. T. Hudden	L	Printed design
Jan 26	16	S. Fielding & Co	S	Printed design
Jan 27	8	Craven Dunnill & Co Ltd	J	Tile form
Jan 30	2	Hollinshead & Kirkham	T	Printed design
Jan 30	3	Grove & Stark	L	"Cora" print
Feb 1	1	Edge, Malkin & Co	B	Jug
Feb 3	4	Brown-Westhead, Moore & Co	Sh	Tureen forms
Feb 4	10	Minton, Hollins & Co	S	Tile design
Feb 6	4	Campbell Tile Co	S	Tile designs
Feb 7	2	William Mills	H	Jug

Feb 8	7	Wardle & Co	H	Jug
Feb 15	4	Grove & Stark	L	Blossom print
Feb 16	6	Mintons	S	Tile designs
Feb 18	5	J. F. Wileman & Co	F	Bird print
Feb 20	6	W. B. Simpson & Sons	Ln	Tile design
Feb 23	17	Minton, Hollins & Co	S	Tile designs
Feb 24	3	Taylor, Tunnicliffe & Co	H	Floral print
Mar 1	11	Worcester Royal Porcelain Co Ltd	W	Printed border
Mar 1	12	Minton Hollins & Co	S	Tile design
Mar 7	7	Minton Hollins & Co	S	Tile designs
Mar 13	3	J. T. Hudden	L	Floral print
Mar 15	3	Powell, Bishop & Stonier	H	Jug
Mar 15	4	Murray & Co	G	Teapot
Mar 20	5	W. A. Adderley	L	Jug
Mar 23	2	W. & T. Adams	T	Mark device
Mar 23	15	T. A. Simpson	H	Teapot
Mar 27	3	D. Chapman	L	Printed swan design
Mar 27	10	Shorter & Boulton	S	Jug
Mar 28	12	Ambrose Wood★	H	Tile design
Mar 28	16	A. Bevington & Co	H	Printed designs
Mar 28	16	A. Bevington & Co	H	Cheese dish
Mar 29	9	Oetzmann & Co★	Ln	Printed design
Mar 30	13	J. Rose & Co	Cpt	Floral dish form
Mar 30	17	S. Fielding & Co	S	Jug
Mar 31	3	A. Bevington & Co	H	Floral print
April 4	2	W. Brownfield & Sons	C	Jug
April 4	2	W. Brownfield & Sons	C	Basket flower holder
April 11	6	G. Jones & Sons	S	Strawberry dish
April 11	7	Minton, Hollins & Co	S	Tile designs
April 14	14	Oetzmann & Co★	Ln	Floral print
April 21	7	Sampson Bridgwood & Son	L	Coffee pot
April 27	14	New Wharf Pottery Co	B	Print for Greece
May 2	5	G. L. Ashworth & Bros	H	Toiletwares
May 3	1	Samuel Radford	L	Floral print
May 5	2	Wood, Hines & Winkle	H	Jug
May 6	5	Powell, Bishop & Stonier	H	London print
May 6	6	Whittaker, Edge & Co	H	Jug forms
May 8	18	Davenports Ltd	Lpt	Toiletwares
May 8	18	Davenports Ltd	Lpt	Tureen
May 9	3	Henry Alcock & Co	C	Tureen forms
May 9	4	Whittaker, Edge & Co	H	Printed border
May 9	7	W. Brownfield & Sons	C	Cup form
May 9	11	Minton, Hollins & Co	S	Tile design
May 10	4	John Edwards	F	Tureen
May 10	4	John Edwards	F	Jug
May 10	14	S. Fielding & Co	S	Jug
May 13	6	G. Jones & Sons	S	Dish
May 17	2	Edwin J. Bodley	B	Printed designs
May 24	4	Minton, Hollins & Co	S	Tile design
May 24	21	Doulton & Co	B	Coffee pot
May 25	11	W. A. Adderley	L	Printed design
May 27	3	Samuel Lear	H	Teapot

May 30	5	W .H. Grindley & Co	T	Printed design
Jun 5	6	Mintons	S	Tile design
Jun 5	7	Wood, Hines & Winkle	H	Printed design
Jun 9	3	Hall & Read	B	Teapot
Jun 9	4	W. A. Adderley	L	Toiletwares
Jun 13	11	A. Shaw & Son	B	Shakespeare print
Jun 13	14	Wardle & Co	H	Jug forms
Jun 17	3	A. Boyd & Son★	Ln	Tile design
Jun 21	4	William Lowe	L	Printed design
Jun 21	5	Sampson Bridgwood & Son	L	Teawares
Jun 21	11	Old Hall Earthenware Co Ltd	H	Brighton print
Jun 23	1	J. Wedgwood & Sons	E	Tureen
Jun 23	1	J. Wedgwood & Sons	E	Jug
Jun 23	5	Burgess & Leigh	B	Printed design
Jun 28	2	Derby Crown Porcelain Co Ltd	D	Printed design
Jun 29	11	J. Defries & Sons★	Ln	Teawares
July 1	8	Taylor, Tunnicliffe & Co	H	Menu tablet
July 3	2	Mintons	S	Tile design
July 3	3	Edwin J. D. Bodley	B	Printed design
July 4	3	Wright & Rigby	H	Jug
July 6	4	W. Brownfield & Sons	C	Floral print
July 6	4	W. Brownfield & Sons	C	Printed border
July 14	3	G. Jones & Sons	S	Ornaments
July 14	10	Wardle & Co	H	Teapot
July 14	10	Wardle & Co	H	Jug
July 14	14	Beech & Tellwright	C	Figure box
July 17	8	Wood & Son	B	Tureen
July 18	13	Shuffrey & Co★	Ln	Tile design
July 19	7	Wardle & Co	L	Floral jug
July 20	1	John Edwards	F	Coffee pot & jug
July 20	1	John Edwards	F	Tureen
July 22	8	G. Jones & Son	S	Jug
July 25	3	Frederick Grosvenor	G	Bird fountain
July 25	9	Brownhills Pottery Co Ltd	T	"Hizen" print
July 25	9	Brownhills Pottery Co Ltd	T	Water set
July 25	9	Brownhills Pottery Co Ltd	T	Jug
July 26	4	Adderley & Lawson	L	Floral print
July 28	3	Hawley & Co	F	Teapot
July 31	2	Sampson Bridgwood & Son	L	Teawares
July 31	9	Mintons	S	Jardineres
Aug 5	4	W. Brownfield & Sons	C	Dish – fish
Aug 5	4	W. Brownfield & Sons	C	Printed design
Aug 10	5	Wright & Rigby	H	Teapot Gen. Booth
Aug 11	10	Oetzmann & Co★	Ln	Printed designs
Aug 21	2	John Tams	L	"Rangoon" print
Aug 21	8	Adams & Bromley	H	Jug
Aug 25	2	Mintons	S	Figure lamp base
Aug 26	4	W. Wood & Co	B	Teapot
Aug 28	2	Belfield & Co	Sc	Fluted jardinere
Aug 28	9	Mintons	S	Toiletwares
Aug 29	12	W. Brownfield & Sons	C	Flower tray
Aug 29	14	Shuffrey & Co★	Ln	Vase

Aug 30	14	Worcester Royal Porcelain Co Ltd	W	Dish
Aug 31	3	A. Bevington & Co	H	Jug
Sept 6	2	Hawley & Co	F	Jug
Sept 8	5	Mintons	S	Tile design
Sept 8	5	Mintons	S	Toiletwares
Sept 9	3	Taylor, Tunnicliffe & Co	H	Lamp base
Sept 11	4	Adams & Bromley	H	Jug
Sept 16	2	Hulme & Massey	L	Printed designs
Sept 19	2	W. H. Grindley & Co	T	Printed design
Sept 28	4	Brown-Westhead, Moore & Co	Sh	Printed designs
Sept 28	22	Bridgett & Bates	L	Leafage print
Sept 29	2	Brownhills Pottery Co	T	Printed designs
Oct 6	2	Mintons	S	Tile designs
Oct 9	3	W. T. Copeland & Sons	S	Jug
Oct 9	4	Dean, Capper & Dean	H	Teapot
Oct 11	3	Sampson Bridgwood & Son	L	Toiletwares
Oct 11	4	Wood & Son	B	Printed design
Oct 12	17	T. Furnival & Sons	C	Jug
Oct 16	4	Wood & Son	B	Floral print
Oct 19	4	Lowe, Ratcliffe & Co	L	Printed design
Oct 31	2	William Lowe	L	Beehive print
Nov 1	14	Stonier, Hollinshead & Oliver	H	Jug
Nov 1	14	Stonier, Hollinshead & Oliver	H	Savoy print
Nov 4	19	Worcester Royal Porcelain Co Ltd	W	Printed design
Nov 8	2	Mintons	S	Printed design
Nov 10	10	Ridgways	H	Jasper jug
Nov 10	12	Pratt & Simpson	F	Jug
Nov 10	12	Pratt & Simpson	F	Printed designs
Nov 11	2	Powell, Bishop & Stonier	H	Floral print
Nov 13	1	Edge, Malkin & Co	B	Jug
Nov 13	2	Sampson Bridgwood & Son	L	Printed design
Nov 14	3	Edward Steel	H	Falstaff jug
Nov 14	3	Edward Steel	H	Frog jug
Nov 15	7	S. Fielding & Co	S	Jugs
Nov 16	3	Taylor, Tunnicliffe & Co	H	Menu stand
Nov 21	4	Joseph Holdcroft	L	Jug
Nov 21	8	Gildea & Walker	B	Printed design
Nov 22	11	S. Fielding & Co	S	Floral print
Nov 24	19	Minton, Hollins & Co	S	Tile design
Nov 27	3	Henry Alcock & Co	C	Jug
Nov 27	4	Derby Crown Porcelain Co Ltd	D	Printed design
Nov 27	5	James F. Wileman & Co	F	Blossom print
Dec 2	8	Minton, Hollins & Co	S	Tile design
Dec 4	7	A. Bevington & Co	H	Leafage print
Dec 6	2	Brown-Westhead, Moore & Co	Sh	Tureen
Dec 6	2	Brown-Westhead, Moore & Co	Sh	Octagonal plate
Dec 6	11	G. Jackson & Son★	Ln	Relief plaques
Dec 9	5	W. H. Micklethwaite & Co	Y	Tile design
Dec 13	4	Mintons	S	Tile designs
Dec 13	4	Mintons	S	Jug
Dec 13	5	J. Wedgwood & Sons	E	Jug
Dec 14	6	Samuel Lear	H	Jug

Dec 15	3	Old Hall Earthenware Co Ltd	H	"Farm" print
Dec 18	9	John Lockett & Co	L	Toilet pan
Dec 19	3	Henry Kennedy	G	Figure print
Dec 21	4	Edwin J. D. Bodley	B	Jug, tusk
Dec 21	5	Wood, Hines & Winkle	H	Toast rack
Dec 22	2	Grove & Stark	L	"Rubus" jug
Dec 22	14	L. Hutschenreuther	Ger	Printed design
Dec 23	4	James F. Wileman	F	Floral print
Dec 23	12	New Wharf Pottery Co	B	Printed border
Dec 23	14	Worcester Royal Porcelain Co Ltd	W	Figure group
Dec 23	14	Worcester Royal Porcelain Co Ltd	W	Single figures
Dec 27	1	New Wharf Pottery Co	B	Jug

1883 (K at right)

Jan 2	2	Derby Crown Porcelain Co Ltd	D	Printed border
Jan 3	1	William Hines	L	Printed design
Jan 3	14	T. Furnival & Sons	C	Tureen
Jan 3	18	J. Rose & Co	Cpt	Fluted teawares
Jan 4	5	Brown-Westhead, Moore & Co	Sh	Printed design
Jan 8	5	W. T. Copeland & Sons	S	Tureen
Jan 8	12	Worcester Royal Porcelain Co Ltd	W	Flower holder
Jan 9	3	Powell, Bishop & Stonier	H	Toiletwares
Jan 9	4	Edward F. Bodley & Son	L	Printed design
Jan 9	5	Hall & Read	H	"Tokio" print
Jan 9	5	Hall & Read	H	Tureen forms
Jan 9	11	Davenports Ltd	Lpt	Tureen form
Jan 10	17	Gildea & Walker	B	Printed design
Jan 12	3	Holmes, Plant & Madew	B	Printed design
Jan 13	6	Moore & Co	L	Printed design
Jan 13	17	T. & R. Boote	B	No entry
Jan 16	1	Blair & Co	L	Printed design
Jan 17	3	W. H. Grindley & Co	T	Printed design
Jan 17	11	Alfred Clark★	Ln	Jug
Jan 22	1	W. H. Micklethwaite & Co	Y	Tile design
Jan 23	8	Edward F. Bodley & Son	L	Tureen
Jan 23	10	W. T. Copeland & Sons	S	Toiletwares
Jan 24	1	Sampson Bridgwood & Son	L	Tureen
Jan 24	2	W. Brownfield & Sons	C	Tureen
Jan 25	3	Brownhills Pottery Co	T	Trinket set
Jan 26	8	William Lowe	L	Printed design
Jan 27	8	G. W. Turner & Sons	T	Tureen
Jan 29	6	W. Brownfield & Sons	C	Umbrella stand, bear
Jan 29	7	W. H. Grindley & Co	T	Printed design
Jan 29	7	W. H. Grindley & Co	T	Tureen
Jan 30	1	Edward F. Bodley & Son	L	Tureen
Jan 30	12	Wedgwood & Co	T	Printed design
Jan 31	14	Minton Hollins & Co	S	Tile design
Feb 1	3	Sampson Bridgwood & Son	L	Tureen
Feb 1	17	Edwin J. D. Bodley	B	Cup form
Feb 2	4	S. Hancock	S	Printed design
Feb 2	17	Wedgwood & Co	T	Tureen
Feb 3	3	Mintons	S	Tile design

Feb 5	2	Joseph Holdcroft	L	Teapot
Feb 6	1	Wood, Hines & Winkle	H	Toilet jug
Feb 7	4	Hawley & Co	F	Jug
Feb 7	5	Mountford & Thomas	H	Jug
Feb 9	9	Edwin J. D. Bodley	B	Oyster plate
Feb 12	3	Dunn, Bennett & Co	H	"Marlborough" print
Feb 13	11	Baw & Dotter	Fr	Oval tureen
Feb 14	3	W. H. Grindley & Co	T	Printed design
Feb 15	5	J. H. Davis	H	"Chatsworth" print
Feb 16	11	G. Jackson & Sons★	Ln	Figure plaques
Feb 17	13	G. W. Turner & Sons	T	Jug
Feb 17	13	G. W. Turner & Sons	T	Printed design
Feb 19	1	W. A. Adderley	L	Coffee pot
Feb 20	13	Davenports Ltd	Lpt	Printed design
Feb 20	14	G. Siebdrat★	Ln	Toast rack, condiment
Feb 20	17	Gildea & Walker	B	Printed design
Feb 21	3	G. Jones & Sons	S	Leaf dish
Feb 22	6	Hall & Read	H	Printed design
Feb 22	6	Hall & Read	H	Tureen forms
Feb 22	6	Hall & Read	H	Jug
Feb 22	20	Worcester Royal Porcelain Co Ltd	W	Welled dish
Feb 22	21	Old Hall Earthenware Co Ltd	H	Tureen
Feb 24	12	J. Wedgwood & Sons	E	Toiletwares
Feb 24	13	Worcester Royal Porcelain Co Ltd	W	Small vase
Feb 26	6	Williamson & Sons	L	Blossom print
Feb 27	18	W. B. Simpson & Sons	Ln	Tile design
Feb 28	3	T. Till & Sons	B	Tureen
Mar 2	12	G. Richardson & Son★	Ln	Figure plaque
Mar 8	5	M. Massey	H	Jug
Mar 8	20	Edward F. Bodley & Son	Lpt	Jug
Mar 8	20	Edward F. Bodley & Son	Lpt	Teaset on tray
Mar 14	3	Derby Porcelain Co Ltd	D	Printed design
Mar 15	3	T. Furnival & Sons	C	Printed design
Mar 16	6	J. Broadhurst	F	Printed design
Mar 17	7	Carron Company	Sc	Tile designs
Mar 17	8	Mintons	S	"Wynn" tray
Mar 20	3	Elizabeth Wood★	H	Jug
Mar 20	4	J. Wedgwood & Sons	E	Jug
Mar 24	3	Sampson Bridgwood & Sons	L	Teapot
Mar 30	1	Mintons	S	Tile design
Mar 30	9	Minton, Hollins & Co	S	Tile design
April 2	3	T. & E. L. Poulson	Y	"Raikes" print
April 3	3	Emelius Warburton★	L	Jug
April 6	14	G. & J. Hobson	B	Baking dish
April 10	1	Banks & Thorley	H	Jug
April 18	13	W.B. Simpson & Sons	Ln	Tile designs
April 19	3	R.H. Plant & Co	L	Floral print
April 21	1	James F. Wileman & Co	F	Printed design
April 23	8	W. B. Simpson & Sons	Ln	Tile design
April 24	7	G. L. Ashworth & Bros	H	Tureen
April 25	14	Pratt & Simpson	F	Tureen
April 27	17	C. Littler & Co	H	Dinnerwares

April 27	18	J.H. Davis	H	Tureen
April 27	19	Powell, Bishop & Stonier	H	Floral print
April 2	4	Brown–Westhead, Moore & Co	Sh	Jug forms
May 5	4	Whittaker, Edge & Co	H	Tureen
May 7	8	S. Fielding & Co	S	Jug – "Avon"
May 8	6	T. G. & F. Booth	T	Tureen
May 8	6	T. G. & F. Booth	T	Printed design
May 11	5	R. H. Plant & Co	L	Fruit print
May 16	12	T. A. Simpson	S	Tile design
May 16	13	Ambrose Wood★	H	Printed designs
May 22	11	Powell, Bishop & Stonier	H	Teapot
May 23	7	T. G. & F. Booth	T	Centrepiece
May 23	7	T. G. & F. Booth	T	Covered box
May 23	8	Elizabeth Wood★	H	Jug
May 24	3	Brownhills Pottery & Co	T	Printed design
May 25	4	W. A. Adderley	L	Tureen
May 28	2	O. G. Blunden	Sussex	Cooking vessels
May 29	14	W. B. Simpson & Sons	Ln	Tile designs
May 31	7	Wardle & Co	H	Jug
Jun 2	9	Minton, Hollins & Co	S	Tile designs
Jun 4	8	Clementson Brothers	H	Tureen
Jun 4	8	Clementson Brothers	H	Printed designs
Jun 8	2	H. Alcock & Co	C	Tureen
Jun 9	2	Sampson Bridgwood & Son	L	Tureen
Jun 9	6	Mintons	S	Floral print
Jun 11	2	Grove & Stark	L	Tureen
Jun 11	8	J. Mathews	WsM	Flower pot
Jun 11	9	J. Mathews	WsM	Slug trap
Jun 13	3	Belfield & Co	Sc	Teapot
Jun 13	7	Pratt & Simpson	F	Printed design
Jun 14	2	Grove & Stark	L	Printed designs
Jun 18	11	J. Tams	L	Jug
Jun 18	12	W. Brownfield & Sons	C	Tureens
Jun 18	12	W. Brownfield & Sons	C	Jugs
Jun 18	12	W. Brownfield & Sons	C	Cruet
Jun 20	3	T. & R. Boote	B	Teapot
Jun 20	4	Mintons	S	Printed design
Jun 20	16	W. & E. Corn	B	Tureen
Jun 21	22	Wardle & Co	H	Jug
Jun 23	4	J. Wedgwood & Sons	E	Flower pot
Jun 25	5	Ford & Riley	B	"Florence" print
Jun 25	10	W. Brownfield & Sons	C	Figure candlesticks
July 2	4	Edge, Malkin & Co	B	Tureen
July 2	4	Edge, Malkin & Co	B	Printed design
July 3	3	J. Aynsley & Sons	L	Teawares
July 3	4	Moore Brothers	L	Leaf dishes, plates
July 4	4	Wittmann & Roth★	Ln	Lamp bases
July 4	7	W. Brownfield & Sons	C	Ice tray
July 5	6	Grove & Stark	L	Tureen
July 5	19	T. Furnival & Sons	C	Jug
July 5	21	Owen, Raby & Co	Lpt	Tureen
July 6	2	Blackhurst & Bourne	B	Printed design

July 10	9	Ambrose Wood★	H	Tile design
July 10	10	J. Macintyre & Co	B	Inkwells
July 11	1	J. Wedgwood & Sons	E	Lobster salad bowl
July 19	4	Davenports Ltd	Lpt	Jug
July 19	21	G. Jones & Sons	S	Jug
July 19	21	G. Jones & Sons	S	Printed design
July 20	11	Hollinshead & Kirkham	T	Tureen
July 21	3	Bridgett & Bates	L	Floral design
July 23	3	J. Wedgwood & Sons	E	Printed design
July 26	1	W. A. Adderley	L	Jug
July 27	4	Brown-Westhead, Moore & Co	Sh	Printed design
July 27	13	W. Bennett	H	Printed design – birds
July 30	10	W. Brownfield & Sons	C	Lamp base
July 31	3	T. & R. Boote	B	Tile design
Aug 1	3	Wagstaff & Brunt	L	Printed design
Aug 1	4	G. Jones & Sons	S	Coffee pot
Aug 1	4	G. Jones & Sons	S	Jug
Aug 1	9	Brown-Westhead, Moore & Co	Sh	Printed design
Aug 2	3	Davenports Ltd	Lpt	Toiletwares
Aug 3	17	Edward F. Bodley	B	Jug
Aug 8	9	J. & E. Ridgway	H	"Variety" print
Aug 9	15	Haviland & Co	Fr	Tureen forms
Aug 17	5	Edwin J. D. Bodley	B	Jug
Aug 20	8	Worcester Royal Porcelain Co Ltd	W	Double dish
Aug 22	1	Brownhills Pottery Co	T	"Kioto" print
Aug 22	1	Brownhills Pottery Co	T	Tureen
Aug 23	2	Grove & Cope	H	Garden seat
Aug 23	2	Grove & Cope	H	Basket
Aug 24	12	Mountford & Thomas	H	Jug
Aug 25	11	W. Brownfield & Sons	C	Jug
Aug 29	3	J. Aynsley & Sons	L	Cup form
Aug 31	6	W. & E. Corn	B	Tureen
Aug 31	7	J. F. Wileman & Co	F	Printed design
Sept 1	10	S. Fielding & Co	S	Thistle print
Sept 5	3	W. Brownfield & Sons	C	Toast racks
Sept 7	4	Derby Crown Porcelain Co Ltd	D	"Arab Star" print
Sept 7	16	Haines, Batchelor & Co★	Ln	Burmese print
Sept 7	19	Powell, Bishop & Stonier	H	Tureen
Sept 11	4	J. Wedgwood & Sons	E	Jug
Sept 13	17	H. Aynsley & Co	L	Printed designs
Sept 14	1	W. & T. Adams	T	Printed design
Sept 14	2	Mintons	S	Tile designs
Sept 17	14	Derby Crown Porcelain Co Ltd	D	Floral print
Sept 20	12	Hall & Read	H	Toiletwares
Sept 20	12	Hall & Read	H	Printed designs
Sept 20	13	Derby Crown Porcelain Co Ltd	D	"Pembroke" print
Sept 21	4	Brown-Westhead, Moore & Co	S	"Florette" print
Sept 24	9	Jones & Hopkinson	H	Jug
Sept 25	4	Grove & Stark	L	"Rosebud" print
Sept 25	5	Sampson Bridgwood & Son	L	Comport
Sept 25	5	Sampson Bridgwood & Son	L	Covered box
Sept 27	21	Meigh & Forester	L	Printed design, fish

Sept 28	4	Blair & Co	L	Printed design
Sept 28	5	Edwin J. D. Bodley	B	Printed design
Sept 29	4	Sampson Bridgwood & Son	L	Footed bowl
Oct 2	15	Mellor, Taylor & Co	B	Tureen
Oct 2	22	Meigh & Forester	L	Printed design
Oct 2	22	Meigh & Forester	L	Shell cruet
Oct 4	4	Sampson Bridgwood & Sons	L	Teapot
Oct 4	5	Whittaker, Edge & Co	H	Printed design
Oct 4	24	Worcester Royal Porcelain Co Ltd	W	Fish dish–plate
Oct 6	2	W. H. Grindley & Co	T	Printed design
Oct 8	1	Hollinson & Goodall	L	Jug
Oct 8	2	T. G. & F. Booth	T	Tile designs
Oct 8	3	Hall & Read	H	Printed designs
Oct 9	9	A. Bevington & Co	H	Cruet
Oct 9	9	A. Bevington & Co	H	Covered dish
Oct 9	9	A. Bevington & Co	H	Egg cup stand
Oct 11	2	Wittmann & Roth★	Ln	Bird ornament
Oct 12	13	Bridgett & Bates	L	Floral print
Oct 13	3	Wood & Son	B	Tureen
Oct 13	11	W. Brownfield & Sons	C	Teapot
Oct 13	11	W. Brownfield & Sons	C	Jug
Oct 17	5	New Wharf Pottery Co	B	Tureen
Oct 17	6	Hall & Read	H	Floral print
Oct 17	6	Hall & Read	H	Tureen
Oct 20	3	W. A. Adderley	L	Stratford prints
Oct 20	4	W. Brownfield & Sons	C	Oyster trays
Oct 20	4	W. Brownfield & Sons	C	Candlelabra
Oct 23	8	J. Dimmock & Co	H	Jug
Oct 24	11	Minton, Hollins & Co	S	Tile designs
Oct 25	17	Taylor, Tunnicliffe & Co	H	Menu card
Oct 25	17	Taylor, Tunnicliffe & Co	H	Ash tray
Oct 26	7	Jones & Hopkinson	H	Jug
Oct 27	1	Brownhills Pottery Co	T	Printed design
Oct 30	2	J. Marshall & Co	Sc	Jug – dog pattern
Oct 30	3	New Wharf Pottery Co	B	Printed design
Oct 30	7	Joseph Robinson	B	Printed design
Nov 1	1	A. Bevington & Co	H	Jug
Nov 1	25	Wood, Hines & Winkle	H	Jug
Nov 1	26	S. Fielding & Co	S	Jug – thistle
Nov 1	27	Davenports Ltd	Lpt	Jug
Nov 2	19	Worcester Royal Porcelain Co Ltd	W	Vase forms
Nov 5	13	Henry Alcock & Co	C	Printed design
Nov 6	3	E. & C. Challinor	F	Tureen
Nov 7	2	W. & E. Corn	B	Tureen
Nov 10	9	Taylor, Tunnicliffe & Co	H	Lamp base – swan
Nov 10	10	W. Brownfield & Sons	C	Plate form
Nov 13	10	T. G. & F. Booth	T	"Sandringham" print
Nov 14	3	Stonier, Hollinshead & Oliver	H	Tureen
Nov 15	17	T. Furnival & Sons	C	Bowl form
Nov 17	2	Derby Crown Porcelain Co Ltd	D	"Chandos" print
Nov 21	3	F. J. Emery	B	Teapot
Nov 22	3	S. Fielding & Co	S	"Lattice" print

Nov 23	7	Minton, Hollins & Co	S	Tile design
Nov 24	3	Powell, Bishop & Stonier	H	Floral print
Nov 26	2	W. A. Adderley	L	Jug
Nov 26	3	Sampson Bridgwood & Son	L	Pierced dish
Nov 28	12	Worcester Royal Porcelain Co Ltd	W	Pair candlelabra
Nov 28	12	Worcester Royal Porcelain Co Ltd	W	Four basket figures
Dec 1	3	Worcester Royal Porcelain Co Ltd	W	Printed border
Dec 3	10	James Wilson	L	Printed, rope, design
Dec 5	2	Malkin, Edge & Co	B	Tile design
Dec 5	3	Derby Crown Porcelain Co Ltd	D	Gladstone design
Dec 8	8	James F. Wileman & Co	F	Cup form
Dec 14	4	Brownhills Pottery Co	T	Nations print
Dec 15	13	T. G. & F. Booth	T	Antique teapot form
Dec 15	14	Hollinson & Goodall	L	Jug
Dec 29	4	Powell, Bishop & Stonier	H	Oval tureen

The 1842–83 registration system ended at this point. There had been well over 5,000 basic shapes or designs registered. Any one of these could be produced in different sizes, adorned with different patterns or appear on various objects. Of these registrations some 85 per cent related to Staffordshire firms, a fact that underlines the importance of the Staffordshire Potteries as the centre of the world ceramic industry.

REGISTRATION NUMBERS 1884–1999

In January 1884 a new system of simple numbering of designs, patents and trade marks commenced, giving a five-year coverage. The first ceramic design was number 130, a printed design issued by J. Dimmock & Co., of Hanley. This numbering system continued in sequence until 1990 when it was rebased to 2,000,000. These post-1883 registered numbers are found prefixed $R^d N^o$ (or similar abbreviations). They should not be confused with earlier entry numbers, or with patent numbers or with numbered trade marks. (A design registration is quite different from a patented novel process or object. Objects bearing patent references, whilst normally indicating the earliest possible date of introduction, do not link with registered design records. British patents can be researched at the Patent Office.) Whilst one cannot list all these entries – there were 19,753 in 1884 alone – I do publish the approximate number reached by January of each year. This enables one to at least discover the year of registration and therefore the earliest possible date of manufacture. It should be noted, however, that some manufacturers extended their official coverage by registering one object, say a relief-moulded jug, but then used that design or elements of it on other articles, using the original registration mark!

This table shows the approximate number reached by January of each year.

1	=	1884	224720	=	1894
19754	=	1885	246975	=	1895
40480	=	1886	268392	=	1896
64520	=	1887	291241	=	1897
90483	=	1888	311658	=	1898
116648	=	1889	331707	=	1899
141273	=	1890	351202	=	1900
163767	=	1891	368154	=	1901
185713	=	1892	385180	=	1902
205240	=	1893	403200	=	1903

424400	=	1904	876067	=	1955
447800	=	1905	879282	=	1956
471860	=	1906	882949	=	1957
493900	=	1907	887079	=	1958
518640	=	1908	891665	=	1959
535170	=	1909	895000	=	1960
552000	=	1910	899914	=	1961
574817	=	1911	904638	=	1962
594195	=	1912	909364	=	1963
612431	=	1913	914536	=	1964
630190	=	1914	919607	=	1965
644935	=	1915	924510	=	1966
653521	=	1916	929335	=	1967
658988	=	1917	934515	=	1968
662872	=	1918	939875	=	1969
666128	=	1919	944932	=	1970
673750	=	1920	950046	=	1971
680147	=	1921	955342	=	1972
687144	=	1922	960708	=	1973
694999	=	1923	965185	=	1974
702671	=	1924	969249	=	1975
710165	=	1925	973838	=	1976
718057	=	1926	978426	=	1977
726330	=	1927	982815	=	1978
734370	=	1928	987910	=	1979
742725	=	1929	993012	=	1980
751160	=	1930	998302	=	1981
760583	=	1931	1004456	=	1982
769670	=	1932	1010583	=	1983
779292	=	1933	1017131	=	1984
789019	=	1934	1024174	=	1985
799097	=	1935	1031358	=	1986
808794	=	1936	1039055	=	1987
817293	=	1937	1047479	=	1988
825231	=	1938	1056078	=	1989
832610	=	1939	2003720	=	1990
837520	=	1940	2012047	=	1991
838590	=	1941	2019933	=	1992
839230	=	1942	2028115	=	1993
839980	=	1943	2036116	=	1994
841040	=	1944	2044227	=	1995
842670	=	1945	2053121	=	1996
845550	=	1946	2062149	=	1997
849730	=	1947	2071420	=	1998
853260	=	1948	2080158	=	1999
856999	=	1949			
860854	=	1950			
863970	=	1951			
866280	=	1952			
869300	=	1953			
872531	=	1954			

Collectors' Clubs, Societies and Groups

It is natural and healthy that groups of collectors and others sharing like hobbies should get together to share interests, carry out research, hold meetings, publish magazines or journals and in general help to further the study and understanding of their chosen field of collecting.

I list here the various clubs and societies that relate to different aspects of British ceramics. I am unable to give the addresses of the various secretaries or other officials as these change and out-of-date information can be embarrassing. However, leading museums may well be able to supply details. Some magazines such as the *Antique Diary* (P.O. Box 30, Twyford, RG10 8DQ) also publish details of such clubs. If you wish to write to any source for information do remember to enclose a stamped and self-addressed envelope. Public libraries should have details of any local collectors' clubs, of which several exist.

National organizations such as NADFAS (National Association of Decorative and Fine Art Societies) hold monthly lecture meetings to broaden your understanding of the arts in general. The specialist speakers may include from time to time ceramic subjects. Details of your nearest local society may be obtained from their head office, 8 Guilford Street, London, WC1N 1DT (S.A.E. please).

The most senior of the societies devoted to the study of British ceramics is the English Ceramic Circle formed in May 1931, from the English Porcelain Circle which was formed in February 1927 by a group of private collectors 'seeking to increase the knowledge of early English porcelain by communications and discussions at meetings'. Various well-researched members' papers have been published in the society's *Transactions* which are available on subscription. The ECC is based in London and its interests tend to be confined to pre-1820 ceramics.

The club with the widest interests and the largest, international, membership is undoubtedly the (mis-named) Northern Ceramic Society. Their lecture meetings are usually held in the northern part of the country but reports, research papers and other information are circulated by regular *Newsletters* and a *Journal*. The NCS also holds educational exhibitions and seminars. Details regarding the Northern Ceramic Society can be obtained from the Ceramics Department at The Potteries Museum, Hanley, Stoke-on-Trent, ST1 3DW. Membership is open (by subscription) to all, not only to northern collectors.

More specialist groups include the following. Each of these may be expected to hold meetings and to publish or at least circulate details of their deliberations and research to their members.

Aynsley Collectors' Society

Belleek Collectors' Group (UK)
Beswick Collectors Club

Carlton Ware Collectors' Club
Clarice Cliff Collectors' Club
Cornish Ware Collectors' Club

Derby Porcelain International Society

Friends of Blue (mainly blue-printed earthenwares)

Goss Collectors' Club

Honiton Pottery Collectors' Society
Hornsea Pottery Collectors' & Research Club

Langley Collectors' Society

Mason Collectors' Club
(The Potteries Museum, Stoke-on-Trent)
Moorcroft Collectors' Club
Moore Brothers Club
Morley College Ceramic Circle (London)

Paragon International Collectors' Club
Pilkington Royal Lancastrian Pottery Society
Pinxton Porcelain Society

Royal Doulton Collectors' Club
(Minton House, London Road, Stoke-on-Trent, ST4 7QD)

Scottish Pottery Society
Shelley Group
SylvaC Collectors' Circle

Tiles & Architectural Ceramics Society
Torquay Pottery Collectors' Society

Wade Collectors' Club
Wedgwood Society
Worcester, Friends of
XYZ Study Group

Some societies and individuals also hold annual Seminars or specialist meetings, with helpful slide-illustrated lectures. These are listed for the late 1990s. Corrections or details of other Seminar-type meetings of interest to collectors of British pottery and porcelain would be welcomed by the author (for address see Godden Seminars, page 249).

Academy of Antiques & Fine Arts
P.O. Box 18, Lydney, GL15 4YJ

Bridgnorth Seminars
M. Berthoud, 64 St Mary's Street, Bridgnorth, WV16 4DR

Godden Seminars
G. Godden, 3 The Square, Findon, W. Sussex, BN14 0TE

International Ceramics Fair & Seminar (London, in June)
B. Haughton, 31 Old Burlington Street, London, W1X 1LB

Keele University August Seminar
Dr C. Wakeling, Keele University, Staffs, ST5 5BG

Mercury Antiques evening meetings
Mrs L. Richards, 1 Ladbroke Road, London, W11 3PA

Morley College Ceramic Circle Seminar (London)
Mrs J. Boff, Clarebrook, Clasemont Road, Claygate, Esher, Surrey, KT10 0PL

Sevenoaks Ceramic Seminar
G. Fisk, Hawthorn Cottage, 43 Garth Road, Sevenoaks, Kent, TN13 1RX

Stow-on-the-Wold Ceramic House Parties
G. Godden, 3 The Square, Findon, W. Sussex, BN14 0TE

Selected Bibliography

Several specialist reference books have already been mentioned under the relevant factories in the main section of this book. The following general books listed by date of publication give good background and often detailed information on the subjects suggested by their various titles. All these books should be available in a good reference library even if some are not currently in print and available for purchase.

The Ceramic Art of Great Britain. L. Jewitt (1878; revised 1883; further revised with additional material and illustrations by G. A. Godden, Barrie & Jenkins, 1972).

A History and Description of English Porcelain. W. Burton (Cassell, 1902).

English Earthenware and Stoneware. W. Burton (Cassell, 1904).

Staffordshire Pots and Potters. G. W. & F. A. Rhead (Hutchinson, 1906).

The A.B.C. of English Saltglaze Stoneware. J. F. Blacker (Stanley Paul, 1922).

Guide to Collectors of Pottery and Porcelain. F. Litchfield (Truslove & Hanson, 1925).

Old English Porcelain. W. B. Honey (Faber & Faber, 1928, new edition, 1977).

English Pottery and Porcelain. W. B. Honey (A. & C. Black, 1933, 5th edition, 1962).

English Pottery Figures 1660–1860. R. G. Haggar (Phoenix House, 1947).

English Country Pottery. R. G. Haggar (Phoenix House, 1950).

Nineteenth Century English Pottery and Porcelain. G. Bemrose (Faber & Faber, 1952).

The Concise Encyclopaedia of English Pottery and Porcelain. R. G. Haggar and W. Mankowitz (Deutsch, 1957).

Victorian Porcelain. G. Godden (H. Jenkins, 1961).

Victorian Pottery. H. Wakefield (H. Jenkins, 1962).

English Blue and White Porcelain of the 18th Century. B. Watney (Faber & Faber, 1963, revised 1973).

Encyclopaedia of British Pottery and Porcelain Marks. G. Godden (Barrie & Jenkins, 1964, revised 1991).

An Illustrated Encyclopaedia of British Pottery and Porcelain. G. Godden (Barrie & Jenkins, 1966).

British Pottery and Porcelain: For Pleasure and Investment. H. Sandon (J. Gifford, 1969).

Staffordshire Blue. W. L. Little (Batsford, 1969).

Caughley & Worcester Porcelains 1775–1800. G. A. Godden (Antique Collectors' Club, 1969; new edition, 1981).

Coalport & Coalbrookdale Porcelains. G. A. Godden (Antique Collectors' Club, 1970, new edition, 1981).

Staffordshire Portrait Figures. P. D. G. Pugh (Antique Collectors' Club, 1971, revised edition, 1987).

British Porcelain. G. A. Godden (Barrie & Jenkins, 1974).

British Pottery. G. A. Godden (Barrie & Jenkins, 1974).

Yorkshire Pots and Potteries. H. Lawrence (David & Charles, 1974).

Godden's Guide to English Porcelain. G. A. Godden (Granada, 1978).

Derby Porcelain. J. Twitchett (Barrie & Jenkins, 1980).

18th Century English Porcelain Figures 1745–1795. P. Bradshaw (Antique Collectors' Club, 1981).

The Dictionary of Blue and White Printed Pottery 1780–1880. A. Coysh & R. Henrywood (Antique Collectors' Club, 1982).

English Brown Stoneware 1670–1900. A. Oswald, R. Hildyard & R. Hughes (Faber & Faber, 1982).

Chamberlain-Worcester Porcelain 1788–1852. G. A. Godden (Barrie & Jenkins, 1982).

An Anthology of British Cups. M. Berthoud (Micawber, 1982).

Staffordshire Porcelain, edited by G. A. Godden (Granada, 1983).

Eighteenth-Century English Porcelain. G. A. Godden (Granada, 1985).

Art Deco Tableware. J. Spours (Ward Lock, 1988).

Encyclopaedia of British Porcelain Manufacturers. G. A. Godden (Barrie & Jenkins, 1988).

English Decorative Ceramics Art Nouveau to Art Deco. J. Barlett (Kevin Francis, 1989).

Majolica. British, Continental and American Wares 1851–1915. V. Bergesen (Barrie & Jenkins, 1989).

Phillips Guide to English Porcelain. J. Sandon (Merehurst Press, 1989).

British Studio Ceramics in the 20th Century. P. Rice & C. Gowing (Barrie & Jenkins, 1989).

The Concise Guide to British Pottery and Porcelain. G. A. Godden (Barrie & Jenkins, 1990).

Encyclopaedia of British Art Pottery, 1870–1920. V. Bergesen (Barrie & Jenkins, 1991).

English Earthenware Figures 1740–1840. P. Halfpenny (Antique Collectors' Club, 1991).

Collecting Lustreware. G. Godden & M. Gibson (Barrie & Jenkins, 1991).

Collector's History of British Porcelain. J. & M. Cushion (Antique Collectors' Club, 1992).

Printed English Pottery 1760–1820. D. Drakard (Jonathan Horne, 1992).

British Teapots & Tea Drinking 1700–1850. R. Emmerson (HMSO 1992).

Antique Porcelain (Starting to Collect Series). J. Sandon (Antique Collectors' Club, 1997).

True Blue. Transfer Printed Earthenware, edited by G. Blake Roberts (Friends of Blue, 1998).

English Dry-Bodied Stoneware. Wedgwood and Contemporary Manufacturers 1774 to 1830. D. Edwards & R. Hampson (Antique Collectors' Club, 1998).

Godden's Guide to Ironstone, Stone and Granite Wares. G. Godden (Antique Collectors Club, 1999).

Index

It is obviously unnecessary to duplicate here the alphabetical entries in the Mark Section, pp. 40–150, nor the multitude of initials and names found in British ceramic markings in the subsequent two sections, pp. 151–245. The following index is, however, helpful in listing the potters' names, trade-names, types of ware, and other information in this book that is not covered in the main section's headings. For example, the entry 'Denby' refers to a trade-name of J. Bourne & Son on p. 50.

A. Bros 43
Adams 27
Anchor device 51, 60, 61, 62
Arnoux, L. 28
Art Deco 14
Art Pottery 15

Barr, Flight & Barr 148
Basalt 16
Bevington & Co. 132
BL:, B.L. 93
Blue and white 18–19
Biscuit (bisque) porcelain 17
Bisto 48
Bone china 10, 20
Brameld 124
Bretby 134
Bristol 33
Burleigh (Ware) 56

Cambrian Pottery 132
Carlton Ware 144
Castleford type 21
C.C. 22
C Dale 63
Cetem Ware 100
Chamberlain-Worcester 33
Clarice Cliff 14, 62–3
Coalbrookdale 63
Coalport 33
Copyright 10, 168–70
Courtney 75
Creamware 21–2

Crescent device 49, 92, 97, 146, 147, 148–9
Crescent China 92
Cross mark 54
Crossed-swords device 47, 54, 97, 105, 125, 147
Crown Devon 83–4

D 73
D and crown 73, 74, 75
Daisy mark 127
Dawson 131
De Morgan 15
Deer device 137
Delft (delft) 23
Denby 50
Derby 17
Design Registry 246
Dillwyn (& Co.) 132
Disguised numeral marks 58, 147
Dixon & Co. 131
Dixon, Austin & Co. 131
Dixon, Phillips & Co. 131
Doultons 35, 37

Eastwood 44
Edwards, J. 168
Edwards, J. & T. 168
Egyptian black 16
England (in mark) 9
English Fine Bone China 80
English Translucent China 80
Evans & Co. 133

Evans & Glasson 132

Flight 147
Flight & Barr 147–8
Flight, Barr & Barr 148
Foley 144

G. L. A. Bros 43
Grainger–Worcester 30
Granite China 25

Harp device 45
Hybrid hard-paste porcelain 33

Impressed marks 8
Incised marks 8, 51
Initial marks 10, 151–67
Ironstone 24–5, 33

Jackfield type 25
Jasper 26–7
Jones, G. 29, 30

Kerr, W. H. & Co. 148
Kerr & Binns 148
Kidston & Co. 168

Ls (two crossed) 95
L^B 93
Lessore, E. 140
Letters, impressed 74, 116
Locker & Co. 75
Longton Hall 95
Ltd 9
Lustre 27–8

Made in England 10
Majolica 28–9
Marks, general guidelines 8–11
Mason, C. J. 24
Mason, M. 24, 33
Meigh, C. 168
Minton(s) 28, 29, 30–1
Moore (& Co.) 131
Moore, B. 110–11

N incised 73
Neale 27
Neale & Palmer 113
Neale & Wilson 113
New Hall 33, 113
Nottingham stonewares 37
Numbers in blue 51, 97
Numbers, impressed 64

Oriental ivory (body) 48
Opaque porcelain 33
Owl mark 137

Pad mark 73
Painters' marks 146
Parian body 29–30
Pâte-sur-pâte 30–1
Patent Ironstone China 101–2
Pattern numbers 113, 116
Pearlware 31–2
Phillips (& Co.) 131
Plymouth 33
Porcelain 32
Pratt, F. & R. 38
Public Record Office 170, 246

Queen's Ware 130

® 10
R^D N^O 245
Regent China 59
Registered designs 33–4, 171–245
Registration device 9, 33–4, 168–70
Registration numbers 245–6
Retailers' marks 11
Ridgway, J. (& Co.) 121, 168
Ridgway, Bates & Co. 122
Ridgway & Morley 123
Rose, J. & Co. 34, 63
Royal prefix 9
Royal Arms 9, 58
Royal Windsor 83
Royal Worcester 30

.S. (impressed seal) 93
Sadler 95

Salopian 58
Salt-glaze 34–5
Scott (& Co.) 131
Scott & Sons 131
Scott Bros 131
Semi China 33
Sèvres mark, copied 65
Shelley 144
Ship device 87
Slip decoration 35–6
Solon, M. L. 30–1
Spode 20
Square or seal mark 147
Staffs and crown 59
Staffordshire Potteries 10, 170
Statuary porcelain 29
Stevenson, Sharp & Co. 75
Stone China 25, 91
Stoneware 37
Stylecraft 104
SylvaC 127

Terra-cotta 38

T° 51, 54, 134
Tin-glaze 23
Toft, T. 36
Tooth, H. 134
Tooth & Ault 134
Triangle mark (incised) 60
Trident and crown 60
Trade mark 8–9
Turner 27
Turner's Patent 135

Victoria, Victorian (marks) 48

W and vase mark 142
W(★★★) 22, 137
Wade Heath (& Co.) 138
Warburton's Patent 114
Wedgewood 130
Wedgwood, J. 16, 26, 31
Wedgwood & Bentley 140, 142
Wemyss 90
West Pans 95
Worcester 18, 19, 146–50